THE
KENNEDY
PROMISE

THE
KENNEDY
PROMISE

The Politics of Expectation

BY HENRY FAIRLIE

Doubleday & Company, Inc., Garden City, New York
1973

The author wishes to express his thanks to the following:

Atheneum Publishers and André Deutsch Limited for material from *John F. Kennedy, President* by Hugh Sidey, copyright © 1963, © 1964 by Hugh Sidey. Used by permission.

Doubleday & Company, Inc., for excerpts from *Children and the Death of a President*, edited by Martha Wolfenstein and Gilbert Kliman. Copyright © 1965 by Martha Wolfenstein and Gilbert Kliman. Reprinted by permission of Doubleday & Company, Inc.

Doubleday & Company, Inc., and Robert Lantz-Candida Donadio Literary Agency for excerpts from *To Move a Nation* by Roger Hilsman. Copyright © 1964, 1967 by Roger Hilsman. Reprinted by permission of Doubleday & Company, Inc., and Robert Lantz-Candida Donadio Literary Agency, Incorporated.

Doubleday & Company, Inc., and The Sterling Lord Agency for excerpts from *With Kennedy* by Pierre Salinger. Copyright © 1966 by Pierre Salinger. Reprinted by permission of Doubleday & Company, Inc., and The Sterling Lord Agency.

Harper & Row, Publishers, Inc., for material from *A Proposal: Key to an Effective Foreign Policy* by Walt W. Rostow and Max F. Millikan. Used by permission of the publishers.

Holt, Rinehart and Winston, Inc., Jonathan Cape Ltd., and the Estate of Robert Frost for lines from "For John F. Kennedy, His Inauguration" from *The Poetry of Robert Frost*, edited by Edward Connery Lathem. Copyright © 1961, 1962 by Robert Frost. Copyright © 1969 by Holt, Rinehart and Winston, Inc. Reprinted by permission of Holt, Rinehart and Winston, Inc., Jonathan Cape Ltd., and the Estate of Robert Frost.

Houghton Mifflin Company and André Deutsch Limited for material from *A Thousand Days* by Arthur M. Schlesinger, Jr. Copyright © 1965 by Arthur M. Schlesinger, Jr. Reprinted by permission of the publishers, Houghton Mifflin Company and André Deutsch Limited.

Houghton Mifflin Company, The Tweedsmuir Estate, and Hodder & Stroughton Ltd., for material from *Pilgrim's Way*, published in Great Britain by Hodder & Stroughton Ltd., under the title *Memory-Hold the Door*. Used by permission.

The Nation for excerpts from "The Students Take Over" by Kenneth Rexroth; *The Nation*, July 2, 1960. Used by permission.

Newsweek for "Caroline in the White House" from the May 15, 1961, issue. Copyright Newsweek, Inc., 1961. Reprinted by permission.

Southern Illinois University Press for material from *A Diplomat Looks at Aid to Latin America* by Willard L. Beaulac, 1970. Used by permission of the publishers.

United States Naval Institute for excerpts from "Contrasting Strategic Styles in the Cold War" by Charles O. Lercher, Jr., Proceedings, May 1962. Reprinted from *Proceedings* by permission; Copyright © 1962 U. S. Naval Institute.

University of California Press for material from *Party Politics in the Age of Caesar* by Lily Ross Taylor, originally published by the University of California Press; reprinted by permission of The Regents of the University of California.

Contents

THE
KENNEDY
PROMISE

CHAPTER ONE

Politics of Expectation

THE MOMENT HAS clearly arrived when different hands will begin the task of evaluating the political method of the Kennedys and the impact which it has made on our time. This book is concerned primarily with the administration of John Fitzgerald Kennedy, to some extent with the promise of Robert Francis Kennedy, and only incidentally with the potential importance of Edward Moore Kennedy. They should be considered separately, but it is impossible not to consider them also as one. At five successive conventions of the Democratic Party since 1956, the three brothers have in turn been prominent in the national lists, representing not the hope of a few, but a national expectation.

John Kennedy held the office of President of the United States for only "a thousand days"; Robert Kennedy was killed when he was only the junior senator from New York and had not completed his first term. It could be persuasively argued that John Kennedy's achievements were less significant than those of James K. Polk, and that Robert Kennedy's contribution to the political life of his country did not match that of Jacob K. Javits, the senior senator from New York at the time. Yet the Kennedys are legendary figures, and their names will be sung as long as men tell stories to each other

about their past. The legend is today being questioned, but
it is likely to remain the source of a powerful mythology, if
for no other reason than that the lives of the two brothers
were cut short. Both the Unfinished Presidency of the one
and the Unachieved Presidency of the other may tempt the
American people to believe that, just as their country was deprived of two unusual chances of salvation in the past, so
their best hope in the future, as trials beset them, is to find
and to follow another deliverer. It is the *promise* of the Kennedys, unrealised but remembered, which is itself a source of expectation.

The lives of John Kennedy and Robert Kennedy need un-
worshipful retelling, but this book does not pretend to be so
ambitious. A vast number of documents at the Kennedy Library, trivial as well as significant, have been opened to the serious student, but they will require lengthy and critical examination before the biographer can make honest use of them;
and he will require at least as many documents from other
sources to set beside them. Moreover, when the definitive biographies are attempted, they will best be written by Americans,
for only an American can explain the two graves in the National Cemetery at Arlington, bitten into its hillside, their pomp
and their circumstance; not Winston Churchill, not Charles de
Gaulle, has such a resting place, or is even buried in his nation's
capital, yet each was the saviour of his country; not George
Washington, not Abraham Lincoln, not Franklin Roosevelt. At
least to an outsider, the graves pose a question, which in various forms runs through the whole of this book. They are not
simple graves, they are rhetorical; yet we have been told again
and again, of John Kennedy in particular, that the reason why,
in the words of Arthur M. Schlesinger, Jr., he "voiced the dis-
quietude of the post-war generation" was that he expressed "the

mistrust of rhetoric, the disdain for pomposity," which they felt; that the mark of the man was "a skeptical mind, a laconic tongue"; that he was "contained and ironic" in his manner; that he was cool, and that his coolness "was itself a new frontier." All of this we are told, yet the graves are there, immense in their sweep, ample in their design, commanding in their situation, like the tombs which in a vanished age were erected only for the proudest dynasts.

Only an American can explain why, in the twentieth century, they are there: pavilions of splendour among the ranks of equal headstones which mark the deaths of equal men, and which stretch as far as the eye can see on the hillside of Arlington, "as though Cadmus had reversed his myth, and had sown living men to come up dragon's teeth." To an outsider, it seems as if the American people, for the first time in their history, have buried an emperor and, alongside him, his rightful but deprived heir. If the American people are today resisting the imperial role for which they were cast in the 1960s, they must be ready to ask themselves under which President, and under which candidate for the Presidency, the rhetoric of imperialism—of personal emperorship—was so exalted that they grew to cherish it.

One senses today a growing perplexity as people try to place the administration of John Kennedy in the light of subsequent events, and each to form his own judgement of it. The questions are familiar, and are in fact one question. How did such rational and cool men, how did the precise mind of Robert S. McNamara and the prim intellect of McGeorge Bundy, how did an administration of "all the talents" take the United States "waist deep into the big muddy" of Indochina; how did they make the commitment which was then extended and which has since been retrieved with so much pain? As we are told in many accounts, the universities and the foundations were canvassed in order to find a team of "high quality" to conduct the foreign policy of the administration, "people from outside 'unhampered by past loyalties' and committed to the New Frontier," as Arthur Schlesinger puts it. Yet it was they who took America into war, so that I. F. Stone could write in his newsletter, on 23 October 1963, "On every major aspect of the war the Kennedy administration has sought to deceive the country." This was less than a month before the assassination of John Kennedy, and now that everyone knows what I. F. Stone and a few others then perceived, it is not surprising that the people are vexed.

In 1960, so the legend tells them, so the graves at Arlington tell them, they elected the good guys, the good and intelligent guys, the intelligent and cool guys; and in 1968, the legend continues, they would have done so again, if they had not been deprived of the opportunity. Yet, as the evidence is at last frankly debated, it becomes clear that it was these men, these good guys, these intelligent guys, these cool guys, who initially took the United States into an occasion so hostile that it has turned into a domestic tragedy. No wonder a people are disturbed when they are told to regard their politicians, not as politicians at all, but as saviours, and then find, even as they take photographs of the graves, disembarking from their Tourmobiles to snap-snap-snap with their shutters at the Eternal Flame, that these saviours were only men like themselves, capable of error and of deception, politicians who fumbled.

It is necessary, when the issues are so close, to make one's own position clear. I can find no sensible way of regarding the United States today except as an imperial power, with interests and responsibilities which stretch across the globe; and it is equally clear to me that such interests and responsibilities exist

in South-east Asia, and will continue to exist. In short, I am
not shocked by the effort which the United States has made in
South Vietnam, but I am dismayed by the manner in which it
was made. In the company of many international lawyers, I do
not regard the American involvement in the war as illegal; and
I doubt whether there is much reality in trying to determine
whether it has been immoral. In so far as it is the subject of
this book, my concern is with political error; and to demonstrate
that the character of that error was true to the character of the
administration which made it. I have tried to free myself from
an obsession with the war, in part because that obsession has
already distracted the American people too much, but also because the lessons to be learned from the political method of
John Kennedy and of those whom he gathered to his service
are of much wider consequence. We can learn from the failure
of the method something of the proper realm of politics.

There was a fault—in the geological sense—in the political
method of the Kennedys, a fracture to which they were oblivious. They wished to act—of this there can be no doubt—as rational men, unbemused and cool, sceptical and laconic, ironic
and contained, the adjectives which persistently recur in the
literature of the administration; and they had the equipment
with which to do so. But the very energy, the very conviction,
the very zeal, with which they pursued their purpose fatally
contradicted it. Unbemused—yet bemused by the opportunities
of power; cool—yet hot for action; sardonic—yet eager to move
a nation; laconic—yet given to majestic periods in their utterances; ironic—yet surrendered to their own zeal; contained—yet
exuberant performers in the public arena. The panoply of the
graves is only the most striking symbol of the contradictions in
their attitudes. Here was the fault; here was the unmendable

fracture; here was the flaw. Here is the true source of the illusions and disillusions of the politics of expectation.

Energy and activity; conviction and zeal. "Would he sit *still* upon the Woolsack?" asked Walter Bagehot when a man whom he regarded as having a restless temper and an agitating intellect was appointed Lord Chancellor; and the Kennedys would not sit *still* in the White House, neither the two brothers nor those whom they persuaded to serve them; and one catches in a remark of Robert Kennedy, as one often does, a rare note of that genuine irony which was needed in the company of such zealous men, when he remarked of the early months of the administration: "Those were the days when we thought we were succeeding because of all the stories on how hard everybody was working." But this self-depreciation was not, even though they may have believed it, the manner or the method of the Kennedys; activity *was* their method. Again and again, we are told that John Kennedy's enthusiasm for activity was infectious in his administration; indeed it was and fatally so, as this book will argue. When we recognise this, we can understand why rational and cool men, with a justified pride in their intelligence, were capable of extravagant error. The zeal contradicted the coolness, the exuberance contradicted the intelligence; and, at the same time, each influenced the other, and for the worse. An acute mind in a zealous man increases the zeal rather than correcting it; and, in return, the zeal gives the intelligence an incentive to act, converting it into a weapon which is as restless as it is formidable. This was the mark of the administration.

The interest of the last years of Robert Kennedy's life, and of his brief campaign for the Presidency, was that the zeal which in his brother had been concealed beneath a "contained and ironic exterior" burned for all the world to see; and, as one watched him at some of those last meetings, and listened to his impassioned words, one could not help wondering what such a zealot might do—*what he might not do*—if he were elected to the most powerful office in the world. The zeal and the intelligence, the ardour and the conviction, were combined in a single frame as never before; and the result was as inevitable as before. Although his object was to put himself at the head of all individuals and groups who opposed the American involvement in South Vietnam, he concluded the announcement of his candidacy with the proclamation: "At stake is not simply the leadership of our party and even our country. It is the right to the moral leadership of the planet." If he had lived to see an American walk on the moon, as his brother had ordained, how far would the claim have stretched?

It must be noticed that Robert Kennedy did not talk of *an opportunity* to exercise the moral leadership of the planet, even though that would have been a claim which was almost without limit, but of *a right* to it. One cannot ignore this messianic rhetoric, or brush it aside, as some of the supporters of the Kennedys would like us to do. It was the essence of the whole of what came to be known as their style. The moral leadership of the planet may be an uncertain ambition, but the moral leadership of an entire society can be commanded. They would rule its arts, they would rule its science, they would rule its letters, they would rule its fashion, they would rule its taste; and all to create in the society an elevated sense of national purpose. The one required the other. The style was needed to create the sense of purpose, the sense of purpose was needed to justify the style. If the zeal and the intelligence of the Kennedys were not to appear to be harnessed to personal ambition alone, they must be seen to be consecrated to a loftier and more strenuous ideal; and the nation, ennobled by their example, must consecrate itself in turn.

One has some sympathy with the complaint of Theodore Sorensen that, by paying too much attention to the style of the Kennedys, people have sometimes given too little attention to the substance of what they did. On the other hand, it is not clear that such a separation can be made. What is called the Kennedy style was not something added to their political method; it was not just a public display of the external attributes with which they had been bountifully endowed. It was a part of the method, a reflection of its intention, not a decoration of it. An entire people was to be governed by keeping it in a constant state of expectation of the achievements which would be made possible, not merely by political action, but by the actions of a single ruler. They were to be persuaded to believe that the limits of political action could be transcended by exalting the power of their Chief Executive, and to this end they would be moved to discover in him—in the images of excellence with which his actions were arrayed—the embodiment of an elevated sense of national purpose, beyond their own purposes, to which they would commit themselves without question.

But it is a habit of our rulers to try to excite an elevated sense of national purpose in us only when they want us to do battle for them, to kill and to be killed. It is sometimes necessary, of course; and, when England was threatened by the Armada, even the most feckless poetaster might have been in the ranks of the army at Tilbury which cheered Elizabeth I as she rode among them on horseback and cried: "I know I have the body of a weak and feeble woman, but I have the heart and stomach of a king, and of a king of England too, and think foul scorn that Parma or Spain, or any prince of Europe, should dare to invade the borders of my realm; to which, rather than any dishonour shall grow by me, I will myself take up arms." But, of course, she did not take up arms; it was her soldiers who were to die for the national purpose which she had proclaimed in language fit to make a man die for her.

In the summer of 1963, when Harold Macmillan was being accused of failing to give a sense of purpose to Britain, he replied to an inquiry: "If the people want a sense of purpose, they should get it from their archbishops." This delimitation of the field of politics is essential if they are not to exercise too extensive a sway over our lives, if a leader is not to create in us so elevated a sense of national purpose that we will unthinkingly "pay any price, bear any burden, meet any hardship, support any friend, oppose any foe" to achieve it. Even if it does not come to this, the milder danger is that so strenuous a sense of purpose will keep a nation standing on tiptoe, and nothing is more exhausting; day by day craning its neck towards the seat of power, in eager expectation of deliverance at least, and of exaltation at most.

One of John Kennedy's most persistent themes was clearly stated on 6 September 1960, at Pocatello, Idaho, as he began his national campaign:

> I do not accept the view that we can be influential abroad, that we can be a source of leadership abroad, unless we are also a source of leadership at home.
>
> I think the administrations of Wilson, Roosevelt, and Truman prove the point. It is a fact that in those administrations the vitality of the American system was mostly developed, and it has been in those administrations which have stood still at home that we have stood still abroad.

But it was under the three administrations which he praised that the United States found itself at war in the first half of the twentieth century; and it was under the equally active administrations of John Kennedy and Lyndon Johnson in the second half of the century that it found itself at war again.

Moreover, they were all Democratic administrations. It is clear that there is here an historical fact to be explained: that, under every Democratic administration of this century, the United States has been at war, and that each of these administrations has been distinguished, as John Kennedy correctly said, for its activity at home as well as its energy abroad. Indeed, the question may be taken further back than the beginning of this century, as Walter Lippmann explained in the two lectures which were later published as *Isolation and Alliances:*

> The Democratic Party is descended directly from the party which was in office when by diplomacy and by war the United States acquired the Middle West and the Far West. Throughout American history it has been the party of bold designs. The Democrats made the Louisiana Purchase. They declared the Monroe Doctrine. They annexed Texas. They occupied the Southwest and California.

Whatever these facts suggest, and they are beyond the subject of this book, it should at least be obvious that John Kennedy's praise of Democratic administrations of "bold designs" requires at least a little reflection.

Naturally enough, his praise of active administrations was accompanied by his conviction that the Presidency must be an active institution. Until very recently, of course, all Democrats in this century have believed in strong Presidents and an active Presidency; and the Republicans whom they have been willing to include in their pantheon of great Presidents—such as Abraham Lincoln and Theodore Roosevelt—have been as strong and as active as any Democrats. "In this received formulation," as Marcus Cunliffe wrote in the February 1968 issue of *Commentary*, "the growth of Presidential power is historically associated with the assertion of federal against state sovereignty, and of executive as against legislative initiative. . . . On the whole, it has come to be associated with the role of the Democratic Party."

But he then noticed a change: "In the last few years, this kind of interpretation, seemingly so self-evident to men of goodwill, has been jarred by events. Americans who were once so sure that strong leadership was necessarily wholesome leadership no longer take the belief as axiomatic." In September of the same year, there was a revealing symptom: Murray Kempton, who had been one of the most acidulous reporters of the Eisenhower years, published an article in *Esquire*, asking if the talents—the quietude—of Dwight D. Eisenhower had not been undervalued. One of the clearest reactions—not least among Democrats—to the active policies, at home and abroad, pursued for eight years by John Kennedy and Lyndon Johnson has been a demand that the power of the Presidency should be checked, and its activity limited. The movement is unlikely to succeed: even Richard Nixon has demonstrated the freedom of executive action which he enjoys. But one should pay attention to the first straw in the wind as well as to the last straw which breaks the camel's back. It seems improbable that, for many years to come, the American people will be willing to take as exalted a view of "the burden and the glory" of the Presidency as they were persuaded by John Kennedy to do.

The arousal of an elevated sense of national purpose and the activity of the Presidency which accompanies it create what I call the politics of expectation. The people are encouraged to expect too much of their political institutions and of their political leaders. They cease to inquire what politics may accomplish for them, and what they must do for themselves. Instead, they expect politics to take the place which religion once held in their lives; and their politicians to be, not just archbishops, as Harold Macmillan suggested, but cardinals; not just cardinals, but popes; not just popes, but saviours. This was the inevitable end of the political method of the Kennedys; and it was impossible to watch Robert Kennedy among the mobs in the streets in 1968, without realising that most of the people who surged around him would not have been in the least surprised if he had walked upon the waters. As he rode above them on the roofs of cars, and they reached to touch his garments, it seemed an invitation to a crucifixion; and so it tragically was to be.

For three years after 20 January 1961, the American people were persuaded that, metaphorically as well as literally, they could shoot for the moon. The language in which John Kennedy put forward his space programme was designed to excite a national will to conquer. "I believe that this nation should commit itself to achieving the goal, before this decade is out, of landing a man on the moon and returning him safely to earth," he said on 25 May 1961. "No single space project in this period will be more impressive to mankind. . . . In a very real sense, it will not be one man going to the moon; if we make this judgment affirmatively, it will be an entire nation. For all of us must work to put him there." In fact, there was little that the majority of the American people could do to place a man on the moon, and there was no real way in which they could, as a nation, commit themselves to the task. The government of the United States was undertaking a scientific experiment; with the resources, tangible and intangible, at its disposal, there was little doubt that it would succeed. But this experiment was transformed into a national mission, and the national mission into a personal commitment on the part of countless individuals. The programme could not succeed, he said, "unless every scientist, every engineer, every serviceman, every technician, contractor, and civil servant, gives his personal pledge that this nation will move forward, with the full speed of freedom, in the exciting adventure of space." The decision to shoot for the moon, in this kind of language, became a metaphor.

When the expectations of a people—that they may accomplish anything—are so aroused, and are then not realised, frustration grows and disillusion follows. This was to be, in part, the story of the United States during the 1960s. Poverty and discrimination, ignorance and disease, could all be conquered as easily as the technology could be mastered to take a man to the moon, or as the military establishment could be organised to send half a million men across the face of the globe. At home or abroad, what could not be done? All that was required was a national will, an elevated sense of national purpose, received from a single ruler, and then returned to him in the form of a "personal pledge" of support from every citizen. But the manna did not fall from heaven, and the people, in various guises, took to the streets. The mediation of the single ruler on behalf of the people, which was the politics practised at first by John Kennedy and then continued by Lyndon Johnson, had not fulfilled its promise. The people had been taught to expect too much: above all, that their traditional political processes could be transcended by the exercise of a spectacular personal leadership which manufactured, so that it might be sustained by, an elevated sense of national purpose.

Neither the Unfinished Presidency of the one, if finished, nor the Unachieved Presidency of the other, if achieved, would have been likely to succeed. It is difficult to argue this point, since it carries us into the realm of speculation; but we are not

altogether helpless in that speculation. When he was assassinated, John Kennedy was already campaigning vigorously for
his own re-election, and we are entitled to regard the words
which he uttered, almost to his last breath, as witnesses to the
character of his administration if he had enjoyed a second term
in office. However, one is here trying to make a deeper point.
As has been forcefully argued by the able social critic, Midge
Decter, the supporters of the Kennedys cannot both make them
the central figures of the 1960s and then excuse them from
responsibility for the nastiness of the decade. The truth is that
they practised a method of politics which is too exacting for a
free society to bear without grievous dislocation. They called the
American people—Robert Kennedy during his brief campaign
as much as John Kennedy while he was in office—to a feverishness of expectation which had prepared their imaginations only
for crisis; each crisis to be met only by confrontation.

The politics of expectation—the politics of crisis—the politics
of confrontation: the progression is all but unavoidable. The
people are aroused to a high expectation, not only of what
politics may accomplish, but of their importance; in such a
strenuous climate, problems are magnified into crises; in the still
more strenuous atmosphere of crisis, solutions are sought in
confrontation. In the second half of the 1960s, in various causes
and in various guises, the American people took their problems
into the streets, there to confront each other, eyeball to eyeball. It was a period to dismay any American or any friend of
America, for the country seemed to have lost its political good
sense. But this was how, from 20 January 1961 to 22 November
1963, the American people had been taught to regard their
politics. They had been exhorted to transcend the limits of
politics, to exalt the spectacle of personal leadership over the
working of their political institutions. The leaders in the streets

who, in the second half of the 1960s, tried to turn politics into theatre were only following the example of the leader in the White House who, in the first half of the 1960s, had shown the way.

John Kennedy was fully aware of the adjustments and the compromises which are the proper business of politics, and in their memoirs both Arthur Schlesinger and Theodore Sorensen are at pains to explain the restrictions on his freedom of action. In his own foreword to Theodore Sorensen's lectures, *Decision-Making in the White House*, Kennedy explained that, although the President "is rightly described as a man of extraordinary powers . . . , it is also true that he must wield these powers under extraordinary limitations." But in practice he exalted the "extraordinary powers" of his office: in word and in deed, he inflamed the people with an exaggerated promise of what a politician—what the President—what politics—what the Presidency—could achieve. The disillusionment, when it came, was turned against his successor, but it is a reasonable assumption that, if he had been elected for a second term, it would have been turned with some force against him. He had strained the American people too far with the politics of expectation which he practised, and at some point they would have confronted him eyeball to eyeball, asking that the promise should be realised; and one does not know how he would have reacted.

Against the expectations of politics which he aroused, one may put a more limited view of their scope. It was stated most clearly by Michael Oakeshott in 1951, in his Inaugural Lecture on "Political Education" at the London School of Economics: "In political activity, then, men sail a boundless and bottomless sea; and there is neither harbour for shelter nor floor for anchorage, neither starting place nor appointed destination. The enterprise is to keep afloat on an even keel; the sea is both

friend and enemy; and the seamanship consists in using the
resources of a traditional manner of behaviour in order to make
a friend of every hostile occasion." It may be objected that this
is too English a statement, but an echo of it may be found in
the words of Fisher Ames, the eighteenth-century American conservative, when he described the absolute regimes of Europe:
"Monarchy is like a splendid ship, with all sails set; it moves
majestically on, then it hits a rock and sinks for ever. Democracy is like a raft. It never sinks but, damn it, your feet are always in the water."

John Kennedy was not satisfied to use the resources of a
traditional manner of behaviour; he sought to transcend them.
He did not try to make a friend of every hostile occasion; he
defied the occasion. He did not like to have his feet in the water,
or to believe that he was standing only on a raft; he sailed the
ship of state with splendour and with majesty until, at his
death, it was already headed for a rock, its course all but irre-
versible. As the American people recover from this experience,
the reflections of a sympathetic outsider may be of some assistance, if only because he can tell them that their problems are not
unique. The political method which is examined in this book
has been familiar enough since the days of Julius Caesar. From
generation to generation, it keeps recurring, employed by new
men, and is once more found attractive, and once more breeds
disillusion. In our own time, the Kennedys have been the most
vivid exemplars of it; and this book will succeed in its intention
if, starting from the men, gifted and honourable, skilful and intelligent, as they were, it in the end turns the attention of
men of good will away from them to the consideration of a
political method which is always bound to mislead even as it
fatally attracts.

CHAPTER TWO

The Misleading Challenge

A THEORY OF Arthur Meier Schlesinger had an important influence on his son, Arthur Meier Schlesinger, Jr.; and, through the son, an even more important influence on John Kennedy as he sought the Presidency. The father's statement of the theory is to be found in his essay, "The Tides of National Politics"; and his argument is that, in American politics, periods of quietude alternate with periods of rapid movement, and that these shifts of mood "can be plotted with reasonable precision." Perhaps such a theory does not require much elaboration; on the whole, one would expect any people, after a period of activity, to require a period of rest, and *vice versa*. Equally, one might say that it is not a theory particularly applicable to the United States alone; certainly the pendulum has swung with a similar regularity in the United Kingdom. All the same, it is the kind of theory which excites political imaginations.

The father believed that a period of quietude had begun in 1947, with the severe defeats which the Democratic Party had suffered in the Congressional elections in the previous year, an opinion which required drastic revision both when Harry S. Truman was re-elected, and when America found itself fighting a ground war on the Asian mainland. Nevertheless, with the election of Dwight Eisenhower in 1952, it could reasonably be

held that the country had entered a period of rest, if not a
sanitorium; and, with his re-election in 1956, that it wished to
continue to rest. With the approach of 1960, the theory of the
father became immediately interesting once again. Would his
prediction that the next period of rapid movement was due to
start in 1962—give or take a year—prove to be correct? Whatever its actual merits, it was exactly the kind of theory for
which an active young candidate for the Presidency was looking in 1959.

The son took the theory of the father—"The Tides of National Politics"—and put it into a memorandum—"The Shape of
National Politics to Come." The memorandum was given to
Thomas K. Finletter, who passed it on to John Kennedy, who
mentioned that he had been stimulated by it to the son, who
presumably conveyed his gratitude to his father. In his memorandum, the son had made plain his belief that the country
stood "on the threshold of a new political era, and that vigorous
public leadership would be the essence of the next phase": a
point of view, as he tells us, which "evidently corresponded to
things which Kennedy had for some time felt himself." We in
fact have no evidence that John Kennedy had been thinking
of much, since 1956, except how to get himself elected President
in 1960, but it is not difficult to understand why the theory attracted him: a young candidate could convincingly promise to
move the nation under vigorous leadership into a period of
rapid development appropriate to a new decade.

To this end, it had to be shown that the United States was
in the doldrums after eight years of Dwight Eisenhower's leadership; and, since the American people might in fact like the
doldrums, it had further to be shown that they were actually
in danger. Neither of these were arduous tasks. Even if America was neither in danger nor in the doldrums, Dwight Eisen-

hower did little to remove the impression. He had a way with him at press conferences which could not fail to suggest that the ship of state was becalmed, if not slowly sinking. He confided in 1958, for example, that "the carrying on of foreign policy is a very intricate business, and it becomes, you might say, almost an art rather than any science"; and when asked if he could explain what he meant, a frequent request which he bore with soldierly patience, he replied: "That is a very complicated thing. . . . This is so complicated that you have to go—you try to lay out a program, a plan, but it—work it if you have got it here, if you go here you have to defend that, you have to move over here." Perhaps aware that he might not have carried his point, he summed it up: "It is a very difficult, intricate thing, and I don't care what head of state or government has been here or that I have gone to see has acknowledged the intricacies of today in manipulating what, you may say, the foreign policy of any free country."

Perhaps with much of this in mind, Walter Lippmann proclaimed, early in 1960: "Great people can be put to sleep. This can be done if the people's leaders tell them to go to sleep." At the same time, John Steinbeck wrote a letter to Adlai Stevenson, in which he gave his first impressions of the America in which he had been journeying. He had found, he said, "a creeping, all-pervading, nerve gas of immorality," accompanied by "a nervous restlessness, a thirst, a yearning for something unknown—perhaps morality." In hindsight, it seems an acute observation, predicting the climate of the 1960s; but, whatever the reason that was given, there could be no doubt that, as John Kennedy prepared to make his challenge, the United States was ill at ease with itself and with its performance.

Throughout the first half of 1960, intellectuals and journal-

ists, theologians and educationalists, had been engaged in their
own debate about the State of the Union; and in June the
commencement speakers echoed what they had been saying.
"Near and far," cried Robert F. Goheen at Princeton University, "the cheap and the tawdry are glorified over achievements
of solid worth. . . . We find ourselves as a nation on the defen-
sive, and as a people seemingly paralyzed in self-indulgence."
"We must acknowledge," came the answering cry from William C. DeVane at Yale College, "that the loss of faith in our
world, our destiny, our religion, is the cloudy and dark climate
which most of America finds itself living in today." Nathan M.
Pusey at Harvard University was not to be outdone: he found
the whole Western world "adrift with little sense of purposeful
direction, lacking deeply held conviction, wandering along with
no more stirring thought in the minds of the people than the
desire for diversion, personal comfort, and safety." "A general
slackening of will," Samuel B. Gould responded from the University of California at Santa Barbara, "a general tendency to
countenance cupidity and applaud cunning, a general distrust
of intellectual pursuits and those who pursue them, a general
vagueness as to national purpose and resolve." It was as if all
these minds had been drilled.

It was small wonder that the *New Republic* had begun the
year by asking what was the most important question to be decided at the coming election, and gave as its answer: "Who
best understands what needs to be done if this nation is to grow
in power and excellence?" The growing mood could not have
better suited a young and vigorous candidate, who had taken
as his theme the need to move a nation again, and was basing
his campaign, at least in part, on the theory that, after eight
years of quietude, the nation would be ready to respond to such
a call, and to expect great things of him.

Looking back, it is easy to see that the mood was not only feverish but false. It had its origin in the launching of the first Sputnik on 4 October 1957, and in other revelations during the intervening years that the United States no longer held the commanding lead—in armaments, in science, in technology—over the Soviet Union that had given it a sense of security, and therefore of confidence, and therefore of purpose, in the first ten years after the Second World War. Throughout 1960, the debate on the State of the Union found its focus in the alleged weakness of the United States in the face of the growing might of the Soviet Union and, in particular, in the "missile gap" which was supposed to be growing in Russia's favour.

At the very beginning of the year, Nikita Khrushchev told the Supreme Soviet that "it is now clear that the Soviet Union is the strongest military power in the world"; and, by and large, the press and the public in America took him at his word. At the same time, the American newspapers carried the news that a Soviet ballistic missile had travelled 7,762 miles and landed less than 1.24 miles from the pre-calculated target. This piece of information would not amaze the Americans today when they are used to retrieving men from the moon with as much precision; and it should not have disturbed them then. As *Time* had the common sense to point out, the Soviet Union had once again "succeeded in projecting the image of power . . . without altering the realities of power." One of their missiles had merely travelled farther than an American missile.

In this mood, neither the press nor the public was inclined to listen to Thomas S. Gates, the Secretary of Defense, when he appeared before the Joint Armed Services Committee to argue that the defence policy of the administration was adequate, including its expenditure on defence. Indeed, the press gloated when, at a press conference, he said that his optimism was based on an estimate of how many missiles the Soviet Union intended to make, rather than how many it was, and would be, capable of making. As no one would deny today, his standard was the only sensible one: it would have been the height of folly and of wastefulness to enter into a race based on a calculation of how many missiles Russia would be capable of producing if it decided to produce as many as it could. But even the most serious newspapers scoffed at Thomas Gates in language which must today make them blush. "No longer, presumably," wrote the Washington *Post,* "need we worry about the lethal power of the big bruiser next door with the club, once we are told that his heart is pure."

Nothing that Dwight Eisenhower said—calling on his long experience—could stem the hysteria. Yet it is his words which today seem wise. "The real test," he told a Republican audience, "is to provide security in a way that effectively deters aggression and does not itself weaken the values and institutions we seek to defend. This demands the most careful calculation and balance, as well as steadfastness of purpose, not to be disturbed by any noisy trumpeting." But the trumpeting continued, and it could be heard most loudly wherever John Kennedy was campaigning. No matter that Dwight Eisenhower warned that excessive military spending could damage the very values and the very institutions which it was intended to secure; even Walter Lippmann countered by talking of "the prospective world struggle," in which "we shall surely lose if we tell the world that, though we have the richest economy in all history, our liberal system is such that we cannot afford a sure defense and adequate provision for the civil needs of the people." This was the current orthodoxy; and it was wrong.

A week later, at a press conference, Dwight Eisenhower returned to the attack. When asked if Russia's technical gains

would not give it even a psychological advantage, he replied
by expressing his faith in the ultimate victory of freedom and
democracy because "in the long run, men do learn to have the
same belief in liberty," and he added: "I believe that there is
just as much of the seeds of self-destruction in the Communist
system as they claim is in ours." *Time* was so struck by this
reply that it asked various public figures for their comments.
Amongst them was Arthur Schlesinger, who merely retorted
with the theme of John Kennedy's campaign: "The reason we
are falling behind lies in the lack of purpose in our national
life." Yet Dwight Eisenhower had again and again denied that
the United States was falling behind. In wholly understandable
syntax, he had declared: "What you want is enough, a thing
that is adequate. A deterrent has no added power, once it has
become completely adequate."

Neither Dwight Eisenhower's assurances nor his faith would
satisfy Walter Lippmann. "Mr. Eisenhower is mistaken," he
announced. "It is he who lacks faith in our system. It is he
who is saying that our system of liberty is so fragile that it is not
tough enough and durable enough to keep up the pace in the
great contest of national power." The language of the New
Frontier was catching on: "purpose in our national life . . . the
great contest of national power." A mood and a candidate were
beginning to commune; yet, as soon as Robert S. McNamara
became Secretary of Defense, almost his first pronouncement
was to confirm that the "missile gap" was not a threat to American security. In a televised interview on 7 June 1962, Walter
Lippmann said of the supposed gap: "We were the victims, in
part, of mistaken intelligence. Well, we now know that isn't
true. That never existed. The Soviets never built the missiles
that they were supposed to be able to build." But this was exactly the calculation which Dwight Eisenhower had made, and

which Thomas Gates had explained at the time. The fault was not mistaken intelligence but mistaken political judgement on the part of almost everyone except the President and his Secretary of Defense.

"No one would listen to President Eisenhower's denials and assurances," admitted Walter Lippmann again, in the issue of *Newsweek* of 21 January 1963; for he had not listened to them himself. We must ask ourselves why the American people would not, in 1960, listen to the sanity of their President; what it was in their mood which made them respond to so misleading a challenge as the alleged "missile gap"; why they did not have Dwight Eisenhower's faith both in their country's political system and in its technological capacity. For it was in this atmosphere of crisis, generated during 1960, for which there was no warrant, that the politics of expectation, leading to the politics of confrontation, were conceived; in the end to rule a decade.

The more one reads the newspapers and the magazines of the recent past, the more one realises how little they know of the society which they affect to report, and how they understand even less. They seem to pass round each other's information and intimations, until their voice becomes one, and they succeed in creating a wholly artificial national mood, such as the one which we have just been examining. There was no reason why the United States should fear for its security in 1960; yet this fear consumed the press, it was communicated to commencement day speakers, and it informed, as we will see, almost every major speech which John Kennedy made during his campaign and, as we will also see, profoundly influenced his performance as President.

Any extended inquiry into the period must convince the

most reluctant observer that we have a misleading picture of the Eisenhower years, especially of the last four, simply because this was the picture with which we were left, by the newspapers and the magazines, when they came to an end in 1961. It was in the Eisenhower years, after all, that the Beat flourished, heralding the counter-culture of the 1960s: a reminder once more of the limited reach of politics, of how much that is important in society is beyond either their inspiration or their amendment. To find a sense of purpose, the Beat was leading a whole generation to elect its own archbishops, who would tell them that there was none: "and nobody," Jack Kerouac wrote in 1957, in the last sentence of On the Road, "nobody knows what's going to happen to anybody, besides the forlorn rags of growing old." In the year before, Allen Ginsberg had published Howl; and, in the following year, Lawrence Ferlinghetti arrived with his collection, Coney Island of the Mind. In the newspapers and the newsmagazines, the Beat was at first neglected, and then dismissed. "The Beat Generation has finally got what it always wanted—lost," wrote Time in its issue of 10 February 1961. "Essentially the products of a public-relations campaign carried out by amateur flacks in stove-pipe slacks, the untalented Beats picked their own title. . . . the Beats even styled themselves a Movement—but it was one of the great stationary movements of all time, since nothing budges that is fueled by pretension and pot." A year later, on 2 March 1962, it said of them: "They prefer to wear beards and blue jeans, avoid soap and water, live in dingy tenements or, weather permitting, take to the road as holy hoboes, pilgrims to nowhere. Most of them adore Negroes, junkies, jazzmen and Zen. . . . They are, in short, bohemians."

It was only the more serious weekly reviews which appeared to understand that something of significance might be afoot.

In the *New Republic* of 11 January 1960, Frank Getlein distinguished between the bohemian of the past, who "put his principal emphasis on the creation of the work of art, and withdrew from society for that purpose," and the Beat who reversed this relationship, in whom "the withdrawal from society often seems to be the chief purpose—with art or, rather, expression being really an extension of the withdrawal." In a phrase, he had foreseen the 1960s; and it was important, as it is always important, to notice such movements. In so far as the Beat, by his withdrawal, was expressing more than his own alienation, the arousal of an elevated sense of national purpose was not obviously addressed to the needs of the time. It could not satisfy; it could only jar. For it was an irrelevance.

The student of the 1950s, so the conventional reading still asserts, was bland; and, on 25 April 1960, *Newsweek* summarised the portrait of the average college student which had been given in a sociological study from Cornell University, entitled "What College Students Think": "He is idealistic, but often cheats on exams. He believes in romantic love, yet attaches scant importance to chastity. He is religious, but in a hazy uncommitted way. In his business career, he hopes to get ahead through hard work, but not at the expense of family life. He is, over-all, a vaguely detached individual hanging, without much passion, to the middle of the political road. Who is he? A typical college student." As for politics, "the students were plainly apathetic." Yet *Time* had reported in its issue of 22 February 1960 that, at fifteen major universities, students were protesting vehemently against compulsory membership of the ROTC; and, throughout the first half of 1960, as black students began their sit-ins at lunch counters, the white students flocked to join them, unorganised and spontaneous.

Newsweek, reflecting other newsmagazines and the established newspapers, might find the American student as bland and as apathetic as the study from Cornell University suggested. But, in *The Nation* of 2 July 1960, Kenneth Rexroth wrote an article with the title, "The Students Take Over." Again, it is in a small-circulation weekly review that we find the true picture of what was going on, of how the future was taking shape: ". . . an orgy of irresponsibility and lies. That is the world outside the college gates. . . . a society which advances by means of an elite in permanent revolt and alienation is something new. . . . You might as well be a hero if society is going to destroy you anyway. There comes a time when courage and honesty come cheaper than anything else." It is the 1960s announced as they were beginning. Kenneth Rexroth then outlined the hope to which the students were looking, the hope that individual action would make a mark:

> . . . just because the machine is so vast, so complex, it is far more sensitive than ever before. Individual action does tell. Give a tiny poke at one of the insignificant gears down in its bowels and slowly it begins to shudder all over and suddenly belches out hot rivets. . . . Modern society has passed the stage when it was a blind, mechanical monster. It is on the verge of becoming an infinitely responsible instrument.

A false hope it may have been; but it was out of this hope that the students during the 1960s created their strategies. Kenneth Rexroth continued:

> Everything seemed to be going along nicely. According to the papers and most of the professors, 99.4/100 per cent of the nation's youth were cautiously preparing for the day when they could offer their young split-level brains to G.M., I.B.M., Oak Ridge, or the Voice of America. Madison Avenue had discovered its own pet minority of revolt and tamed it into an obedient mascot. According to *Time, Life,* M.G.M., and the editors and publishers of a new, pseudo

avant-garde, all the dear little rebels wanted to do was grow beards, dig jazz, take heroin, and wreck other people's Cadillacs. . . . But what was accumulating was not any kind of programmatic "radicalization," it was a moral demand . . . a great moral rejection, a kind of mass vomit.

These were the students of the 1960s—perceived by Frank Getlein and the *New Republic,* by Kenneth Rexroth and *The Nation,* unperceived by Cornell University and *Newsweek,* by the commencement day speakers and *Time*—who were to play so important a part in shaping the climate of the 1960s, and to whom John Kennedy offered an elevated sense of national purpose. As the young candidate took his campaign to the country, the rhetoric fully blown, Kenneth Rexroth observed: "Literacy is a dubious virtue in politics."

One cannot read of those days without forming the impression that Dwight Eisenhower was presiding over a society which, since it was at peace, had the time for such individual and spontaneous growth: whose members, since they did not feel that they must be committed to, or must challenge, the strenuous ordeals to which their government invited them, were able to make their own adjustments, even their own protests, without feeling the need for confrontation. It was as if a society was developing, with an unusual freedom, without being much harassed by the call of the state—of the government—of the President; without feeling that the answers must, or even could, come from the White House, and finding them instead within itself. It was not a period in which the people asked either what they could do for their country, or what their country could do for them; American life was unusually private.

The search for purpose was beyond politics, as Harold Macmillan said that it should be. In the closing years of Dwight

Eisenhower's regime, the smell of change was everywhere in the air, but it was not, for the most part, the kind of change to which politicians could address themselves. *Time* might offer a conventional portrait of the American suburban housewife in its issue of 20 June 1960: "The key figure in all Suburbia, the thread that weaves between family and community, the keeper of the suburban dream, is the suburban housewife. . . . If she is not pregnant, she wonders if she is. She takes her peanut butter sandwich standing, thinks she looks a fright, watches her weight . . . , paints her face for her husband's return before she wrestles with dinner." But, three months earlier, on 7 March 1960, *Newsweek* had for once grasped the meaning of the phenomenon which it was reporting. "Who could ask for more? The educated American woman has her brains, her good looks, her car, her freedom," it said in a "special science report" on "Young Wives," and then recorded: "Yet she often complains that she is not completely happy." Not completely happy? In fact, it reported complaint after complaint with which we are now familiar. It was noticing the beginning of a profound social change, the spontaneous discovery of a new purpose—or existing lack of purpose—in countless human beings: *The Feminine Mystique* of Betty Friedan and the contraceptive pill were about to be swallowed in one gulp.

The examples could be multiplied; and nothing has been said here, for it requires no emphasis, of the impact on the social imaginations of black and white alike of the decision of the Supreme Court of the United States, in 1954, in *Brown* v. *Board of Education*. It was merely evident to those who would look that American society in 1960 was by its own energy on the move, although in directions and in ways, for the most part, which no politicians could inspire or check. If it was the time to call the society to an elevated sense of national purpose, it

was the time neither to confuse the purpose which it was seeking with trials of national strength between the United States
and the Soviet Union, nor to arouse a popular expectation that
the purpose could be realised by spectacular political action.
American society was perhaps too little political during the regime of Dwight Eisenhower; but the effect of the method of
his successor was that every aspiration of that society was polit-
icized until, by the middle of the 1960s, every need of the
American people, the sacred and the profane, was thought to
be available to a political solution.

The first call made by John Kennedy in 1960 was that the
nation should arm itself both more thoroughly and more ex-
pensively than it had done under Dwight Eisenhower; his second call was that it should support the necessary measures to
expand the national economy. It was again not an arduous task
to demonstrate that the economy at the end of the 1950s was
simultaneously a little torpid and a little racy: that the real
Gross National Product had increased, between 1955 and 1959,
at an average annual rate of only 2.25 per cent, while consumer
prices had risen between March 1956 and March 1958 by
7.5 per cent, a rate which would have cut the value of the
dollar by a half in less than fifteen years, and were still steadily
rising. For two years, in fact, economists had been engaged
in one of their secular (to use a phrase which is familiar to
them) debates which always remind a layman of the old joke
that, when seven economists were gathered together, there were
always eight opinions, two of which came from John Maynard
Keynes. (An up-to-date version of the joke would be that,
when twelve economists are gathered together today, there
are always thirteen opinions, all of which come from John

Kenneth Galbraith.) The truth was that the economists—and not they alone—were hard put to it to explain why prices continued to rise, not only during the sharp recession of 1957-58, but during a longer period in which unemployment had remained at a high level, the highest rate of sustained unemployment since the Second World War.

It was all very puzzling, and there was a lot of talk among the economists about the "inevitability of inflation": talk which was inspired by the fact that, for eight years, two conservative administrations had tried to use the old weapons to fight inflation, but had failed to stop it. It should be noticed that the problem is still with us, and that Richard Nixon's wage-price freeze, and his attempt to establish a permanent form of wage-price regulation, have been designed to cope with it: the discomfiting fact that inflation can continue in a period of recession and unemployment. In 1960, in an essay entitled "Inflation: What It Takes," John Kenneth Galbraith announced that, "During the last two or three years, there has been an increasing measure of agreement on the causes of inflation and, for that reason, one hopes, on the logic of the remedies." This was something of an exaggeration, perhaps another case of all thirteen opinions being adopted as his own, but at least the remedy which he then advocated—a limited form of wage-price setting—has been modified to become a conventional orthodoxy, even in a Republican administration.

There were economists who differed from him, in 1960, both as to the disease and as to the remedy. In particular, there were those who argued that there were new factors at work—not all of them either discerned or understood, in what was still —and how long ago it now seems—simply called a "mixed economy." The ins-and-outs of the debate, although they can have a quaint fascination for a layman who was brought up to enjoy the disputes of the Schoolmen, need not detain us here. For, whereas the conservative and politically minded economists could agree only that they had found no answer, the liberal and politically minded economists had found one answer on which they could all agree: Growth. It became a prominent word about 1958; it was a clean word by 1960; and it remained clean until the conservationists about 1968 began to say that it was not only a dirty word, but the cause of most of the dirt which was suffocating the planet.

It is to the credit of John Kenneth Galbraith that he was never a simple Growth-man; and it was because he fully understood that, in conditions of high employment in the American economy, prices are not stable, that he took the logical step, as he called it, of advocating a limited form of wage-price restraint: "The liberal who wants full use of resources and steady growth and who opposes inflation does not have the additional luxury of deploring proposals such as those here advanced." But for most liberals, Growth was enough, a fine word for a platform: a guttural to start it off, a roll to carry it forward, a long vowel to hold it, and a dental to cut it off. In particular, there could not have been a better word for a young and vigorous candidate who was inviting the people to a new period of rapid development. Moreover, he was already committed to increased expenditures for defence; and other commitments, such as to science and education, were to follow. How would he pay for them? Growth, my fellow Americans.

Of course, the diagnosis on which the remedy was based was not necessarily accurate. It seemed as if the two administrations of Dwight Eisenhower had used the classic weapons against inflation, but this was not altogether true. As Edwin L. Dale, Jr., of the New York *Times*, argued in 1960, they used these weapons only with a faint heart. The pledge given in 1952 was that the budget would be reduced to $60 billion; the estimate for fiscal 1959 was $80 billion on a conventional accounting basis, and about $94 billion on a cash accounting basis. The pledge given in 1952 was that expenditure on defence would be drastically reduced, and by fiscal 1955 it had indeed fallen to $35.5 billion; but by fiscal 1959 it had climbed back to $42.1 billion. There were other causes for the large budgets of the 1950s—an increase of $900 million in expenditure on atomic energy between fiscal 1955 and fiscal 1959; the expenditure on the new highway programme, technically outside the budget, which rose from $650 million in fiscal 1955 to $2.6 billion in fiscal 1959—but the general picture was sharp enough. As Edwin Dale wrote: "Before the conservatives could catch their breath, their balanced budgets were out of the window, and they had first a moderate deficit of $2.8 billion in fiscal 1958, and in fiscal 1959 the biggest peace-time deficit in history: $12.5 billion." This was an eccentric record for a President who had promised "security with solvency"; and any conservative economist could be allowed to suggest that the classic remedies had not been tried.

But, with the discovery of Growth as a panacea, the challenge which John Kennedy would make to the old regime was complete. It locked together. The end of a personal regime, the end also of a period of quietude; a time for youth to succeed age, and for movement to follow calm; the need to meet challenges which had been ignored, especially the challenge of an expanding Communist empire; a call to effort, and a spur to Growth. The language, as we have seen, caught on. Walter Lippmann spoke of "the springs of our national vitality"; *Time* proclaimed that "The great question that stalks the '60s is whether the United States has the plan and the purpose to hold its lead against the threats of the Soviet Union"; *Newsweek* found that "the world struggle for power is a total struggle. It will be waged on all fronts, of peace as well as of war, for as long as men can foresee." Sidney Hook said that Americans must exert the effort to cope with "Communism's permanent state of mobilization against the free world." The young and vigorous candidate was there to meet the mood.

As early as 4 January 1960, in a quotation which has already been given, the *New Republic* made the link which was to become the legend of the New Frontier, inscribed on all its pennants. "Power and excellence," it demanded of the next President. An exciting vocabulary was being collected; and it was difficult not to respond to it. But the President who was preparing to surrender his office stuck to his own language. He had already warned his countrymen, again and again, that too great an emphasis on military strength would threaten the very values and the very institutions which it was intended to secure. In his Farewell Address, ripe with wisdom, he gave his warning the power of a simple text: "We must guard against the acquisition of unwarranted influence, whether sought or unsought, by the military-industrial complex." The man who had commanded armies, after all, and the man who had golfed with industrialists, was not easily fooled. The nation might wish to move again, but the record of the President which was now being so vigorously challenged was at the time given two epitaphs which today seem more than adequate. In a farewell column, James Reston said that, during his administration, "nothing had been settled, but nothing vital to the free world had been lost"; and, in the middle of the campaign in 1960, the Chairman of the Republican Party in California paid the simplest tribute of all: "We are in no shooting wars." It may not have seemed much of a tribute to the American people at the time, when they took peace for granted; but within a year they would be shooting again.

CHAPTER THREE

The Conventional Candidate

IN HIS COLUMN on the eve of the election in 1960, Murray Kempton bid adieu to the John Kennedy who had fought so hard. No matter what befell the next day, he said, "you were one hell of a candidate"; and so he had been, to those who came to hear him and to those who worked for him, even to those whom he just happened to pass on the way. There were few who could forbear to cheer. He had carried himself everywhere as if in a tourney; the spirit had been willing, and the flesh had never weakened. He had borne with him an infectious will to win. There are candidates who, at crucial moments, are to be found in their dressing rooms, reciting their lines, "To be or not to be, that is the question," as if they expect the playgoers to hear them from there. This was not John Kennedy's way. "In the words of Edmund Burke," he had exclaimed to the Senate on 19 February 1959, "we sit on a conspicuous stage, and the whole world marks our demeanor." That was John Kennedy's way. "The whole world marks our demeanor": to the very end, it might have been the motto on his crest.

But what did it all mean? We have been told by Theodore
Sorensen that, on the first morning of the Cuba missile
crisis, John Kennedy asked for copies of his previous statements
on Cuba. This is an interesting piece of information. Words
can bind, we are being told, which is something of a reassurance. But they can bind in many ways, not least unconsciously, without the politician having to send for copies of
his previous speeches. It is part of the argument in this and
the succeeding chapter that John Kennedy, by the style and
rhetoric of his campaign, bound himself to a view of politics
of which there had been little hint in his earlier career, and
from which he could not as President escape: a view of his
capacity, of the capacity of the Presidency, of the capacity of
the country, each sustaining the other, which imprisoned him.

The remarkable feature of most of the accounts of the
campaign—including *The Making of the President* 1960 by
Theodore H. White—is that one would barely know from them
that candidates say anything, that they make utterances, and
that these are not always the same. They may seem the same,
but they seldom altogether are. The speeches of John Kennedy
and Richard Nixon during the campaign of 1960 have been
conveniently collected in two thick volumes, each of approxi-
mately twelve hundred pages, issued by the Committee on
Commerce of the Senate. Moreover, the television appearances
of the two candidates occupy a third volume of almost seven
hundred pages. These are primary documents; no other words
about the campaign are as important as these; and, if Theodore
White had been truly writing about the *making*, instead of
merely the *electing*, of a President, he would have given them
more than a glance. For, as one reads the utterances of John
Kennedy, one can observe the way in which *he was making
himself* the kind of President he would be. As he said in

Chicago on 4 November 1960: "I believe the level of the daily speeches tells you something about the level of future White House operations."

He took all but infinite trouble over his speeches. He understood the power of words. He did not use them slackly; he used them self-consciously. For the purpose, he assembled a large team of speech writers—really only two, says Theodore Sorensen, himself and Richard Goodwin, the rest being only speech drafters—one must be careful in these matters not to offend—behind whom stood an even larger team of expert advisers; but he remained master of the process. Even on 31 October, after ten months of uninterrupted campaigning, he issued in Philadelphia a comprehensive statement of his views on the balance of payments problem, having himself hammered out the final draft, we are told, after a long night's work with John Kenneth Galbraith at the other end of the telephone. In more senses than one, he was not a man lost for words. He used them well to his purpose.

Some of the assistants in the campaigns of the brothers have claimed that they devised a new approach to the electors, even that they revolutionised the art of campaigning. This is untrue; the Kennedys merely pushed conventional methods to their limit, which again has been quite a conventional thing to do since the days of Julius Caesar. But, even if it were true, it would be a strange boast. It is not any techniques which were used which make the campaign debates between Abraham Lincoln and Stephen Douglas so memorable even today: debates which flashed across the country, although it was only a campaign for a seat in the Senate, as if they had been carried by television. It is their words; it is the argument. The excellence lies in them. Indeed, it is my reading of the campaign of 1960 that the techniques may have held John Kennedy back. Such

was the clutter and the visibility of his entourage that he
sometimes appeared not to stand in his own right at all. He
was drenched in his family, and drowned in his aides, until
the voters must have wondered if he existed apart from them,
or was merely, as was in fact suggested, of their manufacture.

To achieve the nomination was a genuine triumph. But what
has to be explained, after the nomination, is the narrowness of
his victory in the election. It was the end of two terms of
Republican administration, a natural time for a change; the
two victories of the Republican Party in 1952 and 1956 had
been largely personal, and now the man who had won them
was withdrawing; the mood of the country, as we have seen,
was one of unease at the direction, or absence of direction, in
which it was moving; the Republican candidate was not a
formidable opponent, and it was never entirely clear from start
to finish whether Dwight Eisenhower recognised him. In short,
once John Kennedy had been nominated, and become the stand-
ard-bearer of his party, he should have won substantially. As
it was, he barely scraped home; and, in terms of the popular
vote, it could be argued that he did not even manage that.
This haunted him throughout his Presidency: the knowledge,
as he often admitted, that Nelson Rockefeller would have defeated him. Indeed, if the Republicans had carried the body
of Dwight Eisenhower prone through the streets, as they might
well have done if a third term had been possible, the people
would have shouted their huzzas once more, and John Kennedy
would have been a loser.

The basis of the electoral strategy of John Kennedy was the
early start, the campaign-before-the-campaign. In itself, this
was not a new strategy, and it is always necessary, in observing
the methods of the Kennedys, not to imagine that what they

did with superior organisation or unusual self-consciousness had not been done before. When Caesar and Pompey and Crassus made their compact, they were planning for elections many years ahead. It is possible, all the same, that the early start made by John Kennedy after the election of 1956 may have had some—at least temporary—effect on the nominating process. As soon as the election of 1968 was over, both Edmund Muskie and George McGovern began their campaigns for the election of 1972, and the already lengthy process by which the American people elect a President seems to be in danger of becoming continuous. Not only is the early candidacy a wasteful indulgence; it concentrates attention on Presidential electoral politics when they ought to be forgotten.

There may have always been a sense in which every politician is perpetually campaigning, but with John Kennedy this natural inclination became a method. He had started early in 1946 in order to capture his first Congressional seat, "months before the regular campaign season opened"; and, as he prepared to challenge Henry Cabot Lodge in 1952 for a seat in the Senate, this was again his main weapon. As James MacGregor Burns records: "The Congressman would fly up to Boston late on Thursday for a long weekend on the hustings. . . . [and] the little party might criss-cross the state several times in one weekend. . . . 'I'll bet he talked to at least a million people and shook hands with seven hundred and fifty thousand,' [Frank] Morrisey said later. . . . By early 1952, Kennedy had stumped in almost all the 351 cities and towns of Massachusetts. . . . [By August 1952], he had a network of 286 'secretaries,' backed by several thousand workers." The reward was victory, narrow but impressive, against an entrenched opponent. The cost of the entire campaign, according to this official biographer, was "probably more than half a million dollars"; and this in turn is probably an underestimate. The expense of the weekend visits alone, "the little party" criss-crossing the state for at least two years, is not difficult to calculate.

We may as well deal with the question of money at the beginning, and then not return to it. The influence of great wealth in American politics bewilders an outsider only a little more than the refusal of the American people, at least until recently, to be seriously worried about it. In the early spring of 1968, the editor of a British newspaper asked Robert Kennedy why the American people were so willing, if not actually eager, to put their trust in multi-millionaires. "Because they think that we don't have to cheat," came the reply; and it may well be the case. In a country which takes the corruption of its politics for granted, the populace may indeed be persuaded that at least the Rockefellers and the Kennedys, the Roosevelts and the Harrimans, have nothing to gain; although this does not meet the reasonable presumption that they have something to keep. No matter in how unsavoury a manner the money was originally made, it has been inherited, and is therefore cleansed of its taint, an odd notion for a republic to entertain, and one which would have met with short shrift from David Lloyd George when in 1909 he crushed the political power of the landowners in Britain by the swift device of punitive taxation, a remedy which is available to the American people whenever they choose to employ it.

This is not the place to discuss the problem; one must take the situation as it exists. Given the cost of politics in America, and given a system of taxation which seems actually to have been designed to assist in the preservation of large accumu-lations of wealth, it would be naïve to pretend to any shock at the vast sums which John Kennedy disbursed in all his election campaigns, particularly in 1960, as it also would be naïve to be dumbfounded at the proportionately vast sums which Nelson Rockefeller distributes every four years so that the voters of New York may have the opportunity to touch their caps to him. But it is equally naïve to ask us to accept as the truth, the whole truth, and nothing but the truth, the estimates of election expenditures that are given to us by the Kennedys and their supporters. There is ample evidence that in all of their campaigns each of the three brothers has spent not only substantially more than his rival, but also substantially more than he has acknowledged in his official returns. In an important sense, the family bought its political influence.

What is, and what is not, an election expenditure? This is difficult enough to determine even during the period of the actual campaign. But what of the campaign-before-the-campaign? When we are told that John Kennedy began his campaign for re-election to the Senate in 1958 the day after his 1952 campaign ended, much more is meant than the usually desultory ways in which politicians usually nurse their constituencies. Five determined approaches were used during the next six years, including an annual report, sent to every constituent, recounting the legislative and administrative performance of the senator in protecting and advancing the interests of the state. Theodore Sorensen and his colleagues justified the use of Congressional franking privileges for this document on the ground that a legislator must account for his stewardship to his constituents; and when they were unable to find a suitable quotation to support this interpretation they invented one and attributed it to a Founding Father who was unidentified. Certainly, they would have looked in vain for such a justification in the first inaugural address of George Washington, who declined as "inapplicable to myself any share in the personal

emoluments which may be indispensably included in a permanent provision for the executive department," and prayed that
"the pecuniary estimates for the station in which I am placed
may . . . be limited to such actual expenditures as the public
good may require."

The real advantage which the wealth of the Kennedy family
conferred—and still confers—is not that John Kennedy necessarily spent so much more than his opponents, although he
did, but that he knew that as much as he might ever want
was always there at a moment's call, should he need it. In
other words, no planning to meet any possible eventuality had
to consider whether the money which it would require would
be available; and, if an unforeseen situation occurred, demanding unforeseen expenditure, it could be undertaken without a
moment's hesitation. This was of vital importance in a campaign which was, from the beginning, based on the strategy
of entering all the primaries, winning each of them, and so
going to Los Angeles to be nominated on the first ballot. Only
a very wealthy candidate can adopt such a strategy as early
as did John Kennedy, and then take the measures to make it
succeed. This was the freedom and the advantage which his
wealth gave him, far more important than the fact that his
family was capable of such a device as forming the Ken-Air
Corporation to purchase a $385,000 aircraft, which they then
leased to him at the rate of $1.75 a mile. He could plan ahead
to meet any eventuality.

In the issue of *Life* of 27 May 1966, Richard B. Solley
wrote that the Kennedys "are the best example of the contemporary trend toward very rich men spending vast sums of
their own money, not in order to manipulate governments
behind the secnes, as in the past, but to seek power in public
office." The significance of this trend can be exaggerated, if

only because very rich corporations are today more powerful in American political life than very rich men; and, since it is not yet legal for a very rich corporation to run for public office, it still uses its money to manipulate governments. Nevertheless, no one who knows the history of the Roman Republic will discount the influence of private fortunes which are used for personal advancement. They alter the character of politics by personalising them too much. In the vocabulary of today, the image becomes more important than the issue.

By far the best account of a Kennedy campaign is that provided in *Kennedy Campaigning* by Murray Burton Levin, a political scientist with an intimate knowledge of Massachusetts politics, in which he analyses Edward Moore Kennedy's campaign for a Senate seat in 1962. At the end of a book which is rich in detail, and whose insights may legitimately be transferred to a national level, he reaches his conclusions. The danger of the Kennedy method, supported by the Kennedy fortune, is that the "efficiency, grandiosity, and opulence of the campaign are taken as indications of the candidate's competence." No one who has read the day-to-day reporting of the 1960 campaign of John Kennedy can doubt that this happened. There was hardly a reporter who was not impressed and even invigorated by the scale and the smoothness of the operation. Here was a candidate who could command; why should he not as President command as well? Indeed, even the candidate himself appears to have drawn the same lesson, as is suggested by a remark which he made to Theodore Sorensen during his first months in office, referring to the previous year's campaign: "Last year, in its way, was a pretty tough year, too. I think we can handle whatever hits us." This equation of the qualities of a campaigner with the qualities of a statesman can only be regarded as banal; yet it was exactly this expectation of superior competence which was nourished by the dynamism of his campaigning, and the fortune which made it possible.

The method which the Kennedys used in their campaigns, Murray Levin continues, "may well mean that the distinction between the true and the false, the real and the unreal, the image and the ideal, can no longer be made," and he quotes a sentence from Daniel J. Boorstin: "In this new world, where almost anything can be true, the socially rewarded art is that of making things seem true." These are complaints, in part, against contemporary society as such, and the power of "communications" within it. But no one who cares for the health of American democracy can study the election campaigns of John Kennedy in 1960, or of Edward Kennedy in 1962, or of Robert Kennedy in 1964, each of them overcoming particular disadvantages including that of unusual youth, without wondering at the power of a private fortune to purchase the means by which, in a modern society, "making things seem true" can become an electorally rewarded art.

Whether between 1952 and 1958 on the state level, or between 1956 and 1960 on the national level, the campaign-before-the-campaign of John Kennedy demanded wealth and, with the aid of the wealth, an organisation which no other candidate could emulate. Apart from those who had been with him all the way—Theodore Sorensen, Kenneth O'Donnell, Lawrence O'Brien—he began hiring his campaign staff as soon as the 1958 Massachusetts election was out of the way. Like a fisher of men, he called them away from the jobs which they already held, and they answered the call. He was not concerned only with the highest echelon. As early as January 1959, meeting Jerry Bruno by chance in the underground electric railroad of the Senate office, he remembered him from a

meeting in Wisconsin two years earlier, asked him to his Georgetown home the following morning, and there suggested that
"I go to work full time for him, organizing Wisconsin in case
he decided to run in that state's primary. There was no doubt
that he was running for President."

There was no doubt. He was all over the place. In the
spring of 1959, for example, he went to Hawaii to seek its
votes in the Democratic Convention which was still eighteen
months ahead, and he summoned Lawrence H. Fuchs, who
was in the Islands completing research for a book on their
social and political history, to an audience before he left:

> Kennedy knew me slightly, but he knew my politics well. I was
> a liberal, with political friends in New York City and New
> England.
>
> We talked animatedly for more than half an hour in the
> Senator's hotel room. He sat hunched over the edge of his bed,
> occasionally getting up to attend to a packing chore. He thrust
> questions at me like rifle shots. Why was so-and-so opposed to
> his candidacy? Why was a certain newspaper critical?

The scene, as Lawrence Fuchs recites it in *John F. Kennedy
and American Catholicism*, was constantly repeated, and one
can only wonder what other candidate, eighteen months before the party convention, would have been found putting his
questions to a professor who was completing a book eventually
to be called *Hawaii Pono: A Social History*. He was indeed
"one hell of a candidate"; with money.

The fundamental relationship in American politics at the
state and city level is that between client and patron: favours
are sought, often material ones, and the politician who can
promise to supply them is supported, step by step, from the
ward committee to the state convention, the promise of favours

being exchanged at each stage. At the national level in the nominating process, although the relationship between client and patron is not absent, it is no longer the only, or the most, important one. Politics have at this point moved to a grander scale, and the relationship which counts most is that which the Romans called *amicitia* or "friendship." The best description of it is given by Lily Ross Taylor in her rewarding work, *Party Politics in the Age of Caesar,* where she in fact makes the comparison with the nominating process in the United States today: "*Amicitia* in politics was a responsible relationship. A man expected from his friends, not only support at the polls, but aid in the perils of public life, the unending prosecutions brought from political motives by his personal enemies, his *inimici,* his rivals, in the contests for office and the manifold rewards of public life. Friendship for the man in politics was a sacred agreement. Cicero, in writing to Crassus to clinch their reconciliation, urged Crassus to consider his letter a treaty." Few men in the modern age have understood, and have used, *amicitia* as brilliantly as did John Kennedy in 1960.

He demanded *amicitia* of those with whom he treated, and he returned it. He understood that the sacredness of the agreement lay in the exchange of trust, and that the exchange of trust was made on the basis, on both sides, of a clear-sighted assessment of the realities of a situation. He was a master at this level, and Theodore Sorensen does not assist the reputation of his hero by describing it with a mawkishness which is wholly inappropriate, as when he says that he would describe as "fair" what others consider to be "ruthless." It is meaningless to say that when John Kennedy directly threatened to challenge Michael V. DiSalle, the governor of Ohio, within his own state, his only interest was to demonstrate that the voters in that state supported him. He was twisting the governor's arm in a lock. Cicero and Crassus were not playing marbles, any more than were John Kennedy and Michael DiSalle, or John Kennedy and Charles Buckley as they pulled together 104½ votes in the New York delegation, or John Kennedy and David Lawrence, who held the votes of Pennsylvania back from him until the last moment. Fair or ruthless? It is as absurd to ask the question about John Kennedy as it would have been to ask it about Franklin Roosevelt.

Arthur Schlesinger, as the author of an unfinished biography of Franklin Roosevelt, is at least prepared to admit that the hero of his middle age was as politically adept as the hero of his youth. Pointing out that the selection of a Vice-President "was not a choice Kennedy could sensibly make before the convention, if only for the reason that he might have to use the second place on the ticket, in the manner of Franklin Roosevelt in 1932, as a counter in his own fight for the presidential nomination," he then adds that John Kennedy "had nevertheless set forth certain general specifications." It is a gentle phrase. As he goes on to relate, John Kennedy had on 9 June 1960 told Joseph Rauh, a man of strong liberal attachments, "that his preference would be Hubert Humphrey or 'another midwestern liberal'"; and not much later he "amplified" this—the credit for the word again belongs to Arthur Schlesinger—on "Meet the Press," when he confided that "I would say it would be somebody from the Middle West or the Far West"; and about the same time again, he had taken Clark Clifford aside, and said of Stuart Symington, "Stuart has run a clean campaign, and I'd like to talk with you about having him on the ticket" as a liberal from the Middle West. But this is only a fraction of the story. As far back as February 1960, at a press conference with Grant

Sawyer, the governor of Nevada, sitting beside him, he had said that he would like a Western governor on the ticket with him. A month later in Kansas, he had told reporters that George Docking, then the governor of that state, stood "near the top" of any list of Vice-Presidential possibilities. Moreover, the same Western message was conveyed to Henry Jackson of Washington, to Clinton Anderson of New Mexico, to Clair Engle of California, and to Stewart Udall of Arizona; and the same Midwestern message to Herschel Loveless of Iowa, and to Orville Freeman of Minnesota; and he was still using this counter freely during the early days at Los Angeles.

In the event, of course, he chose Lyndon Johnson, to whom no such message had been conveyed before the Democratic Convention, and who came from neither the Middle West nor the Far West, but from the South. Yet this choice was crucial to his victory, probably the single most important factor in making it possible. As even Theodore Sorensen admits, if the Democratic Party had not won back Louisiana and Texas, and kept the Carolinas, which were expected to defect, Richard Nixon would have won the election, and it was Lyndon Johnson who was responsible for salvaging these southern states. As the candidate for the Vice-Presidency, he fought a campaign which could not have been more hard-working or more selfless, and he did not put a foot wrong; and his leader could therefore all but ignore the South, where he might have entangled himself badly. John Kennedy had formed an *amicitia* of great promise; in Roman terms, he had secured at least a part of a province without using any of his own legions.

"He outsmarted all the pros," said Carmine DeSapio, explaining his own loss of influence in New York. But the whole point is that he had acted throughout as a "pro," and had used conventional methods. He did not defeat Carmine De-

Sapio by relying on Eleanor Roosevelt or Herbert Lehman, the Reform Movement or the Liberal Party; he defeated him by making allies with Charles Buckley and Peter Crotty, whom Arthur Schlesinger properly describes as "old-line bosses in the Bronx and Buffalo." The examples of his conventional approach to politics can be multiplied; and what has to be explained is how he managed at the same time to create the image of a man who was breaking new ground, that he was not as other politicians.

For the moment, however, one must try to explain the mastery of the conventional political process by a candidate who was both unusually young and relatively inexperienced. Lily Ross Taylor describes with considerable verve the education and apprenticeship to which the sons of patrician families in Rome were subjected in order that they might enter public life; for it was assumed, as the saying went, that they had been elected to the consulship in their cradles, much as Joseph Kennedy assumed that one, if not all, of his sons had been born to be President. In Rome, we learn, "The boy's entire education was planned for public life. The chief emphasis was on physical fitness, training of voice and diction, familiarity with public affairs, and the development of ready ease in speaking. To accomplish this last aim, the boy had to store his mind. . . . As the boy grew older, he had daily exercises in speaking under Greek rhetors, who were useful for technique but could of course teach their Roman masters nothing about statecraft. To learn that art, the boy was taken to the Forum to hear the public speeches and orations in the law courts, and he sat at the feet of great Romans who had achieved renown in public affairs. . . . Along with the young man's practice in speaking went his first military service, which began when he was seventeen."

He was then ready for his first candidacy for a minor office, the purpose of which was that "the young noble had to make himself known to the electorate, perhaps to journey about Italy and become acquainted with the men of the municipalities, particularly with the richest men, who were most likely to come to Rome to vote." From then on, he advanced up the ladder, from quaestor to praetor to consul, and whatever might lie beyond, on the assumption that he had already accumulated enough wealth to support a public life, for his house in Rome, as Cicero emphasised, "should be a seemly mansion, with plenty of space in it," where he had to be ready in the morning "to greet the family clients and retainers and friends who came for the daily *salutatio*, and in the Forum he had to appear with a retinue and be always at the call of any friend who might need him."

No one who has read a word of the upbringing and education that Joseph Kennedy gave his sons—and the story is too familiar to repeat any of its details—can fail to respond to this description. Joseph Kennedy was hardly a patrician, but he brought up his boys as if they were the sons of one. When one considers how John F. Fitzgerald and Patrick J. Kennedy pulled themselves out of the tribal life of East Boston into the wider world beyond it, the one becoming the first son of Irish parents to be elected mayor of the city and even buying a home in Concord, and the other sending his son, Joseph Kennedy, to the Latin School and entering him at Harvard College, one realises what an important reflection of the history of the United States is to be found in the story of this one family. But nothing that they did was as calculated as the preparation— the Roman preparation—for public life that was given to his sons by Joseph Kennedy; and, when his second son moved towards the Presidency between 1946 and 1960, by a progress as rapid and as steady as that from quaestor to praetor to consul, he did so, not merely as a professional politician, but as a patrician among professional politicians. The skill was there, learned from rhetors, at the hands of great men, and in the Forum; but so was the patrician command.

Since the time of Andrew Jackson, says Murray Levin, "remarkably few distinguished American families have trained their youth for political careers": in Massachusetts, the Adams family, the Lodges, the McCormacks, and the Kennedys; in New York, the Roosevelts and the Wagners; in Ohio, the Tafts; in Virginia, the Byrds; in Louisiana, the Longs; and with that the catalogue is all but exhausted. There can be little doubt that the self-conscious transformation of the Kennedy family into a political dynasty within the space of three generations had a deep effect on the American people. It was possible to see where they had come from; yet they had travelled further than most. They had begun with no advantages, yet they already seemed to be born to rule. The craving of the American people to be governed by men who are both Everyman and yet better than Everyman could hardly have been better satisfied. Their expectations would be high: such a family, at once themselves and more than themselves, could be expected not to fail them; they would give it their allegiance.

Nourished and educated to such a position, John Kennedy's conventional approach to politics hardly requires an explanation, and it cannot be exaggerated. "Reluctance to amend the Constitution," he had told the Senate on 21 May 1954, "is one of our most valuable safeguards and bulwarks of stability," and the measure which he was opposing was a proposal to extend the right to vote to citizens at the age of eighteen.

Two years later, on 20 March 1956, he made another long speech in the Senate, this time opposing a reform of the Electoral college: ". . . it is not only the unit vote for the Presidency we are talking about, but a whole solar system of governmental power. If it is proposed to change the balance of power of one of the elements of the solar system, it is necessary to consider all the others." His eye was already on the Presidency: he wished to seek it within the context of the conventional politics in which he had been reared.

It might have been either Cicero or Edmund Burke who was speaking that day, as the periods rolled forth from John Kennedy with a traditional conservative defence: "Why should we be in such a hurry to adopt a drastic constitutional amendment which most of the voters do not know we are considering, and which they certainly have not demanded. . . . The world situation does not permit us to take the risk of experimenting with the constitutional system that is fundamental to our strength and leadership. . . . There is obviously little to gain—but much to lose—by tampering with the Constitution at this time. . . . It seems to me that Falkland's definition of 'conservatism' is quite appropriate: 'When it is not necessary to change, it is necessary not to change.' . . . I am very strongly opposed to any change in the Constitution at this time. The present system has served us well." This liking for the conventional processes of politics was deep within him; yet this was not the image of him during his Presidency, and his political method, as has been suggested, was to transcend these processes. We are at the beginning of a puzzle.

He was conventional as a candidate in small ways, yet again managed to give the impression of unconventionality, of trying new ways. In its issue of 4 April 1960, *Time* commented on the "saturation campaign," calling it a "political wonder," which he had conducted in the Wisconsin primary; as it pointed out, few towns with a population of more than three hundred were not visited by some member of the Kennedy family. But the wonder lay in the wealth and the organisation, depending on the wealth, and the family cohesion, providing the wealth, which made the saturation possible; not in any new method that he was employing. Above all, the campaign-before-the-campaign now began to tell. The importance of this preparation was obvious everywhere. In 1959, John Kennedy had made two visits to Indiana, and had finally chosen two men to be the co-chairmen of his state organisation: Marshall Kizer, a state senator from Plymouth, and Albert Deluse, one of the party bosses from Indianapolis. (This division of responsibility between two chairmen was wholly characteristic.) The organisation remained underground, keeping in touch with the headquarters in Washington by telephone; and in the course of one month, Lawrence O'Brien paid eight visits to the state. At last, early in February, John Kennedy announced in Gary that he would enter the Indiana primary; and immediately the underground organisation sprang into open life in every corner of the state, under efficient local leadership, Marshall Kizer and Albert Deluse having earlier briefed forty pro-Kennedy politicians in the Claypool Hotel in Indianapolis. Again, the operation was a "political wonder"; again, it was wholly conventional, except for the driving attention to detail.

He was a candidate, in most respects, like any candidate. We are told by both Theodore Sorensen and Arthur Schlesinger that he avoided the corny gesture and the unnecessary gimmick. It is simply untrue, both of him and of his staff, both in the campaign for the nomination and in the campaign for the Presidency. Those who think that his campaigns did not de-

scend into vulgarity need only read Jerry Bruno's account in
The Advance Man, but the evidence is there, in the day-to-day
accounts in the newspapers and the newsmagazines at the
time: whether, as Murray Kempton reported in his column on
19 October 1960, when he wore his Legion cap at the American
Legion Convention in Miami, "and apologized for having said
in 1949 that the Legion hadn't had a respectable idea for
fifteen years"; or when, as *Time* reported in its issue of 8
February 1960, he visited St. Anselm's College in Manchester,
New Hampshire, and "the college kids dragged out a reluctant donkey (rented for $20 by the efficient Kennedy or-
ganization)"; or when, as the New York *Times* described on
27 February 1960, he told seventy-five farmers at Bloomer,
Wisconsin, that "the American cow is the 'foster mother' of the
human race and a great asset to the nation"; and the examples
could be many times multiplied. This is the stuff of election-
eering, and there can be no complaint against it. The complaint
is against the cultivation of the myth that he conducted his
campaign on so much loftier a level than other politicians, that
he never stooped to conquer, that he was always free of pretence
and humbug.

The pretence was sometimes calculated deceit. On 10 October
1960, a correspondent of *Newsweek* who had just been assigned
to cover John Kennedy's campaign reported: "Newcomers to
the Kennedy entourage receive a mysterious piece of advice:
'Watch out for the "jumpers."' The mystery clears the moment
the Kennedy motorcade gets under way. As Kennedy's car
passes by, the women lining the parade route begin jumping
up and down. Age makes no difference—the jumpers may be
young schoolgirls, mothers with infants, middle-aged matrons,
even prim old ladies. In addition to the standard category of

'jumpers,' there are the 'double-leapers,' women who jump together while holding hands. Then there are the 'clutchers,'
women who cross their arms and hug themselves and scream,
'He looked at me! He looked at me!' Finally, there are the
'runners'—women, sometimes with infants, who break through
the police lines, and run after Kennedy's car." Who break
through the police lines? Let us go to the account of Jerry
Bruno himself, who organised such demonstrations:

> It happened in Detroit. . . . As soon as the plane landed and
> Kennedy stepped out of the doorway, the crowd began to push
> forward. They knocked down the snow fence and swarmed all
> over Kennedy. . . .
> "My God," Kennedy said afterward, "I can't believe that crowd.
> How did you do it?"
> I couldn't believe it either. But it looked so good on film
> and in the press that from then on we made sure that crowds
> surged over Kennedy. I'd have two men holding a rope by
> an airport or along a motorcade; then, at the right time, they'd
> just drop the rope and the crowd would rush close to Kennedy.
> Once again, it was one of those things that just happened.

It did not just happen; it was engineered. Instead of quieten-
ing the hysteria, they stimulated it, and it seems not to have
occurred to these advance men that one result of such hysteria
is, in history, a fast assassination.

Again, in *Kennedy or Nixon: Does It Make any Difference?*,
which he published during the campaign itself, Arthur Schlesinger offers a contrast between the two candidates, which
is repeated in both his and Theodore Sorensen's biographies:
"Nixon . . . is an expert practitioner of 'false personalization.'
He imports histrionics into politics. His rhetoric is vulgar. He
exhorts, denounces, parades emotional irrelevances, even weeps.
Kennedy's political manner, on the other hand, is studiously

unemotional, impersonal, anti-histrionic. He has no scruples about using his family as part of his political organization, but he does not lug them into his serious speeches. Let us try a test: can anyone imagine Kennedy giving the Checkers speech?" Let us, indeed, try a test. On 20 September 1960, John Kennedy and his wife were interviewed by Charles Collingwood on CBS-TV, at 10 P.M. It was a serious political appearance; he was to talk of the policies which he would pursue. At the beginning, a mention was made of their daughter, and the following scene was played:

> MRS. KENNEDY: . . . Would you like to see her?
> MR. COLLINGWOOD: Oh, I'd like to very much. Are you sure it is all right for us to intrude on the young lady?
> MRS. KENNEDY: Well, we will see, Charles, keep your fingers crossed.
> MR. COLLINGWOOD: Hello, Caroline.
> MRS. KENNEDY: Can you say hello?
> CAROLINE: Hello.
> MRS. KENNEDY: Here, do you want to sit up in bed with me?
> MR. COLLINGWOOD: Isn't she a darling?
> MRS. KENNEDY: Now, look at the three bears.
> CAROLINE: What is the dolly's name?
> MRS. KENNEDY: All right, what is the dolly's name?
> CAROLINE: I didn't name her yet.
> MRS. KENNEDY: You didn't name her yet.
> CAROLINE: No.
> MRS. KENNEDY: When are you going to name her?
> MR. COLLINGWOOD: Is that her favorite?
> MRS. KENNEDY: It is her favorite as of this minute.
> MR. COLLINGWOOD: Oh, just like all little girls.
> MRS. KENNEDY: What do you think you will name her tomorrow? What color are her shoes?
> CAROLINE: White. Like mine.
> MRS. KENNEDY: Like yours. What color is your dress?
> CAROLINE: Pink.

> MRS. KENNEDY: And why has she got a hat on?
>
> CAROLINE: [Indistinct]
>
> MR. COLLINGWOOD: I didn't quite get that.
>
> MRS. KENNEDY: She has to have a hat on because the wind blows her hair.
>
> MR. COLLINGWOOD: Oh, Caroline, you are a very, very pretty little girl and I should think, Mrs. Kennedy, that the proud father would get mighty lonesome for her when he is out on the campaign trail.
>
> MRS. KENNEDY: Well, I think he does. We will go down and join him now.
>
> MR. COLLINGWOOD: Oh, that will be a treat for him.
>
> MRS. KENNEDY: Shall we go see daddy?
>
> CAROLINE: Yes.
>
> MRS. KENNEDY: Can you take us to the parlor?
>
> CAROLINE: Yes.
>
> MRS. KENNEDY: And we will go see daddy?
>
> CAROLINE: Yes.
>
> MRS. KENNEDY: All right, let's go see daddy.

As a build-up to a serious political interview at a peak viewing hour, one has to admit that it had its own tension. It was not a solitary occasion. On 2 November 1960, Jacqueline Kennedy and Henry Fonda looked through the family photograph album and ran some home movies before John Kennedy spoke seriously of politics, and the manner was much the same:

> MRS. KENNEDY: . . . Caroline Bouvier Kennedy, aged eighteen months.
>
> MR. FONDA: Formal attire!
>
> MRS. KENNEDY: That's when she was christened.
>
> MR. FONDA: Ah! That's darling! The Senator performing a little additional duty.

Was the Checkers speech any worse? Such things, it may be said, are a part of campaigning, and one can agree. But why pretend, then, that John Kennedy loftily eschewed them, and was always the parfit, gentil knight?

It is now a commonplace to describe John Kennedy as a conventional politician; and in many respects the observation is true, as this chapter has briefly demonstrated. But that can be only the beginning of our inquiry. For, if he had been regarded as a conventional politician at the time, his policies would have been more severely questioned. People would neither have expected so much of him—of the Presidency— of politics; nor would they have followed him so readily in some of his adventures. But, while employing the conventional processes of politics, especially in the conduct of his domestic policy, he gave the impression that they could be transcended, and that he was in fact transcending them. This was one cause of the geological fault in his political method which we noticed at the beginning. A conventional politician, he was nevertheless impatient of the conventional limits of politics. Such a politician would inevitably be driven from improvisation to improvisation, on the one hand, and to spectacular displays of his personal leadership, on the other; never adequately employing the political resources of his country.

In this chapter we have been considering only his performance as a candidate; yet it is not as a conventional candidate that he is remembered today. Part of the explanation lies simply in the attractiveness and the energy and the good humour of the personality; he was without question "one hell of a candidate," as all the brothers have been. If he crisscrossed Massachusetts in 1946, Edward Kennedy did no less in 1962, until one of his opponents exclaimed: "He's been in places like Gill. Who ever goes to Gill? This guy went to Gill to see one delegate they've got there. Most people wouldn't know where Gill was, including Eddie McCormack, including Foster Furcolo, including John Kennedy, or you. . . ." But such energy, such attention to detail, does not account for the impression which John Kennedy left merely by his campaigning. For the deeper explanation, we must turn to the words, for they were indeed his own instrument: forged by himself, no matter how many speech writers or speech drafters or advance men worked at the anvil with him.

CHAPTER FOUR

The Binding Promise

THEY WERE JOHN KENNEDY'S words, and we should treat them as such, with a single reservation. It is difficult to read the almost confessional writings of Theodore Sorensen, or listen to him make a political speech of his own as it was possible to do during his election campaign in 1970, without realising that, in spite of an apparently taciturn nature and a lack of flamboyance appropriate to his Unitarian inheritance, he is a passionate man, and deeply emotional. No one can question that he had a "special relationship" with John Kennedy, which was of importance to them both; but, for the moment, it is enough to suggest that he put something of his own self into the words which he prepared, which were as often as not accepted, and which were then uttered with an unusual command. Arthur Schlesinger may say that, in his public appearance, John Kennedy was "unemotional, impersonal, anti-histrionic"; but this is untrue. A statesman who can travel to West Berlin and cry on its walls, *"Ich bin ein Berliner,"* is being emotional *and* personal *and* histrionic. Many of the speeches over the years, both as candidate and as President, were grandiloquent; and at times, as one reads them again or listens to them on a recording, one stops to ask if the words were in fact his—the words of so cool a man—or were they

Theodore Sorensen's, supplying a need? It is a question to which it will be necessary to return.

On 2 January 1960, John Fitzgerald Kennedy, the junior senator from Massachusetts, at the age of forty-two years, announced that he was a candidate for the nomination of the Democratic Party for the office of President of the United States. At the time, the American people had their noses buried in *The Ugly American,* which they mistakenly read as an essay in self-mortification. Those who looked up from its pages on that day saw a strikingly un-ugly man, whose bearing already displayed what Lincoln Kirstein was to note on the day of the Inauguration, an authority at once "inbred and detached." But he was not yet comfortable with his themes. In preparation for his announcement, he had written the day before: "I believe that we Americans are ready to be called to greatness." The implication of his candidacy was that he was ready to issue the call. But in those nine pages which he wrote on New Year's Day for inclusion in a collection of his earlier speeches, it was clear that he had not yet found the words or the voice or the accent; these were to come later.

It was an important document which he was composing, for autographed copies of the book, *The Strategy of Peace,* were to be mailed to tens of thousands of party leaders and office holders, labour leaders and fund raisers, delegates and supporters, whose names had been collected and filed in the previous years; and then, in another mass mailing, to more thousands of editors and publishers, scientists and clergymen, and other leaders of opinion. But the candidate who, a mere seven months later, would electrify the Democratic Convention with his acceptance speech, could in January find only words which trudged. If the country continued on its present path, its fortunes "would trend in the direction of a slide downhill, into dust, dullness, languor, decay." The words are as dull thuds. He dismissed the Eisenhower years with a sophomore's reliance on heavy repetition: "attitudes, platitudes, beatitudes."

All of this changed as he campaigned. Whether it was the crowds, whether it was the activity, whether it was the exhilaration, whether it was the growing sense of an ambition about to be realised, he developed into a formidable popular orator. It has happened to other candidates during their campaigns, in many countries and in other times, as if standing on "a conspicuous stage," their appeal required to be national and not sectional, they are transformed in part, and in part transform themselves. If one were to put it slyly, one would suggest that they begin to believe what they say. No political journalist who has followed such opponents as Winston Churchill and Aneurin Bevan, Charles de Gaulle and Gaston Deferre, on the stump in great campaigns, can doubt that the interaction between candidate and crowd is of supreme importance to the candidate. It is out of this communion between the candidate and the crowd that the national leader is born; and nothing will replace it. However many millions of eyes and ears a candidate may reach on television, not a single voice reaches him. It is while he is on the stump that a candidate finds himself, that he becomes who he is, so to speak; and of no candidates has this ever been more clear than of John Kennedy as he stormed the country in 1960, and of Robert Kennedy when he took to the streets in 1968.

The first important speech which John Kennedy made in 1960 was not to a popular audience, but to the National Press Club in Washington; with what part of his theme should he begin? He believed that the picture which the press gave of individuals and of events was the picture of them which the people received; he read it assiduously so that he might learn what they were learning. What should he tell the press, then, on 25 January 1960, that it could convey to the people? He would lift his candidacy above the level of a mere candidacy. He had, as *Time* acutely commented at the moment, "worked tirelessly at establishing an image as a strong, tough candidate for the Democratic nomination who would be a strong, tough campaigner in the general election"; and now he "applied an even higher polish to that image, and made a major bid for recognition as one who, if elected, would be a strong, tough President." One way of becoming President is to talk like one.

John Kennedy began to talk in that way to the National Press Club, and then never stopped. His speech was an almost classic recital of the traditional Democratic belief in a strong and active Presidency. He did not have to mention Dwight Eisenhower or Richard Nixon by name; neither of them, for the past or for the future, fitted into the office as he described it. He said that the times and the people demanded "a vigorous proponent of the national interest, not a passive broker for conflicting private interests." He was not satisfied to call the holder of the office simply President, someone who presides, he called him the Chief Executive, someone who acts, and the Commander-in-Chief, someone who orders. "He must above all be the Chief Executive in every sense of the word. He must be prepared to exercise the fullest powers of his office—all that are specified and some that are not." The people demand, he added, "a man capable of acting as the Commander-in-Chief of the grand alliance." This was a sweeping claim; among the purposes which it served, it made any criticism of his youth seem irrelevant and petty. A man of whatever age who could talk of the office which he sought in such terms must be considered ready to hold it.

The phrase—"the fullest powers of his office—all that are specified and some that are not"—was not a sudden thought. Even as a senator, he had not concealed his belief that the unspecified powers of the President were considerable, should be considerable, and ought not to be diminished. In a speech in the Senate on 1 March 1957, on a joint resolution to authorise the President to undertake economic and military co-operation with nations in the general area of the Middle East, in order to assist in the strengthening and defence of their independence, he declared: "It is said that the resolution grants vast powers to the President should he feel an emergency threatens our national security, but practically all constitutional authorities agree that he would possess such power in any event." This is not a claim which would be given a very cordial hearing on the floor of the Senate today, as it tries to retrieve some of the unspecified powers which successive Presidents have exercised since 1941; but it was a claim which was fundamental to the political method of John Kennedy: that the office is, and must be, "the vital center of action in our whole scheme of government." He was still talking of the unspecified powers of the President at the end of the campaign.

From the start to the finish of his campaign, John Kennedy exalted the office of the President, and extended the leadership which it should provide far beyond the constitutional limits of a single country. He may well have been right when he claimed on 3 September 1960, at the International Airport at San Francisco, that the President "is the only one who can speak for the people of the United States," although there used to be a respectable theory that the House of Representatives is the most representative institution in the country. But, on the previous day, at Bangor, Maine, he said that the President "represents all of the people around the world who want to

live in freedom, who look to us for hope and leadership."
There can be no serious objection to the second half of that
statement: many people, then as now, look to the United
States for hope and leadership. But the claim to *represent*
them is an extravagant concept: they did not even have a vote
in the election for which he was conducting his campaign.
Such words cannot be dismissed as if they were only slips
of the tongue.

By his exalted concept of the Presidency, he was inviting
the American people to a most strenuous effort; and there
was scant evidence that they wished to be so excited, to be
wrenched away from their peaceful concerns in order to continue the mission in the world which, they were now being
told, they must pursue. They had to be taught that this was
their wish. The statement which John Kennedy wrote on
New Year's Day was entitled "The Global Challenge"; and
the theme expanded during the months that followed, and
his oratory grew with it. It was still relatively demure on
4 July, in a television broadcast: "For there is a new world
to be won—a world of peace and good will, a world of hope
and abundance; and I want America to lead the way to that
new world." By 17 September, the accent was more martial, as
he declared at Greenville in North Carolina: "Our responsibility is to be the chief defender of freedom at a time when
freedom is under attack all over the globe." Four days later,
at Nashville in Tennessee, he said that this was the substance
of the decision which the voters had to make: "What is at
stake in the election of 1960 is the preservation of freedom
all around the globe." In the issue of *Parade* of 6 November,
he did not appear to find the preservation of freedom a sufficient goal: "In this election," he proclaimed, "the question is

the preservation of civilization." As he put it on the same day
in the Washington *Post*: "The central issue is whether the
United States will actively resume this historic mission," because "the world cannot exist half slave and half free."

Finally, all of this was drawn together in a rich imperial
symbolism, in the November issue of the *Catholic World*:
"Pennsylvania Avenue is no longer a local thoroughfare. It
runs through Paris and London, Ankara and Teheran, New
Delhi and Tokyo. And if Washington is the capital of the
free world, the President must be its leader; our constitution
requires it, our history requires it, our survival requires it";
he must be "a man capable of acting as Commander-in-Chief
of the grand alliance." In short, he had returned to the point
where he had begun in the National Press Club ten months
earlier, to the man and the office. Just as the office must be
"the vital center of action," so he could be heard at the
International Airport at San Francisco on 3 September saying:
"The theme of this campaign is going to be action. . . . I
believe the American people elect a President to act." The
decision of the voters, he said at Portland in Maine on 2 August,
"must make people feel that in the year of 1961 the American
giant began to stir again, the great American boiler to fire
again."

There was nothing manufactured in the exalted vocabulary
which John Kennedy was discovering; it might have been
better if there had been. He was finding himself, as much
as anything else. The idea of a unified national purpose, and
of the leadership which would provide it, was a consistent
part of his political outlook. It is usually unwise to pay too
much attention to the words which a man has uttered in his
youth, but one cannot ignore the general drift of his argument
in *Why England Slept*, a book which he first published as

early as 1940. Most historians today would question his rather
simple explanations of Britain's unpreparedness in 1939, but
that is not our concern. From start to finish, he argued that
Britain's failure to rearm had one primary cause: the lack of
national unity. "To prepare for a war today requires a nation's
united effort," he said; "until this national feeling of unity can
be attained, a democracy is hopelessly outclassed in trying to
compete with a dictatorship. In one country, the effort is
divided and disorganized; in the other, it is united, even though
it is accomplished by propaganda and force." In the end, he
rubbed his point home in startling language:

> The nation had failed to realize that if it hoped to compete
> successfully with a dictatorship on an equal plane, it would have
> to renounce temporarily its democratic privileges. All of its energies
> would have to be molded in one direction, just as all the energies
> of Germany had been molded since 1933. It meant voluntary
> totalitarianism because, after all, the essence of a totalitarian state
> is that the national purpose will not permit group interests to
> interfere with its fulfillment.

One is not for a moment suggesting that there was in John
Kennedy anything which deserved to be called a totalitarian
spirit. But he was not the first dedicated national leader, and
he will not be the last, to listen to the siren of "voluntary
totalitarianism."

It became more and more clear throughout his campaign
that he was asking the American people to submit themselves
to an unusual ordeal. "I think to be an American in the next
decade," he said to a rally of Citizens for Kennedy in New
York on 14 September 1960, "will be a hazardous experience.
We will live on the edge of danger"; and it is sometimes hard
to avoid the feeling that he—and Robert Kennedy—believed
that to "live on the edge of danger" is ennobling both for

individuals and for nations. Danger requires sacrifice; and John
Kennedy did not hesitate to ask it of his countrymen. "I think
the American people," he said in Detroit on 26 August, "are
willing to undergo whatever is necessary for the world's best
defense. They want to know what is needed—they want to
be led by their Commander-in-Chief." He consistently talked
of the Presidency in this manner, as if it were a martial office.
America was at peace, in no "shooting wars"; yet it wished to
be led by its Commander-in-Chief.

To what? To difficulty, to challenge, to confrontation; to
confrontation, in particular, with the Communist world.
Whether at Portland in Oregon on 7 September or at the
Sheraton Park Hotel in Washington on 20 September, he
reiterated his belief that the world cannot exist "half slave
and half free," although that is how it has existed through
most of recorded history. The rhetoric of the Cold War seldom
found more convincing expression. "Across the face of this
globe," he said at Harrisburg, Pennsylvania, on 15 September,
"freedom and Communism are locked in a deadly embrace."
In the October issue of *American Abroad*, he talked of "the
fight between Red imperialism and the world of the freeman";
and at the same time in the *Keystone Catholic Veteran*,
he declared that "the goals of Communism—and its methods
—do not change an iota when Khrushchev talks 'peace.'"
As he had cried on 20 September in his speech in Washington,
"This is no ordinary enemy, and this is no ordinary struggle,"
an observation which he elaborated the following day at the
Tri-Cities Airport at Bristol in Virginia-Tennessee: "Mr.
Khrushchev is not impressed by words, nor is Mr. Castro,
nor are the satellite leaders. They are not impressed by speeches.
They are not impressed by debates. They are impressed by
power. They are impressed by strength." On 24 August, at Al-

exandria, Virginia, he had already declared: ". . . the Communists are determined to destroy us"; and in the issue of *American Abroad* in October he spoke with the disdain of the early John Foster Dulles of a policy of containment:

> Nor is containment an adequate formula by itself for meeting the very active challenge of Communism in the world today. Containment can be one aspect of policy. It is bound to fail if it is the sole policy.
>
> We must move forward to meet Communism, rather than waiting for it to come to us and then reacting to it.
>
> The man who merely builds a fortress of his home will always find in the end that the enemy has devised a way to get in the back door. While we do guard every door, we must move outside the home fortress, and we must challenge the enemy in fields of our own choosing. We must indeed take the initiative again—we must start moving forward again—at home and abroad.

He was advocating a policy of advance.

As a member of the House of Representatives and of the Senate, he had always been a supporter of a vigorous defence policy. During 1948 and 1949, he attacked the administration of Harry Truman for practising economy in the defence establishment, and proposed an Air Force of seventy groups instead of the fifty-five groups which had been requested by Louis Johnson, then the Secretary of Defense. On 16 August 1951, in the House of Representatives, he argued that, "unless Europe is rearmed by the middle of 1952, I think the chances of war are tremendously increased," and on the following day he said that the United States must, if necessary, undertake the task: "Are we going to stop giving Europeans assistance merely because the Europeans themselves are unwilling to make sacrifices to rearm themselves." On 9 August 1952, he returned to the attack again during a debate on the appropriations for the Department of Defense: ". . . the most serious deficiency in our military strength is our weakness in the air. . . . In this critical year in our history, I think we have no alternative but to devote as large a proportion as possible of our national production to our air program." On 17 June 1954, in the Senate, he opposed the reductions in the size of the Army which were being made by the administration of Dwight Eisenhower: "But a budget reduction should be an objective secondary to our national security and our responsible leadership in world affairs." On 23 May 1955, on his return to the Senate after an absence of seven months due to illness, he said that the administration had "guessed short" on the military strength of Russia, and that the further reductions in the strength of the armed services which were being proposed were mistaken. Without a doubt, the record was consistent.

Then, on 14 August 1958, in one of the series of major speeches which he made in the Senate during the years before the 1960 campaign, he turned his attention to the alleged "missile gap," and expanded his warnings:

> In short, the deterrent ratio might well shift to the Soviets so heavily, during the years of the gap, as to open to them a shortcut to world domination. . . . In the years of the gap, the Soviets may be expected to use their superior striking ability to achieve their objective in many ways which may not require launching an actual attack. Their missile power will be the shield from behind which they will slowly, but surely, advance—through sputnik diplomacy, limited brushfire wars, indirect non-overt aggression, intimidation and subversion, internal revolution, increased prestige or influence, and the vicious blackmail of our allies. The periphery of the free world will gradually shift against us.

This was to be the most positive theme of his campaign.

It was not enough for him to say, as he did during the first television debate with Richard Nixon on 26 September 1960,

"I should make it very clear that I do not think we're doing enough" to maintain the country's strength. The concept of a sufficient military establishment, which Dwight Eisenhower had defended, had to be expanded, as in the October issue of the *Keystone Catholic Veteran:* "Let us make certain that so long as the unbridled power of Communism exists, we will have in fact as well as word a military establishment not only second to none, but first. And let us go after it now." He hammered the point home in speech after speech, as at Detroit on 26 August: "I mean first—period. I mean first in military power across the board." His meaning could not be misunderstood. John Kennedy, said Hanson W. Baldwin in the New York *Times* six days before the election, "has put himself on the side of the military 'realists.' His election would seem to mean major changes and a larger defense budget."

But it is not enough to demonstrate that John Kennedy was locked in the ideology of the Cold War—that is well understood by now; or that he was advocating a policy of advance instead of containment against the Communist powers—although the belligerence of his language was striking; or that his emphasis on military strength had been consistent over the years —and the record of that consistency was available to the American public at the time. To demonstrate each and all of these is merely to begin the inquiry. In his campaign, he was already pulling the country onto tiptoe; summoning it to confront great dangers, on the one hand, and to expect great deeds, on the other; teaching it to prepare for a strenuous adventure in which a single ruler would lead it with a united purpose. To an important extent, the ideology of the Cold War and the emphasis on military strength were of only secondary importance, subordinate to his real concern: the exaltation of the power of the state. Moreover, that concern was the creature of a consistent political philosophy: "voluntary totalitarianism" was more than a youthful phrase.

It is hardly surprising that his talk of "the burden and the glory" of the hour at which America had arrived, and of the measures necessary to meet it, aroused the suspicions of the true liberals: those unwearying souls who trudge on, year after year, sceptical of all power and inured to its glamour. They did not, anyhow, much like the style of the campaign. "Kennedy's campaign," said I. F. Stone in his weekly newsletter of 7 November 1960, "gives the impression of being run by technicians who repeat key words on the basis of decibel response"; and, a month earlier, an editorial in *The Nation* observed that "he appears to be waging a campaign based on the principles of market research." But it was not the style alone which bothered them. After the first television debate with Richard Nixon, I. F. Stone observed that "Kennedy is beginning more and more to resemble the late John Foster Dulles," a criticism which, as we have seen, could easily be justified by some of his speeches. "Particularly on Cuba," continued the charge a month later, "Kennedy has been cheap, demagogic, and irresponsible"; and Carleton Beals in *The Nation* in the same week spoke of "Kennedy's wild proposals to promote revolution in Cuba": words which would wash ashore in the Bay of Pigs.

The ambiguous relations of John Kennedy—and later of Robert Kennedy—with the people whom they disparaged as "doctrinaire liberals" were significant. They are a genuine source of perplexity, as one attempts to fit the legend to the reality, and to separate the two brothers so that one may distinguish them as individuals, different characters acting in different situations. For, even as Robert Kennedy in 1968 put himself at the head of a liberal—even a radical—protest against many of the policies of his brother's administration, of which he had been a member, he still disdained the "doctrinaire liberals," and they in turn remained suspicious of him. There was something in the political method of the Kennedys which jarred the political philosophy of the "doctrinaire liberals," and the distance between the two became immediately obvious during the election campaign in 1960.

The record of John Kennedy during the terror of Joe McCarthy had been vulnerable at the time, and it was still vulnerable during the campaign; but it is not revealing. It tells us nothing that we do not otherwise know about him, and nothing that he tried to conceal. He was not a man of keen moral perception; he had no deep care for the independence of the intellectual world which Joe McCarthy was ravaging, and which he himself was to plunder; he was not a liberal of "spontaneous visceral reactions"; the author of *Profiles in Courage* was not himself politically courageous to the point of indiscretion; if hazard could be avoided, he would avoid it. He was neither as brave as some, during the 1950s, nor more cowardly than most. The issue simply did not seem to touch his genuine concerns; and the most serious criticism which can be made of him is that, given those concerns, he did not react instinctively to the terrible injury which Joe McCarthy was doing to the competence and the morale of the Department of State.

The issue dogged him during the campaign. During the first television debate with Richard Nixon, the candidates were asked about "Communist subversive activities in the United States today," and John Kennedy replied: "We should support the laws which the United States has passed in order to protect us from those who would destroy us from within."

It was Richard Nixon who added: "It is also essential, in being alert, to be fair," a remark which drew from many liberals the observation that his reply was more acceptable than that of John Kennedy. It was not the most happy of judgements, because it would be a foolish liberal who, on the basis of such an exchange, was willing to entrust the appointment of, say, an Attorney General of the United States to Richard Nixon rather than to John Kennedy. If for no other reason, John Kennedy had an inborn sense of dignity, perhaps his most remarkable quality, which would not have permitted him to tolerate, under his Presidency, the laws and the institutions of which he was the chief magistrate being used to scurrilous ends; he stood much on protocol.

John Kennedy was, in fact, less concerned to establish himself as a liberal than to distinguish his political position from that of Richard Nixon. It may be hard to believe today, but the distinction in 1960 was not at all clear to many people. It was not only Nikita Khrushchev who could dismiss the two candidates as "a pair of boots—which is the better, the right boot or the left boot?" We have it on the authority of Arthur Schlesinger that John Kennedy was not in the least amused when Eric Sevareid published a column shortly after the two party conventions in which he complained that "The 'managerial revolution' has come to politics, and Nixon and Kennedy are its first completely packaged products." Others made the same accusation, and Arthur Schlesinger, the historian of the Democratic tradition, was moved to take up his pen, and to write a spirited political tract.

Kennedy or Nixon: Does It Make Any Difference? was the title, a question which no liberal had ever had the occasion to ask about Adlai Stevenson. There was apparently a question to be answered, and James MacGregor Burns, the official campaign biographer, had already attempted to explain John Kennedy's slow evolvement into a liberal in terms of a process of self-discovery, not unconnected with his illness in 1955. The comparison with Franklin Roosevelt's affliction was made, and Arthur Schlesinger adopted the theme, reaching the same conclusion: "Once Kennedy resolved the problem of his own identity, his own emotions were liberated for an increasingly forceful commitment to liberalism." One has no doubt, of course, that these evolutions happen; it is merely questionable whether they are as strenuous or as dramatic as is suggested, whether the politician, as he adjusts his opinions, may always be found on a bed of pain, arguing with his soul.

There simply comes a time, as has already been described, when some politicians decide to act on a national level and, both consciously and unconsciously, begin to construct a national appeal; they are translated in the process, and translate themselves. "Some people have their liberalism 'made' by the time they reach their late twenties," John Kennedy once said. "I didn't. I was caught in crosscurrents and eddies. It was only later that I got into the stream of things." It is disarming; but he got into the stream of things only when a high political ambition compelled him to construct a coherent national appeal. A great politician, when he seeks the highest political office, must fit his ambition to the hour. He must become necessary; known to himself, and seen by the people, to be so. It is not his personal identity which he must discover, but his political identity which he must establish.

Neither in his beginnings nor at his end was John Kennedy a liberal; yet he appeared to many to be one. We cannot hope to understand his political method, and the consistent political philosophy on which it was based, unless we resolve this paradox. Not only did he disdain the "doctrinaire liberals" or the "real liberals" or the "professional liberals," as he variously called them, but he preferred, like many of his associates, to be called a "pragmatic liberal" or a "practical liberal." In what, then, did his liberalism consist? The illuminating answer is given by Arthur Schlesinger: he was committed to liberalism "by intellectual analysis," by the "conviction that history requires certain things of the United States, and that these things can be achieved only by programs of the kind which are conventionally known as liberal." In other words, he needed liberalism as an instrument of other purposes; when it was convenient, he used it.

But a liberalism which is so held, by intellectual analysis alone, will neither provide a check, nor point in any clear direction. He had none of the liberal spirit which was unquenchable in Thomas Jefferson. One cannot imagine that John Kennedy would have written at the time of Shays' Rebellion: "The spirit of resistance to government is so valuable that I wish it always to be kept alive. It will often be exercised when wrong, but better so than not to be exercised at all. I like a little rebellion now and then. It is like a storm in the atmosphere." At the root of Thomas Jefferson's attitudes was a theorem, of universal application, which he could work out on a scrap of paper, and it was this which the liberals missed in John Kennedy as he campaigned. They wanted the impersonal theorem which would always do its work instead of the personal gesture which was occasional. The liberalism which John Kennedy reached by intellectual analysis was non-ideological; but can liberalism ever be non-ideological?

The truth is that John Kennedy and the "pragmatic liberals" who served him were men of their time. Even as he campaigned, two significant works were published. First came Seymour Martin Lipset's *Political Man* which, although this was not its object, tended to drain politics of all ideological content. In arguing that a society in which the voters were apathetic is likely to be healthy, he wrote: "A stable democracy may rest on the general belief that the outcome of an election will not make a great difference to a society." Only a few months later came Daniel Bell's *The End of Ideology*, in which a complicated argument could nevertheless be reduced to the simple affirmation of the title. These were important works, signposts of the time, even if they were based, as has been suggested, on a misreading of what was happening in the United States at the end of the 1950s. American politics, which anyhow seem curiously non-ideological to the outsider, were to be celebrated as non-ideological; and the young candidate who was establishing his political identity in his campaign was freed to manufacture an appeal which was constricted neither by ideology, nor by interest, nor by party; in which his personal leadership was without check.

The effect after his election was that he was able, as we will see, to occupy the centre in American politics and so to expand it that he commanded the support of an astonishingly wide range of political opinion. Liberals were reconciled by his aspirations, which he clothed in their vocabulary; conservatives took note of his deeds, which rarely challenged their opinions or their interests. The "pragmatic liberal" would become the leader of all, and each and all could expect satisfaction, if not greatness, from his leadership. Only the "real liberals" continued their battle with him throughout his administration; but, even then, James MacGregor Burns, who had already had the first word, appeared to have the last. In the *New Republic* of 31 October 1960, he defended John Kennedy against the "doctrinaire liberals." In an article significantly entitled "Liberalism without Tears," he concluded: "Kennedy is simply—or at least has been—too successful. If he should die in a plane crash, he would become a liberal martyr." Three years later, his point seemed to be made.

But the campaign which John Kennedy conducted was not political in the sense that mattered to the liberals. Before the voting in the Wisconsin primary, *Time* had observed that "if you were to limit this election to habitual Democrats, Humphrey would probably win; but all the fringe interest has been with Kennedy." To the unpolitical voters, the appeal would be largely unpolitical. Youth and vigour were in themselves a promise; and even political observers took them to be so. After the party conventions, Walter Lippmann proclaimed that "1960 marks the passing of the old political generation, and the appearance of the new"; James Reston perceived a "shift in power from men born in the nineteenth century to the new generation born in the twentieth century"; and Marquis Childs found that a "new kind of party is coming into being under the sponsorship of new men." Indeed, on 11 August 1960, in a television interview, Walter Lippmann, who was born in 1889, found Dwight Eisenhower, who was born in 1890, to be "out of date." But not even a candidate of youth and vigour can offer nothing but them; he must offer some hint of where his youth and vigour are intended to carry the nation.

Where did the Americans want to go? To a frontier, of course, but to what frontier? By the time he gave his acceptance speech at Los Angeles, John Kennedy had found the answer: to a New Frontier. Was the phrase his own? We do not know. But, however the phrase entered his mind, he sent

it forth at Los Angeles arrayed and plumed, a heraldic device
for all to see:

> . . . we stand today on the edge of a New Frontier: the frontier
> of the 1960s, a frontier of unknown opportunities and paths, a fron-
> tier of unfulfilled hopes and threats. . . .
>
> The New Frontier of which I speak is not a set of promises: it
> is a set of challenges. It sums up not what I intend to *offer* the
> American people, but what I intend to *ask* of them. It appeals to
> their pride, not to their pocketbook. It holds out the promise of
> more sacrifice instead of more security. Beyond that frontier are
> uncharted areas of science and space, unsolved problems of peace
> and war, unconquered pockets of ignorance and prejudice, un-
> answered questions of poverty and surplus.
>
> It would be easy to shrink from that frontier, to look to the
> safe mediocrity of the past. . . . But I believe the time demands
> invention, innovation, imagination, decision. I am asking each of
> you to be new pioneers on that New Frontier.

It was magnificent; but what did it mean?

He began his national campaign on 2 September 1960 at an
airport rally at Manchester in New Hampshire, where he told
the crowds: "The New Frontier is in New Hampshire, just as
much as it is in Alaska, just as much as it is in any sector of the
world." Then, on the following day, again at an airport rally at
Anchorage in Alaska, he was a little more positive: "In a very
real sense, Alaska typifies the New Frontier." Three days later,
in Pocatello, Idaho, the theme was becoming involved: "I think
the future of the United States is unlimited, and I say that
after travelling to Maine on Friday, to the last frontier of
Alaska on Saturday, and to the great industrial frontier of
Michigan yesterday. I come today to the frontier of energy."
By the time he reached California, on that first sweep to
the Far West, the metaphor had become something of a mill-
stone around his neck.

But he did not abandon it; he merely abandoned the attempt to place it territorially. "When I talk about the New Frontier," he had already said in Spokane, Washington, "I don't mean just a physical reality, I mean all of those who believe that they want to serve our government and serve our system, who want to join with us, not because of what we are going to do for them, but for the opportunity that they will have to serve our country," and this was to be the form which the theme took for the rest of the campaign. As he exclaimed at Towson, Maryland, "The New Frontier of which I speak is the opportunity for all of us to be of service to this great republic in difficult and dangerous times." He was returning to the theme of sacrifice. "I run for the Presidency in 1960," he said at Oklahoma City almost on the eve of the election, "in the conviction that the people of this country are willing to sacrifice—to give—to spare no effort." The leaders of a free society usually demand such sacrifice of the people only in wartime. But here was an aspiring leader who, as at St. Louis, promised only that "for Americans life will be more difficult and more challenging in the 1960s than it has ever been in the past."

How could such an appeal be made palatable to a people who were in no "shooting wars"? He had to extend the claims of politics. The sacrifice was necessary to recover an elevated sense of national purpose, and the national purpose, as he wrote in *Life* on 22 August 1960, "consists of the combined purposefulness of each of us *when we are at our moral best*: striving, risking, choosing, making decisions, engaging in a pursuit of happiness that is strenuous, heroic, exciting, and exalted." Did no one at the time draw his breath at these words? What part of the private life of an individual, under such a regime, was to be permitted to remain separate from the public domain? But the theme was at the core of the Presidential style that he was already setting.

In an interview on NBC-TV, which was broadcast on 1 October, he called for "the pursuit of excellence in all phases of our national life," and he added: "I think the President can do a good deal in setting that tone." The connection between power and excellence was being made, and it would be carried into every field. "The problems now are so sophisticated and technical that unless you have a partnership or an interrelationship between the intellectual world and the political world, you will not possibly be able to solve these problems which now face us." In the October 1960 issue of *Musical America,* he proclaimed: "And the New Frontier for which I campaign in public life can also be a New Frontier for American art." In harmony with "that creative burst" which would take place in the political field, "there is bound to come a New Frontier in the arts. For we stand, I believe, on the verge of a period of sustained cultural brilliance." This was a heady promise, and it was for some years to make more than one artist a little giddy, as he looked for the rewards.

For the expectation was being extended to all. On the New Frontier there would be built a new city, wondrous to behold, in which all of human endeavour—even scholarship, even art, even music—would have its appointed place, and its opportunity to serve. There happiness would be pursued, strenuously and heroically; there men would risk and strive; there each would be at his moral best. In modern times, the promise was without parallel; the claim was unlimited. Excellence would be sought in all phases of the nation's life, and the President would do a good deal to set the tone. This was the language of personal emperorship, and its motive was to be found in a political philosophy which exalted the power of the state.

Benjamin Bradlee, the journalist, tells us that John Kennedy began "collecting rhetoric in a small, black, leather book before the war," a habit which the aspiring politician would be wise to disdain; it can have the same ill effects as an extended reading of *The Decline and Fall of the Roman Empire* had on the early style of Winston Churchill. After all, what one copies into "a small, black, leather book" when one is a young man are lofty sentences, and one is therefore in danger of imagining that oratory is composed only of wind. It is certainly hard to find a sentence in a major speech of John Kennedy which is flat, which has the impact, not to be despised, of a cracked bell; and one cannot avoid the feeling that, having once read the funeral oration of Pericles, he could not get to his feet without trying to emulate it, forever calling the citizens to witness the sacrifices of their dead by their own dedication, to love their city as a worthy mistress. But it is also hard to avoid the conclusion that this was not the natural style of John Kennedy: that he both forced it upon himself, and allowed it to be forced upon him. Not an inkling of it is to be found in his spontaneous replies to questions at his press conferences; and, although press conferences are different from speeches, there is usually a discernible connection between their styles. We must believe, for the evidence is ample, that in private John Kennedy was laconic and contained, cool and dry in his utterance. But what then happened when he rose to his feet? Whence came the magniloquence? His speeches are not spattered with the popular idiom that, even after the loftiest passages, brought Winston Churchill down to earth. John Kennedy spoke in public as

Byzantine emperors appeared on state occasions: sheathed in gold, suspended between earth and heaven. One must find an explanation.

Theodore Sorensen was, of course, his main speech writer, over many years; and, in the process by which the speeches were manufactured, the relationship between the two men approached a condition of equality. In an acute passage on the oratory which emerged, Patrick Anderson talks of Theodore Sorensen's "mania for contrapuntal sentences," which were balanced and inverted, and alliterative, "often with internal rhymes and formal parallelisms," and he offers such well-known examples as: "Mankind must put an end to war, or war will put an end to mankind. . . . Let us never negotiate out of fear, but let us never fear to negotiate. . . . While we do not intend to see the free world give up, we shall make every effort to prevent the world from being blown up." One notices, in this last example, how close the high-blown style comes to banality, and banality was achieved in the declaration to the United Nations after the death of Dag Hammarskjold: "His tragedy is deep in our hearts, but the task for which he died is at the top of our agenda."

We are told that, in his high school valedictory address in 1945, Theodore Sorensen declared, "To prove ourselves, we must improve the world"; and perhaps we cannot altogether ignore this evidence that, even at so early an age, he felt the need to combine such melodic lines in a harmonious relationship, because the same need is to be found, twenty years later, in his memoir of John Kennedy, a book which was written in a hurry, and which we may therefore take to represent his natural style. The thought is wrenched by the style; and men cease to question; the false parallels are digested without resistance.

The object of the style—banal though it often was, arch
and pompous—was to exalt, not merely the man and his office,
but his every occasion. At no time would the President appear
to act with anything but the full exercise of his authority. It
is doubtful whether he could have announced an increase in
the sugar subsidies without Theodore Sorensen finding words
for him to recite which would bring a noble lustre to men's
eyes. "Let the word go forth from this time and place that
the American people will not permit the growers of sugar. . . ."
The style is all too easy to parody. Yet, even if this was not the
natural style of John Kennedy, it became his public style. By
the end of the campaign, it was his own.

"I believe the nature of the campaign tells you something
about the nature of the candidates," he had said at Chicago
on 4 November 1960; and no one could complain that his
campaign and his speeches had not done exactly that. How
could it all be summarised? Almost a year later, on 16 October
1961, Alexander Welsh reviewed in the *New Republic* a new
edition of *Why England Slept*. His criticisms of it, particularly
in the light of the first year of John Kennedy's administration,
were much the same as those given above. John Kennedy had
been "chiefly concerned with the problem of *collective energy*
in a democracy." What he wished to excite was "the commitment, the responsibility, the obligation of the individual"; this
carried "the contract theory just about as far as it can go." This
was, in short, what he meant by "voluntary totalitarianism."

It had been there, throughout 1960, in the election campaign,
in the style of the speeches as well as in their substance; and
what it amounted to, concluded Alexander Welsh, was that
John Kennedy was elected "in one of the most nationalistic
campaigns in our history." It was in this campaign that the
politics of expectation were born: the American people were

summoned, even while they were at peace, to a sense of their national mission, to meet a global challenge as he called it, on which their reason must have looked with suspicion, but at which his rhetoric persuaded them to gaze with wonder. When the "collective energy" of a free people is aroused, it becomes an unquestioning force. What can a free people, when so elevated, not accomplish? It is only doubtful whether it is in the nature of any free people to wish life to be as strenuous and heroic as John Kennedy had fatally promised.

CHAPTER FIVE

The Crowning of
a President

IT IS SOME TIME since the English people decided that they did not want a sovereign who insisted on rallying them to an elevated sense of national purpose which he had proclaimed without consulting them. So, in the course of forty years, they executed one king, and threw out another, and finally solved the problem by offering the throne to an obscure German prince who could speak not a word of the English language. His son was hardly more proficient and, since they could not communicate an elevated sense of national purpose to the English nation in the German tongue, a tradition was established which has lasted until this day. The sovereigns of the English people may stay on the throne as long as they seek to communicate a sense of purpose only to Welsh corgis, racehorses, and pedigree cattle, a duty which they perform with more conviction than could reasonably be expected of less dedicated a royal family. But, if they try to communicate it to the people, as the luckless Edward VIII did in the course of a visit to the Welsh coalfields, they will not reign for long.

This does not mean that the English people do not value—and enjoy—them as a symbol of national unity, but it is not an oppressive symbol since it does not demand that national unity be accompanied by national purpose. Across the Channel, the French people may still hanker after a national leader who will speak to them of *la gloire;* but from "the little Queen," as Walter Bagehot called her when he was only twelve years old, it would be excessive. Even at the coronation of a new sovereign, no sense of purpose is communicated, other than to conduct the ceremony in faultless style; and it needed Edward Shils, an American sociologist of usually restrained judgement, to observe the coronation of Elizabeth II, and in his excitement to send to the *Sociological Review* of December 1953 an account of the ceremony which assured the startled natives that the pageantry which they enjoyed at its face value had in fact a deeper meaning.

Nevertheless, his account serves the purpose of this chapter. He followed the ceremony through each of its stages, claiming that the literal meaning of each of them has a contemporary significance. First, there is the Recognition, when the Archbishop presents the Queen to the four sides of the "theatre," asking the assembly to reaffirm their allegiance to her. Secondly, there is the Oath, by which the Queen acknowledges that the moral standards embodied in the law and the customs of the realm are superior to her personal will. Thirdly, there is the Presenting of The Bible, which is to go with her always, so that her moral consciousness will be kept alive by means of continuous contact with the Book in which God's will is revealed. Fourthly, there is the Anointing, after the Queen has been stripped of her regalia, and stands before the assembly a frail creature, who is about to be transformed into a Queen who will be something more and greater than the human being who has received the previous instruction. Fifthly, there is the Presenting of the Orb and the Sword and the Bracelets and the Robe Royal, each of them given to her by her people, her authority thus received from them, and each of symbolic importance: the Orb of her temporal jurisdiction, the Sword of her power to enforce the moral law of justice, the Bracelets investing her with sincerity and wisdom, and the Robe Royal enfolding her righteousness. Finally, there is the Benediction, and the circle of obligation, she to her people, and the people to her, is complete. Few ceremonies are more satisfying.

One merely questions the argument of Edward Shils that its literal meaning, reaching back to the earliest days of kingship in Europe, has a contemporary significance. It is too much to claim that the Recognition is "a dramatic concentration of the devotion which millions now feel," or that the reason why it is proper that the Oath should be administered by the Church of England alone is that it "serves the vague religiosity" of the English people, "without raising issues of ecclesiastical jurisdiction or formal representation." To those of us who were in Westminster Abbey in 1953, the power of the ritual lay in the ceremony and the pageantry themselves, faultlessly executed; and for four hours at the centre of it, as faultess in her own performance, stood a single human being. When she was stripped of her regalia before the Anointing, and stood in a white shift among her emblazoned peers and the mitred bishops, one may have gasped with pity as she was then loaded with the symbols of her office. But the power is in the ceremony itself, not in meanings which no longer have any power.

Strangely, the English people are less inclined to read a contemporary meaning into the coronation of their Queen than are the American people into the inauguration of their

President. "America has no more solemn rite than the inauguration of a President," says Arthur Schlesinger in an introduction to a collection of the inaugural addresses of the
Presidents of the United States. "Every four years since 1789,
the austere ceremony has suspended the passions of politics
to permit an interlude of national reunion. . . . Putting doubts
and disagreements aside, the nation listens for a moment as
one people to the words of the man whom they have chosen
for the highest office in the land." Shortly before the inauguration of John Kennedy, there was a lament from "T.R.B."
in the *New Republic*. "The inauguration of a new President,"
he said, "should be a moment of solemnity and consecration;
we have produced a ceremony that is incongruous, tawdry,
ignoble." To an outsider, the adjective used by Arthur Schlesinger seems more just. It is an austere ceremony, and the
austerity is appropriate to the origins of the country. One man
in a black robe administers the oath to another man in a
black coat, as if these were the whole wardrobe which they
had brought with them on the *Mayflower*. The ceremony is
improvised, as was the nation, or gives the impression of being
so; it entirely befits a country which was scribbled into existence
on a scrap of paper.

Even the time of year at which the ceremony is held contrib-
utes to the austerity. Arthur Schlesinger begins his life of
Franklin Roosevelt with a memory of 4 March 1933: it "dawned
gray and bleak. Heavy winter clouds hung over the city. A chill
northwest wind brought brief gusts of rain." It was no different
seven inaugurations later. He begins his memoir of John Kennedy: "It all began in the cold. It had been cold all week in
Washington. Then early Thursday afternoon came the snow.
The winds blew in icy, stinging gusts and whipped the snow
down the frigid streets." It is arranged differently in England,

of course, where even the birthday of the Queen is moved to June, so that she may ride on horseback in the sunshine among her people; and, if it appears that she may be a minute or two late in arriving at the Admiralty, where she will review her soldiers of the Household Brigade as they troop the colour, the hands of the clock above the parade ground are held back, so that it will strike the hour at the very moment at which she rides into the arena, side-saddle on her police horse. In a monarchy, even in a contemporary monarchy, neither calendar nor clock are allowed to rule. There is no reason why the inauguration of a President of the United States should not take place in the spring or in the fall, seasons of unfailing delight in Washington; but this would not be suitable to the austerity of the occasion. In particular, if a nation is to be summoned to an elevated sense of national purpose, in an interlude of national reunion, it is fit that the cold should whip about its ears.

There can be little doubt in whose company one would have most liked to have attended the festivities which accompanied the inauguration of John Fitzgerald Kennedy. On 16 January 1961, as he was later to recount in *The Nation*, Lincoln Kirstein was wakened at 6:30 A.M., to accept delivery of a telegram whose gravity was equal to its length:

DURING OUR FORTHCOMING ADMINISTRATION WE HOPE TO EFFECT A PRODUCTIVE RELATIONSHIP WITH OUR WRITERS ARTISTS COMPOSERS PHILOSOPHERS SCIENTISTS AND HEADS OF CULTURAL INSTITUTIONS STOP AS A BEGINNING IN RECOGNITION OF THEIR IMPORTANCE MAY WE EXTEND TO YOU OUR MOST CORDIAL INVITATION TO ATTEND THE INAUGURATION CEREMONIES IN WASHINGTON ON JANUARY 19 AND 20 STOP RESERVATIONS FOR INAUGURAL CONCERT PARADE BALL ARE HELD FOR YOU STOP ROOM ACCOMMODATIONS AND HOSPITALITY WILL BE ARRANGED FOR YOU BY A SPECIAL SUBCOMMITTEE STOP RSVP

WHICH EVENTS DESIRED AND WHAT ACCOMMODATIONS NEEDED BY
TELEGRAPHING K. HALLE 3001 DENT PLACE STOP
                                        PRESIDENT ELECT AND MRS KENNEDY

As he pondered the invitation, the telephone rang. It was W. H. Auden who, as Lincoln Kirstein puts it, always knows who has received what. Of course they were going, announced the poet without unnecessary ado; it was not an invitation, it was a command; moreover, snow had been promised a year ahead in the *Farmer's Almanac*; so they would leave by car on 19 January at 6:30 A.M.

Lincoln Kirstein's account of the two days in Washington is hilarious. When the two of them eventually arrived in Washington, which was all but immobilised by snow, they trudged through the streets of Georgetown, in obvious good spirits, to find where they should go and what they should do. For the ceremony itself, they were each given a name tag which was marked: PREFERRED STANDING ROOM. In the evening, they made their way to the concert, which began with "a pièce d'occasion. Mr. John LaMontaine had made it or, rather, had it made, with his overture, *From Sea to Sea*, a piece of alarming mediocrity, whose thematic materials, if any, were based on *America the Beautiful*." This was followed by "half the chorus in a horrendous rendition of Randall Thompson's grisly *Testament of Freedom*." The concert hall was almost empty and, far removed from the three hundred or so who were gathered there in his name, sat John Kennedy, his wife, and William Walton, a friend and former correspondent of *Time*.

Wherever the two visitors had gone during the afternoon, they had been told that the President-elect was with William Walton. "And who is William Walton?" W. H. Auden suddenly asked in the middle of the concert; and then, with a reference to the English composer of the same name, inquired: "Any relation to Willie?" He was obviously growing a little restless at the concert, and whispered: "The least they could have done was to ask Stravinsky to write a twelve-tone Fanfare; his late pieces are so nice and short." But there was no Stravinsky, as Lincoln Kirstein commented; no Copland; no Virgil Thompson. So the two of them went from occasion to occasion, meeting other poets and artists. Arthur Miller had spoken on the previous day at a Book and Author Luncheon in New York, and said: "It seems that we will now be looking at, or a least glancing towards, our poets, writers, and men-of-the-mind for more than a laugh." More sharply, Lincoln Kirstein observed: "Mrs. Kennedy had said she was going to redecorate the White House, and every American abstract expressionist had had palpitations."

There was much else to observe and to hear, as power changed hands, the old already forgotten, the new assiduously courted. On a level below the elite who were observed by the two companions, there were the popular songs for the occasion. There was "The New Frontier," with the lines: *Ever free and strong, We will march along.* There was "Jacqueline": *She rides to hounds, She sails the sounds.* There was "Big John," from a different generation: *Big John, now everyone is glad Your home will be that big white pad.* But it was the arrival of twelve dozen writers and artists, composers and philosophers, scientists and heads of cultural institutions that distinguished the occasion from other inaugurations. Most of them had doubts but were able to smother them. Gerald W. Johnson, in the *New Republic* of 30 January 1961, confessed that "a superficial observer is not dismayed by the prospect that the national capital may be relieved of the dullness that has settled upon it," and he looked forward to "a raree-show worth the penny." In this spirit, the new administration began.

On 9 January, John Kennedy had said farewell to the state legislature of Massachusetts. It was an eloquent speech, and it

would have been a poor spirit, on such an occasion, that did
not respond to so young a President-elect, as he quoted the
words of John Winthrop: "We must always consider that we
shall be as a city upon a hill—the eyes of all people are upon
us." He was on the conspicuous stage of Edmund Burke again
—and how similar the quotations are—conscious that the world
was marking his demeanour. In this aspect, he had no cause to
worry: his bearing was beyond reproach. It is there in the cold
print of his words; and it is there in the accounts of those who
knew him. One does not need to have observed Julius Caesar
in person to feel the presence of a man who commanded any
arena in which he chose to aspire; until the presence seemed
too commanding, and he was assassinated. In a Caesar and in a
Bonaparte, in an Elizabeth and in a de Gaulle, the bearing does
not fade, even though the centuries pass. It is an incalculable
force in politics, in the evil as well as in the good; it is natural
to respond to it. But, even as we offer our applause we should
retain the scepticism with which history tells us to treat with
men of power; we should, in a phrase, keep our wits about us.

John Kennedy returned to Palm Beach to prepare his inaugural address. For at least four weeks he had been receiving
those whom he would appoint to his administration, and many
have recorded their excitement. Luther Hodges was determined
not to be late for his appointment, and therefore sensibly took
a train from North Carolina instead of an aircraft. On the other
hand, John Kenneth Galbraith was worried whether he would
obtain a seat on an aircraft during the Christmas holiday, consulted his secretary and, with her advice, "decided that, in the
emergency, name-dropping was in order. It worked. In a democracy, one should scrupulously avoid using influence except when
it is needed." Men of all kinds, with all kinds of rationalisations,

were making their way to Palm Beach, and at least the taxi service profited. Luther Hodges went from his train to the seat of power by taxi; and John Kenneth Galbraith, no doubt wondering whether in a democracy he ought not to take a bus, went by taxi as well. In fact, he informs us that "on the way, [I] heard a call on the cab radio for a cab to go to the address to pick up 'a Mr. Heller.' That told me Walter Heller's appointment to the Council of Economic Advisers must have gone through. I am much pleased for, with others, I have urged him for the post."

If he had not been sent abroad, John Kenneth Galbraith might have been the Samuel Pepys of the administration; as his *Ambassador's Journal* suggests, he has an ear for the importance of tittle-tattle. But the excitment which he records was serious and intended. John Kennedy announced the first appointment to his Cabinet on the day on which, eight years earlier, Dwight Eisenhower had announced his last appointment. The myth of the "great talent hunt" was being manufactured. Day by day, with the aid of television and the press, the nation waited at the gates of the President-elect's home, whether at Palm Beach or in Georgetown, attending to the comings and goings. Once again, the impression was being created that something out of the ordinary was taking place. It was as if no one had ever formed an administration before. "Sometimes they almost sound as if they had invented the town," said *Time* of the Kennedy team on 7 June 1963; and it was indeed in this mood that they had first been gathered. There was, not a hush, but a throb, of expectancy, which again concealed the fact that the appointments which were being made were on the whole conventional.

Amid the excitment, the President-elect, by all accounts, remained cool and even casual. Soon after his election, he had asked Theodore Sorensen to begin collecting suggestions for the inaugural address, and they had arrived, solicited and unsolicited, some only paragraphs, some pages, some complete drafts. The time had come for him to begin working on the speech himself, which he at first did alone at Palm Beach, a yellow legal pad on his knees, telephoning instructions to Theodore Sorensen, who remained in Washington. According to Arthur Schlesinger, "he worked away, scribbling a few lines, crossing out others," and then put the sheets of paper on his desk. One is never quite sure what weight one is meant to attach to such pieces of information, since it would seem to be the natural way to write a speech; our attention being required, one would have imagined, only if he had not scribbled any lines, had not crossed any of them out, and thrown the sheets of paper, not on to his desk, but into the swimming pool where he collected his thoughts.

Other episodes in the writing of the speech are more interesting. He obtained a list of possible Biblical quotations from Billy Graham, and Theodore Sorensen secured a similar list from Isaac Frank, the director of the Jewish Community Council in Washington, neither of them the obvious sources to which one would expect a Roman Catholic to look for scriptural inspiration. But the most important decision was taken, it appears, after Theodore Sorensen had joined him at Palm Beach for the final drafting: the speech would be confined to foreign affairs. He was dissatisfied, we are told, with each attempt to outline a domestic programme; it sounded partisan, or seemed divisive. At last, he decided to make no mention of domestic questions. The decision was revealing but not surprising. Foreign policy was his dominant interest; a weakness in himself which he did not recognise.

As far back as 1953, he had asked Theodore Sorensen which of the Cabinet offices would most interest him, if he should ever have the opportunity to run one. Justice or Labor or Health-Education-Welfare, was the reply. "I wouldn't have any interest in any of those," said John Kennedy, "only Secretary of State or Defense." When he became President, it was the same. After the fiasco at the Bay of Pigs, he asked Theodore Sorensen to give more attention to foreign affairs, saying: "That's what's really important these days." Later in the same year, Stewart Udall remarked, according to Hugh Sidey, "He's imprisoned by Berlin." In 1963, he made a prolonged visit to the countries of the North Atlantic Treaty Organization, although there was little to be accomplished by meetings with their leaders, at a time when the struggle for civil rights was breaking into open violence. This was always his manner.

The work on the final draft of the speech appears to have begun on 16 January, when the decision was taken to confine it to foreign affairs; on 17 January, at Palm Beach in the morning, and on the aircraft to Washington later in the day, he was still polishing; on 18 January in Washington, "he and his staff continued to labor," and other people were still giving advice; on 19 January, the eve of the inauguration, it was finished. In the middle of these four days of concentrated endeavour, Dwight Eisenhower said farewell to the country in a television address in which he warned against spectacular policies; and he held his last press conference. It was the ninetieth press conference of his second term, the first which he had held for four months and ten days. "I came this morning," he said after he had invited the press to be seated, "not with any particularly brilliant ideas about the future"; and the exchanges which followed were as innocent commentaries on the brilliance which was to come:

Q. What I mean specifically, how do you think the transition is
   going?
THE PRESIDENT: Oh! the transition.
Q. Yes, sir.
THE PRESIDENT: I think it's going splendidly, splendidly.

He was departing in his own style; and it made as much impact
on Washington, in a phrase which Everett Dirksen was soon to
make familiar, as a snowflake falling on the Potomac.

The ceremony on 20 January 1961 lasted fifty-one minutes;
the prayers of the four clergymen occupied twenty-eight of
them; and a substantial part of these twenty-eight minutes was
occupied by Richard Cardinal Cushing, who rose to the occasion by instructing the Lord of Hosts in his duties in the coming
four years, while the wires of the lectern smouldered in front
of him. It was clear that twenty-eight minutes of praying and
preaching on such an occasion was more than sufficient; and, a
few months later, in its issue of 22 May, *Newsweek* reported
that the annual convocation of the Protestant Episcopal Diocese
of Washington, D.C., had taken its revenge on the Roman
Catholic excess. It had passed a resolution asking that the prayers at such ceremonies should be limited to a short invocation
and benediction, and it had further resolved that "in the judgment of this convocation, it is not in the best interest of religion,
and it lessens the effectiveness of great national ceremonies, to
have the several major religious groups represented and participating."

After the aged cardinal, in the crowning of the youthful politician, came the aged poet. Little more than three months earlier, Robert Frost had refused to attend a meeting of artists and
writers and scientists in New York to support the candidacy of
John Kennedy, because "he had never in his life signed anything with a lot of other people, and it was too late to begin.

'Ganging up' was contrary to the whole point of his poetry and his life." Uttered to Arthur Schlesinger, these were indeed the words of a poet: withdrawn from the world of power, of "a lot of other people" signing things, determined to keep the language of poetry as distant as possible from the vocabulary of politics, refusing to make the connection between power and excellence. But the candidate whom he had refused to support in public had, it seemed, by the mere fact of his election, been transformed into a figure on whom poetry might decently bestow its laurels. In the bright sunlight, the aged poet stepped forward, to read a verse which he had written for the occasion; and, in the enclosure where they enjoyed the privilege of PRE-FERRED STANDING ROOM, Lincoln Kirstein and W. H. Auden observed that "he tried to deliver some doggerel, grateful and decent, but doggerel"; but he did not finish it. He peered at the manuscript in his hands:

> Summoning artists to participate
> In the august occasions of the state
> Seems something artists ought to celebrate.

But the sun, shining on the snow, had blinded him, and the rest of the doggerel remains for us in print, an unkind memorial. He put it aside, and recited an earlier poem, *The Gift Outright*, with its own measure.

The oath was administered to John Kennedy at 12:51 P.M., and then he gave his inaugural address. As *Time* remarked a week later, "it was destined to be famed within minutes of its delivery"; it was heard in England, where the *Manchester Guardian* commented that he had shown that he "possessed a sense of history and of his place in it," and had given "the inspiring example of a man dedicating himself to great responsibilities"; it was heard in Italy, where *Il Messaggero* said that he had displayed "young resolution." Sam Rayburn, as he left the ceremony, remarked: "That speech he made out there was better than anything Franklin Roosevelt said at his best—it was better than Lincoln. I think—really think—he's a man of destiny." A year later, when he wrote an introduction to a collection of John Kennedy's statements during his first year in office, Carl Sandburg described the speech as "a manner of summons to citizens by the new head of our great Republic. Around nearly every sentence of it could be written a thesis, so packed is it with implications." No one can question this last statement, and we must now turn to the implications. The speech is by no means as much praised today as it was at the time, as people realise the nature of the global mission to which John Kennedy was inviting the American people to dedicate themselves. But, even at the time, some listened to the language and anxiously wondered.

It was brilliant; it was moving; it was dangerous. The rhetoric of politicians has a purpose, especially the rhetoric of emperors and of kings and of presidents. It is to describe an order in which their power is securely established, lawful *under* God and *over* the people, exercised to His greater glory and to their immediate benefit. The more universal the claim, the more readily it will be believed; if what is being described is in fact a universal order, then one may as well accept one's place in it. It was for this reason that Lugalzagezzi proclaimed that he ruled "from the sunrise to the sunset"; for this reason that Hammurabi designed his code; for this reason that Darius wrote of himself that he was "king of countries containing all kinds of men"; for this reason that Asoka declared that "I must promote the welfare of the whole world"; for this reason that the king of Ch'in claimed that he would "lift up the whole world in his arms and tie the four seas in a sack"; for this reason that it was said that the Chinese emperors received "the government of the world from heaven and revolving nature." Wherever great power has been exalted, this has been the liturgy.

So it began on 20 January 1961:

> We observe today not a victory of party, but a celebration of freedom, symbolizing an end as well as a beginning, signifying renewal as well as change. For I have sworn before you and Almighty God the same solemn oath our forbears prescribed nearly a century and three-quarters ago.

The order had been established at the beginning, the power placed between "you and Almighty God," the oath which had been taken before each of them securing its legality. (The coronation is rich in the same mumbo jumbo, of course, but the sovereign who is being crowned has no power, which makes a difference.) The merely political character of the power which he was assuming was then denied by John Kennedy—"we observe today not a victory of party"—although that was exactly what was being observed. Instead, the occasion was "a celebration of freedom," carrying the irresistible implication that all could, and should, rejoice in it. Moreover, the power that was being claimed in the present had its inspiration in the past and in the future as well: "symbolizing an end as well as a beginning, signifying renewal as well as change." The claim that was being made was universal in time and space.

It was now transformed into a universal mission:

> The world is very different now. For man holds in his mortal hands the power to abolish all forms of human poverty and all forms of human life. And yet the same revolutionary beliefs for which our forbears fought are still at issue around the globe, the belief that the rights of man come not from the generosity of the state, but from the hand of God.

There was the sense of mission—the manifest destiny—of the American people locked into the second paragraph of the speech: the conviction that their "revolutionary beliefs" are, and should be, "at issue around the globe." It is not evident, I may be permitted to say, that they are at issue in my own country; and those of other countries may make their own remonstrance. But this is the persistent American conviction: that history began in 1776 and that, wherever men today fight for their freedom, it is because they are inspired by "the same revolutionary beliefs" as were the American people two centuries ago.

The claim and the mission were then expanded;

> We dare not forget today that we are the heirs of that first revolution. Let the word go forth from this time and place, to friend and foe alike, that the torch has been passed to a new generation of Americans—born in this century, tempered by war, disciplined by a hard and bitter peace, proud of our ancient heritage—and unwilling to witness or permit the slow undoing of those human rights to which this nation has always been committed, and to which we are committed today, at home and around the world.

This is magnificent oratory, and it has a meaning. In the first place, the American people were being told that they had no choice. As "heirs of that first revolution," they were by their destiny bound to defend the "revolutionary beliefs" which were "still at issue around the globe." Not only did they have no choice, they were ready for the fearful task; they had been tempered and disciplined to it. The call to sacrifice which had grown to occupy so prominent a part in his election campaign was now trumpeted forth, "to friend and foe alike." In fact, he was turning the eyes of the American people with such ardour to their responsibilities in the world that it came almost as a surprise when he suggested that there were commitments also at home. This sudden concern with domestic affairs, the only one in the entire speech, had been an afterthought. At the last moment, he was worried that he might seem to be avoiding the issue of civil rights, which he was; so he added the words "at home" to his defence of human rights. It was a revealing postscript.

The universal mission was now to be made boundless:

> Let every nation know, whether it wishes us well or ill, that we shall pay any price, bear any burden, meet any hardship, support any friend, oppose any foe, in order to assure the survival and the success of liberty.

As if this were not enough, he added:

> This much we pledge—and more.

These are the words which many of those who applauded the speech at the time now find offensive; and they are offensive. By what right does the leader of any free people commit them —for it was a commitment which he was making—to "pay *any* price, bear *any* burden, meet *any* hardship," when their country is not even at war, and not directly threatened? Even in 1940, Winston Churchill did not say that the English people would go so far; he said only that they would continue to fight, on the beaches and on the landing grounds, in the fields and in the streets. The commitment that John Kennedy was making on a conspicuous stage was without limit.

So the language of universal mission, and the sacrifice required to fulfil it continued throughout the speech: the United States would "oppose aggression or subversion anywhere in the Americas"; as testimony to their loyalty, "the graves of young Americans who answered the call to service surround the globe"; the object was to forge "a grand and global alliance, North and

South, East and West"; there would be danger, because "only a few generations have been granted the role of defending freedom in its hour of maximum danger"; there would be the endurance needed to meet it, "to bear the burden of a long twilight struggle," to be "patient in tribulation," to meet the challenge with "high standards of strength and sacrifice." It was John Kennedy's wish, we are told, to set the tone for a new era. The tone was martial.

The words of the inaugural address, magnificent but terrible, were not suddenly found; they had been building up, he had been building them up, during most of the previous year. He had been working his way, for example, in several speeches, towards the sentence which was to become the most famous in the whole inaugural address. "We do not campaign," he had said in Washington on 20 September 1960, "stressing what our country is going to do for us as a people. We stress what we can do for the country, all of us." He had said as much at Anchorage and at Detroit as well; and, as he worked on his inaugural address, these three passages were beside him. They were at last refined into one magnificent phrase:

> And so, my fellow Americans, ask not what your country can do for you; ask what you can do for your country.

As far back as 1945, he had written down a similar sentiment from Rousseau: "As soon as any man says of the affairs of state, 'What does it matter to me?' the state may be given up as lost."

Is this not the point? Among the mostly unfortunate contributions which Jean-Jacques Rousseau made to the modern age was the development of a theory of political obligation in which the citizens of a state were held to subordinate their individual wills to a general will because the general will was, although they might not know it, their real will. Something of this theory lurks in all modern forms of totalitarianism; and the "ask not" sentence of John Kennedy is only a powerful statement of the "voluntary totalitarianism" to which he was attracted as a young man, and never altogether forsook. In the inaugural address, as from the start to the finish of his career, his concern was, in Alexander Welsh's acute observation, "the problem of *collective energy* in a democracy." His solution of the problem—the attempt to transcend the limitations of the conventional institutions of a free society by providing spectacular personal leadership—largely determined the character of his Presidency. This was the meaning of the inaugural address. Coupled with the performance which followed it, and elaborated it, this will be its abiding interest for years to come.

As has been suggested, Dwight Eisenhower, in his farewell address of 17 January, appeared to have answered the inaugural address in advance. He was addressing himself to the same problems:

> We face a hostile ideology. . . . Unhappily, the danger it poses promises to be of indefinite duration. To meet it successfully, there is called for, not so much the emotional and transitory sacrifices of crisis, but rather those which enable us to carry forward steadily, surely, and without complaint, the burdens of a prolonged and complex struggle.
>
> Crises there will contrive to be. In meeting them . . . there is a recurring temptation to feel that some spectacular and costly action could become the miraculous solution to all current difficulties. A huge increase in newer elements of our defense . . . ; a dramatic expansion in basic and applied research. . . .
>
> The need [is] to maintain a balance . . . between our essential requirements as a nation and the duties imposed by the nation upon the individual.

This last sentence might have been a direct reply to the "ask not" sentence of John Kennedy. The dangers which the retiring President foresaw were to confront everyone a few years later:

> In the councils of government, we must guard against the acquisition of unwarranted influence, whether sought or unsought, by the military-industrial complex. The potential for the disastrous rise of misplaced power exists and will persist.
>
> . . . [In the universities] a government contract becomes virtually a substitute for intellectual curiosity. . . . The prospect of domination of the nation's scholars by federal government, project allocation, and the power of money, is ever present, and is gravely to be regarded. We must also be alert to the equal and opposite danger that public policy could itself become the captive of a scientific-technological elite.

But the scholars and the scientists were not listening. Too many of them were on their way to the Department of Defense, where Robert McNamara had already recruited a "scientific-technological elite," and to the Department of State, which they wished to rationalise, and to the offices of the National Security Council. "Let us begin," John Kennedy was to say; they had begun.

The latter-day criticism of the inaugural address is too narrowly confined to its implications for the foreign policy of the United States: its summons to a universal mission; its preparation of the public mind for foreign adventure; its commitment of the nation to what can best be described as Total Cold War. All of these were important, but its meaning lay deeper than any of them. "Government at all levels has certain obligations to you and me," Dwight Eisenhower had told the National Rural Electric Co-operative Association not long before his retirement. Perhaps only he, while still holding the highest office in the land, could have made this distinction between the government and himself; but the important distinction was that between the government and the people, to whom it had certain obligations. Ask, he was in effect saying, what the government should do for you, and the first of his answers was "security from external attack," the most restrained military objective which it is possible to imagine.

The political philosophy of John Kennedy was altogether the opposite. The energy of the government was the energy of the people; and *vice versa*; and the two together would magnify the energy of the country. He made no distinction between the nation (which is a society) and the people (who are individuals) and the government (who are temporary officeholders). The three would be made one, a trinity, by the creation of a general will, an elevated sense of national purpose, the energies of each being released by all, and of all by each. Any people, when addressed in so exalted a manner, is likely to believe the myth for a time. "The energy, the faith, the devotion which we bring to this endeavor," he had proclaimed, "will light our country and all who serve it, and the glow from that fire can truly light the world": or, as a sceptic observed at the time, set it alight.

When we turn to the speeches which John Kennedy was making as he died, we will find the same strenuous political ambition; and we will find it still, although used to different political ends, in the brief campaign of Robert Kennedy. It rests on the belief that there is a source of energy in a society which is greater than its parts, that the people may be exhorted to transcend, not only the limits of their politics, but their own limitations. This is a religious belief, and the inspiration of the inaugural address was religious. In its exhortations, even the language was scriptural: "Let the word go forth . . . Let every nation know . . . Let all our neighbors know . . . Let us be-

gin anew . . . Let us never negotiate . . . Let us never fear
to negotiate . . . Let both sides explore . . . Let both sides
formulate . . . Let both sides seek . . . Let both sides unite
. . . Let both sides join." This reiteration had the power of liturgy; it was an invocation to the energy and the faith and the
devotion—his own words—of a whole people; and in this invocation the politics of expectation received its most splendid expression. In his one direct quotation from the scriptures, he referred to the "command of Isaiah . . . let the oppressed go
free," and summoned the people in the end with the exhortation, "Let us begin."

CHAPTER SIX

Outward Bound

"IN TOTAL WAR, there is only one prime object of policy, the achievement of total victory. To that object, all other aims are subordinate, by that criterion, all special operations must be judged," because it is assumed that, "if there is no victory, there is no future." These are the words of Lionel Robbins, a distinguished English economist who lent his services to his government during the Second World War. As soon as he had left the government, he wrote a valuable essay, *The Economic Problem in Peace and War*, in which he explained why the economic measures which were employed in war could not be used in peace. In peace, "you can no longer express the object of economic policy in terms of a single concrete objective. Gone is the yardstick of military effectiveness. Gone is the willingness of the citizens to be clamped down to a minimum standard of consumption." In war, policy can be easily determined, because it responds to "the peculiar simplifications arising from concentration on a single strategic plan"; in peace, "we have no objective measure either of the conflicting ends or of the effectiveness of alternative means." But at least some people, especially active people, long for the simplifications of war: "Hence the demands for strong men, planning committees, new organs of government, and so on and so forth"; and to these he might have added the attempt to excite a unifying sense of national purpose.

In the total wars of the modern age, we are willing to surrender our individualism for the period of a war, because we are persuaded that, "if there is no victory, there is no future"; and the danger is that this totalitarian spirit is then carried into peace. "If we can perform such miracles in war, why cannot we perform them in peace?": such is the plausible cry. If we can build Pluto and Mulberry—the improvised pipeline and the artificial harbour which were constructed for D-Day—why cannot we build schools and hospitals? The answer lies—and we should be grateful for it—in the people themselves, who have recovered at least some of their individualism. They no longer have a single objective; some want schools, others want automobiles; some want colour television, others want hospitals; even those who want schools and hospitals may want universities or libraries even more. Which of these is the nobler aspiration is a matter of subjective preference, and the people cannot, with the return of at least some measure of their freedom, be confined to any one of them. In a free society, when it is at peace, a government cannot override the variety of people's choices; it can only marginally influence them. In that margin, the politician works.

This is what is galling to those, like John Kennedy, who are concerned with the problem of collective energy in a democracy; and it is they, whether leaders or followers, who will reach to strong men and planning committees, new organs of government and a sense of purpose, in an effort to recover in peace the simplifications of war; it is they, whether leaders or followers, who will try to make the purpose as single as that which exists in war, in an effort to replace the myriad of individual purposes which have returned with peace. There is no doubt that the collective energy of a democracy in war is impressive. "The reason you won and we lost," said Albert Speer after 1945, "was that you made total war and we did not." When one has recovered from the shock of the remark, one can recognise its truth. The voluntary totalitarianism of a democracy in war is more formidable and more efficient than the coercive totalitarianism of a dictatorship, because "the will to cooperate and the sense of responsibility" are spontaneous and freely given; and the extraordinary power of the democracies, especially of the United States, during the Second World War had a profound influence on an entire generation. It was this generation of Americans who determined in 1961 to restore to the United States an elevated sense of national purpose. They were the first American leaders born in this century, it was boasted, and no one observed that it had been a century of total war. This had been their experience; they had known no other.

"Another thing that defined the New Frontiersmen," writes Arthur Schlesinger, "was that many had fought in the war"; and he proceeds to inscribe on his pages a roll of honour of some twenty members of the administration who had served with unusual distinction and bravery in the armed services in some quarter of the globe after 1941. "The war experience," he concludes, "helped to give the New Frontier its casual and laconic tone, its grim, puncturing humor, and its mistrust of evangelism." But it is exactly this conclusion which needs to be challenged. The vocabulary of the New Frontier makes it seductive: this repeated insistence that the men around John Kennedy were laconic and sardonic, cool and casual, puncturing their own and each other's pretensions with their humour. The experience of the Second World War was indeed formative, but not as Arthur Schlesinger represents it.

The effort which the United States made in the First World

War had been astonishing enough. Its manpower and its industries were mobilised so rapidly that it was hard to believe that
it was the first great war which the country had fought overseas.
But it was all over almost before it had begun, and the de-
mobilisation which then took place was as rapid and as complete
as the mobilisation. Few documents in the history of the United
States are more moving than the first cable which John J.
Pershing sent to Washington soon after his arrival in Paris in
the early summer of 1917, asking that preparations should be
made to send one million men to Europe, and the second cable,
following in a week, in which he revised his estimate, and asked
that preparations should be made to send three million men. In
the event, two million combat troops were sent to Europe—a triumph of organisation—and more than one million of them saw
action. So the United States entered history, but only partially
and only briefly. Little more than a year after men of the First
American Division took part in their first action, the war was
over. The military role of the United States—decisive as it was
—occupied only one year and was enacted in only one continent. Moreover, its diplomatic role was almost as confined: indeed, the attitude of Woodrow Wilson toward both the Treaty
of Versailles and the League of Nations could fairly be described as anti-diplomacy: an effort to replace diplomacy, and to
avoid the need for the United States to become engaged in it.
In its impact on the American people, the First World War was
absorbed as a once-and-only experience, an abnormal occurrence,
an exception to their history.

The experience of the Second World War was altogether
different. The country was at war for almost four years. Its men
were in action during the whole length of them, and they fought
or stood guard in every continent and in every ocean. Moreover,
the country was deeply engaged in the diplomacy of the war: not

only in the summit conferences of the Big Three or the Big
Five, but in choosing whom it would recognise as the leader of
the Free French, in deciding whom it would support in Italy
after the fall of Mussolini, and in numberless other situations
which offered similar challenges. The war was immediately followed by a second demonstration of the efficient power of the
United States—its rescue of Western Europe after 1946—and
many of those who had fought in the war were as deeply engaged in the second operation. This was the generation which
seized power with John Kennedy, and they were acutely described at the time by one of their own number. "Most of the
men have had experience in government operations before,"
Walt W. Rostow said to Hugh Sidey. "They know what discipline is. Most of them are about the same age as the President,
a generation which saw a lot of war and diplomacy."

A lot of war and diplomacy: few self-descriptions could be
more illuminating. What is more, one can find in it at least a
part of the explanation of the unusual sense of camaraderie
which seemed to inspire the members of the administration. The
playful sense that they were "a band of brothers . . . we happy
few" was profoundly important, both in the reality and in the
myth; and it is interesting, in this connection, that one of John
Kennedy's favourite books, as we are told on every side, was
Pilgrim's Way, the rather slight autobiography of John Buchan.
To an Englishman, at least, this is a clue, and one which is
worth following. As a schoolboy in England, it was sometimes
hard to escape the impression that one was being raised on
John Buchan, by John Buchan, for John Buchan. He had two
public lives, and both of them are pertinent in the context of
this book. It is necessary to introduce him.

He was one of "Milner's Young Men," a group of self-
consciously gifted individuals who were recruited by Alfred Mil-

ner when he was the Governor General of South Africa at the beginning of this century. They formed a comradeship which lasted their lives, they were always writing letters to each other with much more frequency than they ever wrote to any woman, and they were possessed by a conviction, which their comradeship and their letters reinforced, that they were an elite. As such, they stand as an awful warning to any who are possessed by the same conviction, because the majority of them, after lives of conspicuous (but not equally significant) public service, ended their careers in some ineffectual post on the margins of what has since been identified as "the Establishment." Robert Lowell, in his poem *Washington in Summer*, talks of "the elected and the elect," who arrive there "bright as dimes" and stay until they are "soft and disheveled." He might have been talking of public servants of the breed of John Buchan and most of "Milner's Young Men."

The public servant was also a popular novelist. The theme of his novels was the imperial mission, the upper class who scarcely believed in it but felt bound to serve it, and the secret agents who did its dirty work. Alan Sandison, in his brilliant work of literary criticism, *The Wheel of Empire*, demonstrates how the imperial theme, which was used with such sensitivity by Rider Haggard and Joseph Conrad and Rudyard Kipling, had become corrupt in the stories of John Buchan; and, in much the same way, in our own time, the most vivid of John Buchan's characters, Richard Hannay, has been further corrupted in the character of James Bond. (It is worth noticing again that the novels of Ian Fleming were also among John Kennedy's reading.) Again and again, the camaraderie of the administration which took power so eagerly in 1961 is illuminated in the novels of John Buchan, as in this exchange in *Huntingtower*, an exchange which one has heard repeated on summer evenings in Washington, as the ice melts and clinks in a glass:

"You were a friend of Captain Kennedy?"
"His oldest, we were at the same private school, and he was at m'tutors, and we were never much separated till he went abroad to cram for the Diplomatic and I started to shoot things."

It is a lot of war and diplomacy in another idiom; and no one who has read the literature of the Kennedy administration, or spent an evening with any of its members, can fail to respond to the parallel. For twenty years, by 1961, the "band of brothers" had conducted the wars and the diplomacy of their country in "government operations"; now they were the government.

We must learn what we can from *Pilgrim's Way;* we cannot afford to neglect such clues. The book is a reverie. It is a re-creation—a celebration—of an England which, if it ever existed, perished in the trenches of the First World War; and it is a strange book for an American—and an Irish-American at that—to have taken to his heart. Yet, as one reads it again, with this in mind, one begins to understand its appeal. In proportion to their numbers, it was the junior officers who were most savagely cut down in the trenches: the flower of their country—and of their class—the bloom of youth still on them; "debonair and brilliant and brave," as John Buchan describes one of them, they went from the ease and the gentleness of the England in which they had been raised to the slime and the blood and the sickness and the death of Flanders. We have their letters; we know their poems. Those who survived did not forget, and they created an idyll in remembrance of their friends who had become "part of that immortal England which knows not age or weariness or defeat."

It was an idyll of youth: but of youth which could never end precisely because it had been cut off before it had run its course. It was an idyll of promise: but of promise which was celebrated as performance. These lives had not been tested; they were tested in their deaths; and each of them passed, one almost expects to read, *summa cum laude*. For, to some of us who were reared with the idyll sung in our ears, it became increasingly objectionable. It seemed as if the survivors felt no anger at the slaughter of their friends, as if their sorrow at these vanished lives was sweet to them. They did not seem to remember how their friends had died—"the riddled corpses round Bapaume"— and instead recalled them as eternally young: "They march on into life with a boyish grace, and their high noon keeps all the freshness of the morning." So the idyll preserves them for us: "great beauty of person; the gift of winning speech; a mind that mastered readily whatever it cared to master; poetry and the love of all beautiful things; a magic to draw friends to him; a heart as tender as it was brave. One gift only was withheld from him—length of years." But is that to be regretted when the remembered youth is without flaw? For does not John Buchan himself tell us how "the promise of youth dulls into a dreary middle age of success, or, it may be, of failure and cynicism"?

At the core of the idyll was the comradeship: the circle of friends—"that happy circle"—made at Oxford. "A careless good-breeding, an agreeable worldliness, were its characteristics"—a description which is very close to that which tells us that the mark of the Kennedy administration was that its members were cool and laconic and unbemused—and the comradeship was carried into the law, into the army, into the government, as they pursued their careers amidst a lot of war and diplomacy. As John Buchan says of Alfred Milner:

> He had a vision of the Good Life spread in a wide commonalty; and when his imagination apprehended the Empire, his field of

vision was marvellously enlarged. So at the outset of his career he dedicated himself to a cause, putting things like leisure, domestic happiness, and money-making behind him. In Bacon's phrase, he espoused the State.

A more usual way of remarking that a man has "espoused the state" is to say that he has "gone into politics," but this is hardly enough for men who have put away leisure and domestic happiness—for what?

> Slowly I began to see the war as a gigantic cosmic drama, embracing every quarter of the globe and the whole orbit of man's life. Though it lacked the epic fervour and simplicity, it had an apocalyptic splendour of design. The prospect, and my work, which lay largely in the study of the mind of other nations, gave me a new intellectual interest.

This was John Kennedy's favourite reading, and must we not point out that there is in it the same geological fault which we noticed at the beginning: the comradeship of men claiming to be cool and casual—a careless good breeding, an agreeable worldliness—yet entranced by power, and by the opportunity to shape great events, by diplomacy and in war, in a "splendour of design"?

This was the bond in 1961; and John Kennedy and the men around him were, in this, true children of their time. We all carry our landscapes with us, and their landscape was a word-view in which there was hardly a degree of longitude or of latitude where one of them did not feet at home. If they had a "mistrust of evangelism"—these men who were ready to "pay any price, bear any burden, meet any hardship" in the cause of freedom around the globe—then it was not evident in their sense of their country's mission.

A number of them had been members of the Office of Strategic Services during the Second World War, a brilliantly improvised organisation that was responsible for many of the clandestine operations of the allies. One of its tasks, especially of the Research and Analysis Branch, was to gather information about the occupied countries so that, when they were liberated, the United States would not be at a loss in coping with their economies and their politics. The catalogue of the Library of Congress bears witness to the extent and thoroughness of their work; and many of the scholarly analyses deserved at least doctoral awards. But it was heady work, as was most of the business of the OSS, and it encouraged the illusion that, by accurate intelligence and rational analysis of it, the United States could successfully intervene in local situations, from the sunrise to the sunset, from the tropics to the snows, with a confidence which far surpassed that of the colonial empires of Europe; and they were not alone in this conviction.

For the first decade after 1945, the power and the influence of the United States were extraordinary, and they were regarded, rightly, as a liberal force. It was the Social Democrats in post-war Europe who looked with hope to the United States, and anti-Americanism was as often as not an extreme right-wing, as well as an extreme left-wing, phenomenon in Europe and Asia and Latin America. The mood was the same in the United States; never before had the intellectuals felt so little alienation from their country. They read de Tocqueville again and found that he had understood the United States better than they had done. His prediction seemed to have come true, that in the century to come America and Russia would confront each other, two vast empires, one representing the principle of absolutism, the other the principle of liberty, and that they would contend for the mastery of the world in an epic struggle. It was the expansive mood which Dwight Eisenhower seemed to have dissipated.

But it had been dissipated, of course, because the balance of power in the world had become more complex: as Russia drew abreast of the United States in strategic power, as the satellites or dependents of both of them recovered from the war and began to assert their independence or at least their longing for it; as the significance of Mao Tse-tung's victory in China made itself clear; and as the dissolution of the colonial empires of Europe introduced the unknown quantity of what the French christened the Third World. All these movements happened in a short time at the same time; and none of them appears as threatening today as they did then. The world gives every sign of shaking itself down after a violent quarter of a century. But that was not how it seemed while it was all happening, and the foreign adventures of John Kennedy and Nikita Khrushchev, each feeding the apprehensions of the other, were in part a response to the disarray into which the world had fallen.

The exaggerated interest in foreign affairs of John Kennedy and of many of those in his service was part of the landscape in which they had grown. *Newsweek* was strikingly close to the truth when it observed of the new administration on 9 January 1961, that they were "men of the 50s and 60s." They could not rid themselves of the landscape of the 1950s. They came to power too late. These young men were old before their time. They had seen too much of war and diplomacy too early. When they should have been fooling about in their youth, wasting the years which are most precious in one's life because one can afford to waste them, they were always on missions, pushing into the jungle of Burma, parachuting into Europe, organising the Marshall Plan, conducting the air lift to Berlin. The habit was ingrained in them. There was always another mission to ready, more intelligence to gather, a lot of war and diplomacy to pursue. If they were not in the Situation Room, moving counters across their maps and charts, if there was not a crisis to manage somewhere, it was no longer the world as they could recognise it; or shape it.

The historians and others, of varying degrees of competence, who are today engaged in revising the history of the Cold War have a story to tell which is plausible, and some of which is even true. But it has very little to do with what it was like in Western Europe between 1946 and 1950, and it was Western Europe which was the battlefield. They write, from the documents, about the motives of Joseph Stalin, on the one hand, and of Harry Truman, on the other, but they forget the condition of the continent whose future was in the balance. They forget it all: the cold and the hunger and the disease; the factories which were in ruins, the others which had been dismantled, the rest which were idle because there was no fuel; the unemployed and the refugees—they forget even these, the displaced persons, as we learned to call them, for whom there was no room, indeed no inn; they forget that scavenging had become a way of life. They even forget the weather, the terrible winter of 1947, which seemed to have no end; when I could walk, if a personal memory will be allowed, over the hills of Northumberland in what ought to have been the warmth of a new spring, but which was instead still a freezing cold, kicking the carcasses of the sheep which had frozen to death, and that I could as easily have walked through the cellars of Europe, kicking the unburied corpses of human beings.

Europe in that winter was a hell frozen over; and they forget the hopelessness; they forget what Hajo Holborn, in his classic work of that title, calls "the political collapse of Europe"; they forget that a few thousand votes in Marseilles or in Lyons, in Milan or in Turin, might have tipped an election in France or in Italy to the Communists; and, if they think that such an event would not have mattered, they forget what happened to Czechoslovakia; they forget that the intellectual life of Europe was scattered, that its intellectual cohesion—so diverse in its expressions, so rich and so vital, for so many centuries—seemed at last to have been broken. They forget that this is what faced men like Dean Acheson.

As he writes in his memoirs, "the life of Europe as an organized industrial community had come well-nigh to a standstill and, with it, so had production and distribution of goods of every sort. Only in Britain and Russia did people have any confidence in government, or social or economic organization, or currencies." Then, as he goes on, "came that awful winter. . . . The one before had been bad enough, a winter of freezing drought. This was one of freezing blizzards. . . . It is enough to say of it that perhaps its most crushing blow fell on Britain"; and that, as the industry of the country came almost to a standstill, its workless people confined to their homes, for much of the time without light and without heat, it was compelled to inform the government of the United States that it could no longer guarantee the security of Greece and Turkey.

Whatever the *raisons d'état*—the considerations of political strategy and military need—which then impelled the United States to accept the Truman Doctrine and adopt the Marshall Plan, no European can deny the saving power which at last arrived from the New World. Ortega y Gasset once described the Europeans as a swarm: innumerable bees, but a single flight. Without the assistance of the United States, the swarm might have died, the flight might have ended. The energy and the creativity of the European peoples is one of the most remarkable phenomena in the history of the world. But in 1947, they needed time, and they had nothing with which to buy it. With a foresight beyond measure, and a magnanimity beyond praise, the American people gave it to them. The revisionist histories of the Cold War—with their omissions and elisions—must therefore gall any European whose memory is not short; and, as one turns to criticise the Cold War ideology as it eventually seized the American people and their leaders, it must be made clear that the memory does not fade.

At first after 1945, the United States created a world-wide system of alliances, whose object was to protect those countries which were considered to be directly threatened by the military power of the Soviet Union and, after the Korean War had revealed its strength on the ground, of Communist China. This was the original policy of "containment," which then, as Anthony Hartley has put it, "evolved into something far more dispersed." With the proclamation on 5 January 1957 of what came to be known as the Eisenhower Doctrine, the United States undertook to "assist any nation or group of nations . . . in the development of economic strength dedicated to the maintenance of national independence"; and to provide military assistance to any nation which desired it for that purpose. This commitment was at first made only to the Middle East, but it was then extended. The motive for American intervention throughout the globe had ceased to be the clear determination to protect any nation which was directly threatened by Communist military power, but the diffuse need to preserve the general stability of a nation or a region. But, although this was the doctrine proclaimed by Dwight Eisenhower, he in fact applied it hesitantly, and appeared to bequeath a legacy of frustration, if not of failure. The reaction of John Kennedy and his administration to this legacy was not to question the policy, but to substitute for the hesitancy and the indirection with which Dwight Eisenhower had pursued it their own dynamism, single-minded and confident.

At no time during his administration did John Kennedy or his advisers give any indication that they fundamentally questioned the mutation in American policy which has just been described. He had shackled himself to the ideology of the Cold War, in part by his oratory, as we have already seen, but also by the appointments which he made. Every reliable source tells us that, in making these appointments, and especially in his choice of a Secretary of State and a Secretary of Defense, he relied heavily on the advice of Robert A. Lovett, who had earned from Henry M. Jackson the sobriquet of Mr. National Security. In fact, Robert Lovett is taken by such keen observers of American defence policy as Samuel P. Huntington and James M. Roherty as the most typical member of the Cold War cadre who, in stiffening American policy after 1946, had themselves become frozen in their attitudes. America was soon to hear a lot of hardened nuclear missiles, sunk deep in their concrete silos; and, as men such as Roswell Gilpatric and Paul Nitze were pulled into the administration, in key positions in the defence establishment, they seemed like hardened missiles themselves, called from the Cold War silos in which they had been emplaced a decade earlier.

The first act of the President-elect had been to retain J. Edgar Hoover as Director of the Federal Bureau of Investigation and Allen Dulles as Director of the Central Intelligence Agency; and, when Allen Dulles had to take his leave after the fiasco at the Bay of Pigs, he was replaced by none other than John A. McCone, of whom the *New Republic* commented on 9 October 1961, "He is the kind of man who hates Communism, not because it betrayed the revolution, but because he assumes it *is* the revolution. That is a flaw beyond correction." But the choice of John McCone was no more remarkable than the appointment of John McCloy to take charge of disarmament policy, and his replacement by William C. Foster, both of them hand-picked from the silos of the Republican Party and intricately involved in the development of American policy during the period when it mutated into a global commitment to regional stability. Having been told by Richard Neustadt that the Treasury was "a major foreign policy post," it was not surprising that John Kennedy appointed to it Douglas Dillon who believed that, as *Time* put it on 18 August 1961, the American economy "is a dynamic weapon of the Cold War . . . an active, shaping force"; and he was used in such a role.

In a way most revealing of all, when the situation in Berlin in 1961 appeared to be dangerous, John Kennedy turned instinctively to Dean Acheson to prepare a special report, and to Lucius Clay to be his personal representative in West Berlin: two men of unusually strong personalities, closely identified with the defence of West Berlin during the iciest days of the Cold War. In much the same manner, for the same reason, at the same time, he appointed Curtis LeMay to be Chief of Air Staff: in the words of Hugh Sidey, he "had the toughness Kennedy felt the country needed most." Indeed, his defence of the appointment—even with the important qualification—is illuminating: "It's good to have men like Curt LeMay and Arleigh Burke commanding troops once you decide to go in. But these men aren't the only ones you should listen to when you decide whether to go in or not. I like having LeMay at the head of the Air Force. Everybody knows how he feels. That's a good thing right now." The important words are the final "right now." He was looking at the situation in Berlin within a frame of crisis and of confrontation, a legacy of the Cold War from which he could not escape.

He could not escape from it, certainly, in the company which he had chosen to keep. The wagons were being loaded to go to

the New Frontier—to borrow a phrase which Richard Rovere
used in January 1961—but they were to be driven by teams of
old warriors who were also Cold Warriors. In key positions,
John Kennedy placed men who had not merely seen a lot of
war and diplomacy but had seen it in the conditions of the Cold
War, with its peculiar simplifications. All of this is today well
understood and has been much explored. But some of the analyses are themselves marked by a peculiar simplification. The
ideology of the Cold War was not single; there was not even
a single Cold War; as we have just seen, the policy of the
United States to meet it suffered a mutation during the second
half of the 1950s. It was now to suffer a further mutation as
John Kennedy and his administration determined to wage Total Cold War. For this expansion there had to be a new reason,
and it was one which was popular at the time, not least in intellectual circles; and it was an intellectual who gave the new
doctrine its most powerful expression.

Ideas and men: of such are administrations made; and they
interact, the ideas confirming the men in their actions, the men
reinforcing the ideas. In the mind of Walt Rostow—the man
whom Dean Rusk at first refused to take into the Department
of State, and whom John Kennedy then took into the White
House, only later to send him to Dean Rusk after all—the
ideology of the Cold War was translated into an all-embracing
doctrine such as would have been sufficient, in an earlier age,
to sustain the church militant. It is not easy to exaggerate his
influence, witting and unwitting. With intelligence and industry
and zeal in equal parts, he took the ideology of the Cold War,
which had been appropriate to a brief period, and converted it
into a motive for a crusade of limitless extent and of endless
duration. By his thesis, he supplied the rationale by which the

Cold War, just as it was ending, was transformed from a national exigency into a national purpose; he gave to the Total Cold War a sense, not only of mission, but of inevitability. He caught the mind and the temper of his time, and his most influential work, *The Stages of Economic Growth*, which he published in 1960, was based on a series of lectures which he had given earlier, and which had then received a wide publicity when they were serialised by the *Economist* in Britain, and by *Fortune* in the United States.

Moreover, the broad themes which would be—and were—drawn from the work to become the imperatives of American foreign policy during the 1960s were being canvassed by other writers with a voguish influence on the public mind, and the quick mind of John Kennedy responded to them. They were being hawked, for example, by Barbara Ward, a public figure of considerably less intellectual power than Walt Rostow, whose hold on educated opinion during the decade which concerns us is inexplicable except in terms of the vagaries of "the Establishment." Although an Englishwoman, she commanded the ears of both John Kennedy and Lyndon Johnson; and someone once suggested that her rise to such prominence on the basis of economic journalism of a decent competence could be explained only by the fact that, whenever a government in Britain had to appoint to a royal commission, or to some other advisory body, (a) a woman and (b) a Roman Catholic (c) a liberal and (d) an economist, Barbara Ward was a most convenient package deal. With an irreproachable generosity of spirit she tirelessly urged the United States to pour its treasure into the farthest regions of the world. On at least one such occasion, as Arthur Schlesinger recounts it, John Kennedy was "impressed by Barbara Ward's several interventions" on behalf of Ghana; and, if the reader cares to travel a few years ahead, he will find in the memoirs of Lyndon Johnson that, as late as March 1968, she was one of "a group of British intellectuals"—she is the only one whom he mentions—who sent a memorandum to him proposing, among other measures, that the United States should even then "mobilize more men for Vietnam . . . reinforce its armies in the South and continue the talk of 'pacification.'" With such friends, is there need of enemies?

Barbara Ward's main message was quoted by John Kennedy in a speech which he gave at Lincoln, Nebraska, as early as 13 October 1959: "The profoundest matter at stake in Africa is the quality and capacity of Western society itself." Rudyard Kipling, after the annexation of the Philippines, had addressed his famous exhortation to the American people—"Take up the White Man's burden"—and here was Barbara Ward offering the same invitation, and John Kennedy accepting it. (There is no way of denying that the English have been ready with this advice since they found their own dominion over palm and pine too much for them, and I freely admit that I have sometimes tended it myself.) But behind the advice of Barbara Ward lay the power of an idea, and it was to this idea that the work of Walt Rostow gave a formidable intellectual construction, by which it worked its influence on the administration.

"The stages of economic growth" are five:

1. *The traditional society,* in which men have not yet come to know that it is possible to manipulate the environment through knowledge of the laws of the external world.

2. *The preconditions for take-off,* in which the idea spreads, not merely that economic progress is possible, but that it is a necessary condition for the achievement of broader purposes.

3. *The take-off,* in which the old obstacles and resistance to steady economic growth are finally overcome.

4. *The drive to maturity,* in which the economy grows stead-

ily over a prolonged period, and modern technology extends over the whole economy.

5. *The age of high mass consumption,* in which the economic emphasis steadily shifts to the supply of goods and services to the consumer.

This steadily articulated progression bears a strong resemblance to the method of argument which was used by Winnie-the-Pooh, who made his way by a process of ponderous—but, in his case, beguiling—ratiocination from the empirical observation that there were bees in the vicinity, to the rational speculation that where there were bees there was likely to be honey, to the positive resolution that where there was honey there he had a right to be; and in this manner succeeded in achieving a high level of personal consumption and even, on occasions, an accelerated rate of physical growth. On a level which some will regard as more serious, it would be as treacherous for any state, developed or undeveloped, to construct its policies on the model of Walt Rostow's stages of economic growth as for it to build them on the model of Arnold Toynbee's cycles of civilisation.

Even if it could be shown that the economies of our own civilisation have passed through the stages of growth which he describes—with only the most casual references to other factors which have influenced their development—these stages cannot be found in other civilisations of high (if non-Western) achievement and equal (if non-Western) maturity. Yet he formulated these stages as if they were a law of universal application. It was, he said, "my alternative to the system of historical analysis developed by Karl Marx." But the only reliable alternative to the system of Karl Marx is to have no system: to appreciate the untidiness and the unpredictability, the chances and the digressions, of the actual historical world; to learn to live within it, not as a system, but as a narrative. The politics of expectation was nourished in part by the illusion that an answer could be found to the systems of Marxism or of Communism, other than the spontaneity of free societies.

In its impact on the foreign policy of the United States, the doctrine of Walt Rostow could be reduced to three propositions: that, in their present stage of economic growth, the countries of the underdeveloped world require the support and the assistance of the United States in the pressing task of nation-building; that this task can best be performed within a framework of regional stability, to which the United States must also give its support and assistance; and that both these tasks need to be performed, by the iron law of economic growth, throughout the underdeveloped world. In short, the need for the support and the assistance of the United States exists in much the same form across the face of the globe. America must regard itself as committed to intervention in numerous individual nations, in a wider frame of regional stability, within the ultimate context of global responsibility. This is a policy to which no limits can be set. The hesitant example of the Eisenhower Doctrine, in guaranteeing the stability of individual nations and of regions, had been transformed by a powerful intellectual construction, to which Walt Rostow still fundamentally holds in *Politics and the Stages of Growth*, which he published in 1971.

The practical effect of this construction was necessarily militarist, as Walt Rostow himself made clear when he spoke on 28 June 1961 to the Special Warfare School at Fort Bragg:

> Our central task in the underdeveloped areas, as we see it, is to protect the independence of the revolutionary process now going

forward . . . We are committed by the nature of our system to
support the cause of national independence. . . .

Finally, the United States has a role to play in learning to deter
guerrilla warfare, if possible, and to deal with it, if necessary. . . .
We are determined to destroy this international disease. This requires, of course, not merely a proper military program of de-
terrence, but programs of village development, communications,
and indoctrination. . . .

I salute you, as I would a group of doctors, teachers, economic
planners, agricultural experts, civil servants, or those others who are
now leading the way in the whole southern half of the globe in
fashioning the new nations.

From the idea which he had demurely formed as an economic
historian, he had reached the point where he was ordering the
Special Forces of the United States Army into battle. Doctors
and teachers, economists and agriculturalists, and the Green
Berets going on before! In this way, the ecclesiast and the
missionary and the soldier were joined in the Ignatius Loyola
of the administration.

For some time before he gave it the historical trappings of
The Stages of Economic Growth, Walt Rostow had been at
work on his idea. As early as 1957, he and Max F. Millikan,
who was also to advise John Kennedy on foreign aid, had
presented the theme in *A Proposal: Key to an Effective Foreign
Policy.* "One of the highest priority tasks for United States
foreign policy," they said, "is to use our influence to promote
the evolution of societies" that would become "stable" and
"effective" and "democratic." One must notice, in passing, the
slack vocabulary. If they had written, "in areas of the world
where its national interest is directly engaged, the United
States must provide economic assistance and, where necessary,
military support to governments which are capable of acting
as trustworthy allies," a lot of trouble, of men, and of money,
would have been saved. But who can sensibly question an

abstraction—a "highest priority task"—to be performed in pursuit of another abstraction—"the evolution of societies"? It is these abstractions which are open-ended, which have no limit.

Edward Weintal and Charles Bartlett tell us that Robert Cutler, when he was Special Assistant for National Security Affairs in the administration of Dwight Eisenhower, used to irritate some members of the National Security Council by asking questions such as: "What exactly do you mean by preserving democracy in South Korea?" But it is the question which should have been repeatedly asked in the past twenty years; and it was all too rarely asked in the administration of John Kennedy, infatuated as it was by the concept of nation-building. It was this kind of intellectual construction which was inherently attractive to John Kennedy and to the men whom he gathered to serve him. They needed it to sustain the "splendor of design" of what they did. It was from this design that so much was expected, but it was self-defeating, since it tempted them to neglect the diversity and the intractability of the actual world.

Alongside the concept of nation-building was the concept of regionalism. In an address, "Regional Organization: A Planner's Perspective," which was published in the *Department of State Bulletin* of 21 June 1965, Walt Rostow boldly said of South-east Asia: "Of course, the region itself is at stake. The flank of the Indian sub-continent is at stake." Three pages later, he asserted: "This increasing interest in the building of regional organization is one of the most interesting features in the world scene today." Perhaps it is; perhaps it is not. Certainly, there is little evidence in most parts of the world that regionalism is much of a force. It does not seem to bind India to Pakistan in South Asia; the Cambodians to the Vietnamese, or even the Vietnamese to the Vietnamese, in South-east Asia;

Israel to Egypt in the Middle East, or even Arab to Arab; the new countries of Africa or the old republics of Latin America fondly to each other; and even the Irish on their small island still fight.

Between the two quotations which have just been given, Walt Rostow had spoken once more of the "assertive nationalism" which he said was evident "throughout the world"— everything is seen as global—which he in fact said was "a wave." But, if this assertive nationalism is a wave, it is hard to understand how the regionalism can be much of a wave as well. He went on to speak, for example, of the "thrusts for regional hegemony" which would be the consequence of regional organisation, with the obvious implication that, if the hegemony were established by a nation which was hostile to the United States, it would be a crushing reverse for American foreign policy. But, if nationalism is the wave which he claimed it to be, the chance of any nation's establishing a regional hegemony would seem to be distant. During the 1960s, regionalism became a conventional orthodoxy of American policy, and it is not surprising that Lyndon Johnson, in his memoirs, has a whole chapter entitled, "The New Age of Regionalism." In his prose, the idea may seem banal. The intellectual construction is absent. But it was this construction—this model —which had deluded him, as it had deluded his predecessor. When he proposed to build a Great Society in South-east Asia, the concept of regionalism collapsed under the weight of its own absurdity; yet it had driven two administrations to pretentious undertakings, under the expectation that the world would behave with the predictability of the model.

When a concept becomes as powerful as this, we are likely to find that it has more than one origin, and the concept of regionalism was significantly reinforced by the "area studies" which became fashionable in American universities after the Second World War, and which in turn had a familiar origin. It has been conveniently summarised by none other than McGeorge Bundy in a lecture which he gave at Johns Hopkins University early in 1964, "The Battlefields of Power and the Searchlights of the Academy":

> It is a curious fact of academic history that the first great center of area studies in the United States was not located in any university, but in Washington, during the Second World War in the Office of Strategic Services. In very large measure, the area study programs developed in American universities in the years after the war were manned, directed, or stimulated by graduates of the OSS —a remarkable institution, half cops and robbers, half faculty meeting. It is still true today, and I hope it will always be, that there is a big measure of interpenetration between universities with area programs and the information-gathering agencies of the United States.

This is an illuminating passage, not least in the radical failure to distinguish between the purposes of universities and the purposes of government. In the past twenty-five years in the United States, their "interpenetration" has been carried so far that it can fairly be described as a national calamity; and it is with extreme difficulty that the universities are today trying to disengage themselves. But "half cops and robbers, half faculty meeting" was a part of the spirit of the New Frontier: physical bravado joined to intellectual bravura.

Once again, in noticing their ideas, we are brought back to the experience of the men themselves in a lot of war and diplomacy, particularly in the Office of Strategic Services; and it is when Arthur Schlesinger is discussing the economists who assisted in creating the foreign aid policy of John Kennedy, especially as it affected the underdeveloped countries, that he also takes us back to the OSS: "Another common experience was wartime work in such agencies as the Office of Strategic Services (Edward S. Mason, Walt Rostow, Carl Kaysen) or the Strategic Bombing Survey (J. K. Galbraith), where economists, whether in order to pick out bombing targets or to assess the significance of the damage wrought, had to think in terms of the leverage points within the economic system." But the one fact about the bombing in the Second World War which is today universally acknowledged is that it had only a marginal effect on the economies of the countries which were bombed. If in war, when the life of a country is fixed on a single objective, it is hard to identify the leverage points in an economy, one can be sure that in peace, when the life of a country is again diversified, it will be even more difficult: that the effort to expand an economy by concentrating on them will prove to be as misconceived as the effort to destroy an economy by reducing them to rubble. But this was exactly the kind of misconception which these men drew from their experience in the Second World War.

It was to agencies such as the OSS that many academics were attracted—or directed—during that time; and it must have been as inspiriting as it was novel for them to find that the business of war and diplomacy, so it seemed, could be managed by their kind of intellectual expertise. The gathering of information and the rational analysis of it: this was what they had been accustomed to do in their own profession. The branch of OSS in which many of them toiled was called Research and Analysis. It was no wonder that they became confident that their intellectual tools could manipulate political problems, in their own country, in other countries, in entire regions, in the world. But the precision of their tools, which was the source of their confidence, was also their undoing: it led them to ignore the imprecision of political judgement, the intractability of all human affairs; it led them to erect systems and construct models, and to try to make local situations obedient to their method.

Once the leap had been made from nation-building to the concept of regionalism, it was only a hop and a skip to global commitment, the confidence not failing. They were taken, in a breath-taking phrase, by Walt Rostow himself when he referred, in *View from the Seventh Floor,* to the Cuba missile crisis as "the Gettysburg of the global civil conflict." His scheme had become self-sustaining. On the one hand, he was saying, the United States and the Soviet Union are involved in local civil conflicts because they are engaged in a global civil war; on the other hand, the evidence that they are engaged in a global civil war is to be found in their involvement in local civil conflicts. This is a game which used to be called, "Here we go round the mulberry bush"; and, at the end of it, we "all fall down." Apart from anything else, it is an exhausting way in which to conduct one's life, and wise grandparents would watch the bright eyes of the children grow brighter still, and mutter sharply that "there will be tears before nightfall"; and there always were. It is much the condition of the American people today. Round and round the mulberry bush they went, between 1961 and 1968, when they all fell down, tired of building nations, tired of stabilising regions, tired of global conflict. But this was exactly what they had been promised when they set out; this had been the expectation.

For all its quickness and its curiosity, the mind of John Kennedy does not appear to have been equipped to cope with complexity. The ideology of the Cold War was simplifying, not least in the intellectual construction with which Walt Rostow provided it; it retained the peculiar simplifications of war; confrontation was simplifying; to think of the globe was simplifying. Louis Koenig at one point describes the attention which John Kennedy gave to "his global constituency"; and not only he but his brothers as well. Time and again, when domestic politics become too complex and too intractable, we find them boarding an aircraft, to visit their global constituents. The virtue of such constituents is that, since they do not pay taxes in the United States, since their domestic lives are not in detail affected by what the President does inside the United States, they do not have any serious grumble. So they can gather in the streets and cheer. They will cheer even more readily if the visiting President, or aspirant for the Presidency, tells them that the United States will always be at their side with money and, if necessary, men as well.

They will especially cheer if the President, or the aspirant for the Presidency, appears to belong to a family of movie stars, and to have a movie star as his wife, whose faces are known. In this manner, when Edward Kennedy has taken himself to places which happen to be in the headlines, and expressed his concern for what is happening in India or Pakistan or Ireland, he has merely been continuing a habit of his two brothers. John Kennedy used the method before 1960; Robert Kennedy used it before 1968. What is more, not only did John Kennedy use it also while he was President, he used Robert Kennedy to the same purpose, as at the beginning of 1962, when he sent his brother on a tour of the world which lasted fourteen weeks. What the Attorney General of the United States was doing on such a tour, at a time when his department was deeply engaged in handling the first serious violence of the struggle for civil rights, is beyond all sensible explanation. But is this not exactly the point? By such a world tour, both the Attorney General and the President, especially since they were brothers, were lifted above the domestic problems at home and their undignified squabbles.

There is a scene in Charlie Chaplin's film, *The Great Dictator*, in which he dances, in the character of Adolf Hitler, an intoxicated ballet, first round the globe which is in his room, and then holding the globe, spinning it on the tips of his fingers, doing anything which he likes with it; until it bursts. They should have played that film, and that scene, in the private cinema of the White House between 1961 and 1963, for the men of the administration were intoxicated by the globe. In their memoirs and in the history books, we too often find men of power bent over their maps of the world; and one wishes that they would turn instead to the long columns which form the indexes of their atlases, to the names of actual places in small print. All the cities, all the towns, all the villages, all the hamlets—population 8,000,000 or population 64—that is the globe, diverse and unknowable. The mind which wishes to conquer it, like that of Napoleon Bonaparte, is uneducated; the mind which would reduce it to a system, like that of Karl Marx, is anxious; the mind which imagines that it is a village, like that of Marshall McLuhan, is narrow; the mind which thinks that it may make a tour of it, and know it, like those of the men whom we are considering, is frivolous. We need to learn again to think our problems small, and so deal with them; and our politicians should not tempt us otherwise.

But the fascination with the globe of John Kennedy and his administration did not allow them to think their problems small. It went against their grain to bother with the complexity of Latin America—the local political situations, the individual national traditions, the different economic problems—and they must instead think big with an "Alliance for Progress" which, as Abraham F. Lowenthal said in the issue of *Foreign Affairs* of April 1970, was marked from the beginning by "the easy optimism and the excessive ardor of the Kennedy administration." As the countries of Western Europe began to recover from the war, and then to assert their independence, the administration seemed once again to feel threatened by the complexity of the new situation, and thought big once more with a "Grand Design," which was described by Joseph Kraft, perhaps its most articulate spokesman outside the administration, as "another spectacular leap in this country's remarkable transit from isolation to international engagement," although there was little that the United States could do to reshape the Atlantic Alliance in the new conditions.

In the book which he published in 1962, *The Grand Design: From Common Market to Atlantic Partnership,* it seemed that Joseph Kraft was flying a kite for the administration. He had been made privy to its earliest, and its latest, debates on the question, beginning with a meeting between Robert Bowie and Henry Owen at the Department of State in September 1961; and he himself says that his book "could not have been written without the kind co-operation of officials in the Kennedy administration, and to a certain extent reflects their views." We are entitled to regard it as a primary document of a kind: a firsthand account of how the Kennedy administration was accustomed to enfold its diplomacy in majestic concepts. It is also interesting because, as anyone who is familiar with the work of Joesph Kraft is aware, his mind is peculiarly gifted to cope with complexity and to avoid the temptations of a "splendor of design." In the quotations which follow we have an outstanding example of what could happen to a subtle mind when it was molested by the bravura of the administration.

As a result of the Grand Design, the West would be tall in the saddle: "The Atlantic Partnership will confront the Soviet bloc with a force such as the world has never known. It—and perhaps it alone—will be of a scale to cope with the tasks of developing Southern continents." The modest adjustments of politics were put aside: "For what is emerging is a unifying intellectual principle for the New Frontier . . . a means of fulfilling the historic mission of the Kennedy administration, which is the squaring of domestic affairs with the requirements of world leadership." This was exactly the problem to which John Kennedy gave only perfunctory attention, for the very reason that his mind was engrossed elsewhere: "The overwhelming problem, of course, is the problem of the underdeveloped countries"; the second problem was the power of the Soviet Union; the third problem was the unity of Western Europe. "The Grand Design is grand precisely because it gives the promise of dealing with all these problems."

One can only imagine the stupefaction of Charles Maurice de Talleyrand-Périgord or Klemens Wenzel Nepomuk Lothar von Metternich if they had read such a variety of claims, and had then been shown the key to the design. For it was nothing more than the Trade Expansion Act of 1962, a measure which was described by Bernard D. Nossiter at the time as "a masterful invocation of nineteenth-century liberal thought." Speaking of the special message on "Foreign Trade Policy" which John Kennedy had sent to Congress in support of the measure, Joseph Kraft said that it was "generously sprinkled with expressions of sweep and grandeur. . . . A map of the world and its troubles had been set before Congress and the American people." A map of the world in a trade policy? It is indeed an engaging nineteenth-century liberal idea. But the Kennedy Round of trade negotiations which followed the Trade Expansion Act only marginally touched the problems of the underdeveloped countries and made no difference to the power of the Atlantic Alliance in relation to that of the Soviet Union. Even as trade negotiations, their achievement was modest. In trade negotiations, countries squabble about chickens—as in the "Chicken War" between 1962 and 1964, which eventually demanded John Kennedy's personal attention—or tomatoes; they do not draw maps of the world. The issue in a Chicken War cannot also be the issue of a Grand Design.

It is true that the Grand Design was to be sustained by a common defence policy as well as by a common trade policy. But the strategy which was developed by Robert McNamara alarmed, rather than reassured, the partners of the United States; and the concept foundered, in any event, on the Nassau Agreement which was reached by John Kennedy and Harold Macmillan after America's cancellation of the Skybolt air-to-surface missile. One of the consequences of the agreement was that Charles de Gaulle was provided with the opportunity for which he was looking to close the door against Britain's entrance into the Common Market; and the whole Grand Design was in ruins, in part because the Kennedy administration had mishandled a single negotiation with a single country about a single weapon. Having launched a Grand Design with a vocabulary of sweep and grandeur, John Kennedy and his administration allowed it to founder because they paid no attention to actual politics, to the little scratchings on any mariner's chart. For want of a nail, someone might have reminded him, a kingdom was lost.

Neither the American people, nor those whose duty it was to interpret the policy of the administration to them, were inclined to question the rhetorical gestures in which the foreign

policy of John Kennedy was so often expressed. All three—
people and commentators and administration—had persuaded
themselves, or had been persuaded, that grand designs were
possible, that the map of the world could be redrawn at the
initiative of the United States. If we look for the reason for
this delusion, we will find a clue in the exclusion by John
Kennedy of any reference to domestic affairs in his inaugural
address. The administration believed that the domestic problems
of the country were largely settled. This was one of the themes
of the "pragmatic liberals," given a characteristically bold expression by Walt Rostow and Max Millikan:

> . . . we need the challenge of world development to keep us
> from the stagnation of smug prosperity . . . to give fresh meaning
> and vitality to the historic American sense of mission—a mission to
> see the principles of national independence and human liberty
> extended on the world scene. . . .
>
> The farm problem, the status of big business in a democratic
> society, the status and responsibilities of organized labor, the
> avoidance of extreme cyclical unemployment, social equity for the
> Negro, the provision of equal educational opportunity, the equitable
> distribution of income—none of all these great issues is fully re-
> solved; but a national consensus exists within which we are clearly
> moving forward as a nation. . . .

The extraordinary optimism of this statement is equalled only
by the narrow definition of the social issues confronting the
United States; but from this platform they could make their
outward leap:

> [American] society has a meaning and a purpose which tran-
> scend the nation. . . . If over the coming decades the United
> States should turn its back on the great revolutionary transforma-
> tions going forward in the underdeveloped countries, devoting
> itself almost exclusively to domestic chores and objectives, American
> society will progressively lose some of those basic spiritual qualities

which have been historically linked to the nation's sense of world mission. The nation will risk the long-term danger of helping to bring about by its own spiritual decline a kind of self-enforced isolation which would further damage the military and non-military bases of national security.

There is a truth lurking in these words; a great nation cannot refuse its historical moment; possessing great power, and therefore great influence, it cannot avoid exercising them. But the words carry the truth into aëry regions, into worlds of the spirit where the mission has an existence of its own which *transcends the nation;* and it is this kind of concept which distorts and then binds.

As has been shown, the evidence was already available to suggest that the United States was, in its own land, about to enter a period of uncertainty, and even of disturbance. Some of its people were already taking to the streets; the administration had barely begun its labours before the Freedom Riders took to the highways. Problems such as racial discrimination and ineradicable poverty, which had appeared to exist only in the South, had already travelled North, or had at last been recognised there: the cities were already decaying, and were known to be decaying; the flight to the suburbs was already well enough understood to be the subject of reports by the newsmagazines; the expansion of the highway programme by the administration of Dwight Eisenhower had begun to alter the manner of living of the people; public transit was already dying; public education was beginning to collapse; public medicine had become a crying need. If, in this condition, a policy of bold designs was to be pursued at all, it was most urgent that it should be pursued at home.

But, as John Kennedy had noticed while writing his inaugural address, domestic issues are divisive. He was in this, once more, a man of his time. Far from challenging the kind of consensus—a word to which we will return—by which Dwight Eisenhower had governed during the 1950s, he in fact wished to preserve it; and then to use it, as his predecessor had not done, in support of a foreign policy of grand designs. It was on this that the politics of expectation was built: the conviction that the country was at home so united, its problems no more than chores, as Walt Rostow and Max Millikan put it, that it could afford the luxury of remaking the world, that it had the right and the duty to do so; that a nation which had so nearly finished its own business could be moved by a spirit which transcended the nation to accomplish in the farthest regions of the world what at home it found too awkward to consider.

CHAPTER SEVEN

Arming the Presidency

JOHN KENNEDY HAD an exaggerated—and simplifying—interest in foreign affairs; and, with it, an exaggerated—and simplifying—notion of the capacity of the Presidency. The two have, by and large, gone together in every Democratic administration of this century, and the connection was made in 1900, appropriately enough, by Woodrow Wilson, writing in *Congressional Government:* "When foreign affairs play a prominent part in the politics and policy of a nation, its Executive must of necessity be its guide; must utter every initial judgment, take every first step of action, supply the information upon which it is to act." This view of the Presidency passed in direct line to Franklin Roosevelt, to Harry Truman, to John Kennedy, to Lyndon Johnson; and it is only with some difficulty that the American people, and in particular their representatives in Congress, are freeing themselves from the mesmerising belief that, in endowing the Chief Executive with the power to govern them for a time, they endow him also with a virtue and a wisdom greater than their own.

During the winter of 1966–67, Arthur Schlesinger took part in a series of debates with Alfred de Grazia on the role of the Presidency, in which he at first outlined the traditional Democratic belief in a strong President, and then declared: ". . .

some of us who in the past have been all-out supporters of the Presidential prerogative have been forced to think again as a consequence of the present involvement in Vietnam"; and he even argued that there may be an exchange of positions between the two parties "comparable to that between the Federalists and the Jeffersonians from 1800 to 1814." This is a remarkable statement to come from the man who is not only the historian of the Democratic tradition, but the historian of it at its most assertive: in *The Age of Jackson,* who "may be said," as he tells us, "to have invented the modern Presidency," in the *Age of Roosevelt,* who "armed the President," as he again tells us, "with new weapons," and in *A Thousand Days,* in which he describes the exaltation of the Presidency under John Kennedy. It is this past which he seems to be repudiating.

John Kennedy's exalted view of the Presidency is given its most vivid expression by Theodore Sorensen in words which dramatically affirm the primacy of the Presidency within the Executive Branch and of the Executive Branch within the federal government, and no less dramatically assert the leadership of the federal government within the United States and of the United States within the world. This is a formidable construction, built on a concept of the Presidency by which Theodore Sorensen sets great store, but which was hard to justify at the time, and which is impossible to maintain in the mood of today.

It is possible that an Englishman does not altogether appreciate the office of the Presidency. At no time in the history of Britain has any direct grant of popular power been made to a single person; and much that is praised in British political life—its stability and its tolerance—may be traced to this fact. Indeed, the grant of popular power to the President of the United States is less direct than the everyday vocabulary of politics makes it seem; and it is to be hoped that, if the proposal to reform, or to abolish, the Electoral College is ever taken seriously, some un-everyday attention will be paid to the complexity of the electoral process which it serves by its ingenious mechanics. Nevertheless, the general idea is that the sovereign people make a direct grant of their power to the President; and, to someone reared in a different political tradition, this is troubling. Wherever, in modern history, a political leader has been able to claim such a direct grant of power from below, he has usually been found acting as if this conferred on him an unhindered right to exercise power from above. Most modern dictatorships—and the drift to "voluntary totalitarianism" in modern democracies—have their origin in this claim.

In this chapter, however, the vast powers enjoyed by the Presidency are taken for granted; as is also the right of every President to organise the office in the manner which he believes will suit his purposes. We are concerned with the manner in which John Kennedy organised the Presidency to his own purposes; and with the illumination which this can provide both of the purposes and of his method. What cannot be denied is that in his campaign, in his inaugural address, in the Presidency itself, he encouraged the American people to have high expectations of the office. He had a gift for popular leadership; he used the Presidency as a platform from which to exercise it; and the people were grateful to be led. But, although a President is justified in using the office as a "bully pulpit," popular leadership is not the whole of political leadership, and not even its greater part.

The main argument of this chapter is that John Kennedy, by confusing popular leadership with political leadership, not only practised, but dignified, the politics of expectation to such an extent that almost no one questioned either his method or his purposes. He relied so much on the direct connection between the President and the people—his regular use of the televised press conference is an obvious example—that he neglected the actual political processes by which his purposes could be achieved, while arousing the expectation that they would be achieved merely by a dramatic expression of the popular will. Whenever there was something which he wished to do, he went before the television cameras and could rely on obtaining the desired popular reaction; the expectation was aroused, and the expectation was supported; but on the following morning the thing had still to be done. There is in fact very little that the people can do to assist a President while he is in office; brought together at a general election, they are dispersed between elections; brought together in the evening by a television address, they are dispersed the next day. Popular leadership can bring only small returns; and it should be used sparingly.

The most obvious requirement of a President, if he is to use his opportunities of political leadership to the full, is to open himself to a variety of advice. There is a myth that John Kennedy welcomed opposing advice and conflicting opinions; and that he created an administration which would provide him with them. There is scant evidence that this was true. The myth is based in part on the questionable belief that, whereas Dwight Eisenhower "institutionalized" the Presidency, John Kennedy "de-institutionalized" it, thus opening his office to a variety of counsels; that he relied on the informal meetings and the direct contacts, the task forces and the personal emissaries, which Theodore Sorensen, from his experience at the centre, is able to describe for us. But there was in all this a legendary element, the more powerful at the time because the men themselves were attracted by it: the "band of brothers" throwing out ideas and suggestions in gay profusion, or with "grim, puncturing humor," while the chief among them, curious and alert, gayer than the rest and more puncturing, absorbed what was said, and made his choices.

It was not quite like that; and we may begin at the beginning. Some time between 1956 and 1959, John Kennedy had been persuaded that there existed beyond the day-to-day world of politics a reservoir of detached intelligence and informed judgement which could be put to political use. It was not a novel idea in the United States, but it was pursued with his usual exuberance. As early as 3 December 1958, at the Hotel Commander in Cambridge, the "Academic Advisory Committee" of the young, and still unannounced, candidate held its first meeting. We have glimpses of many such occasions. In August 1960, Arthur Schlesinger informs us, John Kennedy summoned "to a seminar on the boat off Hyannis Port," the willing crew of John Kenneth Galbraith, Seymour Harris, Archibald Cox, Paul Samuelson, and Richard Lester, "in an effort to learn the secret" of "how to bring the expansion rate up to 5 per cent." They talked and they talked. "They did their best, but there was no philosopher's stone." One must ask how the politician had been persuaded, or had persuaded himself, that it would be fruitful to look for one. But this kind of delusion is one of the hazards of the method.

The more serious danger is that the politician may imagine that he is receiving independent advice from competing points of view, whereas he is in fact choosing the advice which he is willing to hear. The point is well made by Herbert Stein in his ample volume, *The Fiscal Revolution in America*, in which he first quotes a remark made by Paul Samuelson on the influence of Presidential advisers: "And note this: he who picks his own doctor from an array of competing doctors is in a real sense his own doctor." To this Herbert Stein adds: "The key words here are 'array of competing doctors.' As far as ideas on fiscal policy were concerned, Kennedy did not choose from an array of competing doctors; he chose from an array of doctors whose ideas were basically the same." Whether in the advice which he sought while he was a candidate, or in the task forces which he asked to report to him while he was the President-elect, or in the *ad hoc* task forces which he employed while he was the President, John Kennedy usually contrived to receive the kind of advice which he wished.

In themselves, the task forces which he appointed after his election were not important. Almost a hundred men served on them, for the most part drawn from the academic world in what was advertised at the time as an unusual mobilisation of the country's intellectual talent. It was nothing of the sort. It was a recruitment of a minute fraction of the intellectual talent of the nation, a small number of like minds, many of them acquainted with each other, and in some cases recommending each other for their respective appointments. Swiftly recruited after the election, they as swiftly performed. One might have expected men from the intellectual world—interested in the complexity of truth, rather than in the convenience of half-truth—to hesitate, to demur, to wonder, as they wrote their opinions. But why should they? Being of like mind, and knowing what the politician required of them, there was no reason for them to think, and they wrote their innocuous essays for him without much ado.

As one would expect, John Kennedy glanced at their reports, rather than read them, and passed them on to the incoming heads of the departments concerned, who probably read them, never to glance at them again. To the President-elect, they were window dressing. On 5 December 1960, for example, he appointed a task force on depressed areas, under the chairmanship of Paul Douglas; and, when he publicly received its report a month later, he declared that the depressed areas should be assigned "the most important domestic priority," a pledge which a little puzzled those who remembered that, both at the beginning of his campaign on 21 August 1960, and near the end of it in a letter dated 11 October to the Farm Bureau Federations of Arkansas-Tennessee-Mississippi, he had said that "the farm problem . . . the decline in agricultural income" is "the No. 1 domestic issue in this campaign . . . the No. 1 domestic problem in the United States"; or that at Atlantic City on 19 September he had assured the United Chemical Workers that he considered unemployment to be "the No. 1 domestic problem which the next President of the United States will have to face"; or that in the 10 October issue of *Missiles and Rockets* he had told its readers that "Certainly national scientific goals will be our first objective." None of this is of much significance; he was as agile as any politician. But it helps us to weigh the importance which he attached to the informal advice which he sought.

Just as he did not mention civil rights in his inaugural address, so civil rights was the only significant area of domestic policy in which he did not appoint a task force. He might permit Frederick Hovde, the president of Purdue University, to tell him what he should do about education; or Joseph McMurray, the president of Queens Community College in New York, to prescribe what should be done about housing; or Wilbur Cohen, of the University of Michigan, to propose improvements in social security; or Jerome B. Wiesner, of the Massachusetts Institute of Technology, to suggest how the

United States might pursue the Soviet Union into space; but he was not of a mind to allow them, or any like them, into the field of civil rights. In this area, the liberals and the intellectuals were not given the chance to set any awkward standards. They were invited where they could not cause any serious trouble.

When the advice was politically awkward, he managed to overlook it. Thus, the task force on taxation policy came forward with a radical report under the leadership of Stanley Surrey, a genuine expert in the field and a tireless advocate of tax reforms. The report was delivered, and Stanley Surrey was appointed to the Treasury as an Assistant Secretary in charge of taxation policy. But there the boldness ended. A number of severe tax reforms, on the lines proposed by Stanley Surrey, were brought forward by the administration in 1961; but, by the time they finally took shape in the Revenue Act of 1962, there was not much of them still to be seen. It was not only Congress which was responsible for this default; as Hobart Rowen comments, "the administration showed a weak spine, too." John Kennedy was seeking the political support of big business, so the tax reforms could be bargained away. When one reads of his openness to informal advice, which was so much advertised at the time, one must remember that it carries no political weight. It is as cheap to invite as it is easy to reject; it assists in arousing expectations, but the political realities in the end intervene.

As he looked at the appointments to the new administration on 9 January 1961, T.R.B. in the *New Republic* contrasted them sharply with the men who had first arrived with Franklin Roosevelt:

The New Dealers who poured into Washington to take over the government were as gaudy a bunch of amateurs, intellectuals, and crackpots, as this experienced capital has ever seen—men whom FDR set against each other with sometimes unkind virtuosity, catching the sparks in the net.

What a gang!—Hopkins, Wallace, Ickes, Fanny Perkins, Tommy the Cork, Henry the Morgue, Ben Cohen, Adlai Stevenson, General Johnson, Ray Moley, Abe Fortas, Alger Hiss. . . .

The Kennedy Cabinet is competent, enormously, reassuringly, competent, but nothing like this . . . it is all under control, or seems to be. It is disciplined.

Competence was, indeed, one of their measures of themselves; and they now and then remind one of a conversation between Lewie Haystoun and Tommy Wratislaw in John Buchan's novel, *The Half-Hearted*:

> "What would you call the highest happiness, Lewie?" he asked.
> "The sense of competence," was the answer given without hesitation.
> "Right! And what do we mean by competence? Not success! God knows it is something very different from success! Any fool may be successful, if the gods wish to hurt him. Competence means that splendid joy in your own powers, and the approval of your own heart, which great men feel always and lesser men now and again at favoured intervals. There are a certain number of things to be done in the world, and we have got to do them. We may fail —it doesn't in the least matter. We may get killed in the attempt— it matters still less. The things may not altogether be worth doing— it is of very little importance. It is ourselves we have to judge by. If we are playing our part well and know it.

That was the spirit, that was the manner; and, noticing their competence on 7 June 1963, *Time* wryly commented: "They make mistakes—but they make them efficiently." Ten years later, the irony bites deep.

At the core of their discipline and their self-discipline was their single-minded, singlehearted, commitment to their President. They were absolute in their devotion to him; and, as they stood in a cluster, listening to the delivery of the first message to Congress on the State of the Union, an attendant Republican was heard to remark: "All they need now is Eleanor Roosevelt to be den mother." The ill effect of such an atmosphere was that it diminished the likelihood that John Kennedy would receive genuinely conflicting advice: not just different opinions, differing suggestions, different options; but the kind of conflicting advice which, in politics, emerges only when strong men are at loggerheads, when entrenched departments do battle, and when their bruising altercations are carried day by day to the ear of the President.

Most of the gang to whom Franklin Roosevelt gave the opportunities of power—many of them with the manners of cut throats—stood on their own ground, prickly and obstinate and suspicious, and served him from there. It is inconceivable that, even in the dawn of the New Deal, they would ever have referred to themselves as a "band of brothers . . . we happy few"; and, if one of them had done so, it is not hard to imagine the spit in the eye he would have got from Harold Ickes. But it was not in the nature of John Kennedy to enjoy the fussing and the feuding of strong men about him. He wanted to create a Presidency which would be as personal as Franklin Roosevelt's; but, as Richard Neustadt put it in the *American Political Science Review* of December 1963, "without much feuding in the White House staff." The cost to him and to his administration—and ultimately to the country—of this anxiety was to be high.

"Those who did not agree with the Kennedy thoughts or did not like the Kennedy technique, or found other objections, simply did not survive," wrote Hugh Sidey at the time; and, when we are presented with the familiar picture of a man open to differing opinions and opposing counsels, we must not forget how much evidence supports this statement. As the Secretary of the Air Force in the administration, Eugene M. Zuckert had some difficulty in his dealings with Robert McNamara, and he gave a remarkably informative account of them in the issue of *Foreign Affairs* of April 1966. On one occasion, early in the life of the administration, he carried one of these differences to John Kennedy, and was curtly rebuffed: "He wanted my support and, while willing in this instance to stand for a certain amount of 'independent' thinking, that independence must in the future be neither frequent nor important." One senses in the full account of this incident the extreme coolness of John Kennedy to what he took to be any unnecessary interruption of the smooth running of the machinery of the Presidency as he had created it; and he gathered most closely to him men on whom he could rely to stay "cool under pressure."

They prided themselves, either that they were unemotional men, or that at least they concealed their emotions. But what was required was someone to disturb this ineffable self-assurance; someone who would bang the table, and bang it hard; someone who would say—shout, if necessary—"Mr. President, we are going to war, and we are not even calling it a war," and say it again at the next meeting. The foresight of George W. Ball was indeed impressive, when he suggested in the fall of 1961 that the commitment of the prestige of the United States to the war in Vietnam might eventually require as many as 300,000 American troops to achieve a military solution. But his warning was made coolly, and even blandly, and not a hint of it reached the press or the public. In the atmosphere of the administration, it was inevitable that such a vital counsel would be made in less than a whisper.

There is no evidence—either in the literature, or in the personal accounts which one has been given—that any of those close to John Kennedy ever talked back to him as did many of those close to Franklin Roosevelt. One could ransack the memoirs of Harold Ickes for such instances, and it is hard not to smile when one reads, in his entry for 27 August 1935: "I was pretty angry and I showed it. I never thought I would talk to a President of the United States the way I talked to President Roosevelt last night. I think I made it pretty clear that I wasn't going to stand for much more of the same kind of medicine. . . . I am afraid I was a little unbending in the President's office"; as if he were recounting unusual behaviour on his part. But the same entry is lit with the lightning of other battles: "We voted millions upon millions of dollars for Hopkins, all of it absolutely blind. . . . Rex Tugwell is preparing to go ahead with a lot of housing projects in metropolitan areas," and four days later: "But I don't take naturally to fighting such underhand efforts as Morgenthau and Hopkins have been putting in to undermine me and aggrandize themselves. The President certainly has a blind side so far as Morgenthau is concerned, and Hopkins seems to sing a siren song for him." The important point is that they may all have been fighting to aggrandize themselves, but they were fighting also for the agencies and the projects of which they were in charge; and by doing so, in the end, they were fighting for the good performance of the administration and the reputation of the President whom they served.

Louis Howe, quite as devoted to Franklin Roosevelt as Theodore Sorensen was to John Kennedy, was once confronted by a note from his President which drew from him the exclamation: "Tell the President to go to hell." One cannot imagine that the men close to John Kennedy would ever have reacted in such a way; and one is tempted to add that they did not think as much of him as that. He had to be protected; his power had to be protected; his office had to be protected. But the power which needs this protection is likely to be blind. To the end of his life, Paul Cézanne thought that he suffered from defective eyesight and concluded that this was why he could not paint. The art of politics can be taken seriously enough to make the comparison. To the end of his days of power, the politician must believe that he has defective eyesight. He must seek the help, witting and unwitting, not only of a thousand pairs of eyes, but of eyes which see in a thousand different ways, eyes that flash at him, eyes that are suspicious, eyes that seem to sleep, eyes that are open, eyes that wear hoods, eyes that tell him nothing and, in doing so, tell him all which he needs to know. John Kennedy had the same object as Franklin Roosevelt, the accumulation of power to the Presidency; he had a genuine political ability, as did many of those around him; but he and they saw, with few exceptions, with a single pair of eyes; that was how he wished it.

We are told that, in seeking to gather the maximum amount of personal power in his office, John Kennedy did not want a Presidency that was either "institutionalized" or "collective"; and these words are now encrusted in political literature. It would need a jeweller to pry them loose, but those of us with only crude instruments must do our best. One useful task which a political journalist can perform is to dislodge a cliché before it takes root in the mind of a political scientist, where it will wondrously bloom, like a desert flower, however thin the soil. Unfortunately, as the talk of an "institutionalized" and "collective" Presidency was sown, the work of dislodgement was not done. If only the parable were true and, if a seed fall upon stony places, it will wither away and, if among thorns, it will be choked.

It must be clear to the most unadorned mind that the Presidency is, and always has been, an "institution"; and that, since it requires more than a few people to conduct its operations, it is, and always has been, "collective." George Washington appointed his nephew and a former aide-de-camp as his secretaries; and the Presidency was at once an "institution" and "collective." All that is needed to create an institution is someone to write something on a piece of paper, and someone else to look it up as a precedent. But, some time in the 1950s, the idea began to flourish, like a tare, that there had been such an acceleration of the process that there had been a change, not only of degree, but of character, in the organisation of the office. The change could be traced back—put a date where one will—to the New Deal, in general, or to the Government Reorganization Act of 1939, in particular, which established the Executive Office, itself to become the nursery of several new and virile agencies of the President.

No one is going to deny the importance of these agencies, as they grow like coral reefs. But it is worth remembering that their proliferation may "institutionalize" and "collectivize" power, not towards the Presidency, but away from it, as their permanent staffs develop their own procedures and their own interests. It is too early to say, for example, that the Bureau of the Budget, which is today a most efficient arm of the President, will not in time have a life of its own. Such points are worth remembering, because the expectancy with which the American people today look to the President is based in part on the belief that his efficient power has been vastly increased by the addition of the new agencies which are beholden to him. This may not be so. Just as an increase in the activity of government does not necessarily make it more powerful, but may instead, by making it unworkable, make it less powerful, so it may be found that the Presidency, by attempting to control the great departments through an agency such as the Bureau of the Budget, has in the end merely conceded power to it.

But the idea that the organisation of the Presidency had changed its character really only flourished in the 1950s as a result of Dwight Eisenhower's "passion for organization": an eccentric concern which produced the well-worn joke that he was striving to create a Presidency which did not require a President; and the even livelier joke that, when someone expressed his alarm that Dwight Eisenhower might die and be succeeded by Richard Nixon, he was asked to remember the possibility that Sherman Adams might die and be succeeded by Dwight Eisenhower. In fact, the extent to which he organised power away from himself was consistently exaggerated: in part by himself, acting in public the part of a soldier, and attempting to create a military command; in part by those who served him, wishing to demonstate that they had made the emperor's clothes; but above all by the Democrats, who wished to paint a faintly ludicrous picture of him, a partisan effort in which he nevertheless generously assisted them from time to time.

This last is an important point in the context of this book because, out of the legend of the desultory President who was to retire in 1961, grew the legend of the vigorous President who should succeed him; and John Kennedy was quick to seize the point. One cannot help noticing that, as an eight-year Presidency draws to an end, those of the opposing party who have been fretting in their universities and their foundations and their law firms are suddenly impelled to publish their views on what should be the character of the next Presidency; and, somehow or other, their usually vivid evocations of the vigour of the performance which is to come find their way into the hands of one or more of the aspiring candidates.

We have already mentioned the memorandum of the Schlesingers, father and son. Richard Neustadt in 1960 published *Presidential Power,* an academic study in its own right, but with the additional partisan purpose of demonstrating that Dwight Eisenhower was an amateur who had "made the White House his first venture in politics"; and which carried a concluding chapter under the title, strange in an academic study, "The Sixties Come Next." After dinner on 21 November 1960 he handed a copy of his book to the President-elect. Even more remarkable, from the fastness of the Rockefeller Foundation came the voice of Dean Rusk, contributing to the issue of *Foreign Affairs* of April 1960 an article simply entitled, "The President," exalting the office, which we know that John Kennedy read and appreciated, as indeed he might, given exhortations such as this:

> With deep compassion we can acknowledge that his are burdens which no man ought to be asked to bear, that the problems before him may reach beyond the capacity of the mind of man, and we can be grateful that there are men with the temerity to seek the office.

Which of us, if a man talked in that way of the office which we held, or were about to hold, would not find a place for him? Moreover, as we will see, Dean Rusk made one even more telling point.

At the same time, Henry M. Jackson directed the Senate Subcommittee on National Policy Machinery, which he had created almost singlehanded, in a dazzling series of investigations into the structure of government, particularly in the field of national security. In the reports which followed, he was scornful of the elaborate machinery which Dwight Eisenhower had created round the National Security Council; and the brilliance of the reports, combined with the prevailing attitude to the outgoing administration, tended to make his conclusions the current orthodoxy. But we must again observe that it was an election year, that Henry Jackson was candidly seeking the Vice-Presidential nomination, and that John Kennedy in the end heaved him, for the duration of the campaign, into the chairmanship of the Democratic National Committee. All of this must be remembered, because the view which is taken of the structure of the Presidency, actual or ideal, is often determined by partisan leanings; and the particular view which was being nourished as John Kennedy took office was bound to excite the highest expectations of it. The articulate public mind of the country, as well as he, was demanding a Presidency which would be strong and active and personal.

With that in mind, we can turn to consider what it in fact was that Dwight Eisenhower was supposed to have "institutionalized" in the Presidency which John Kennedy is supposed then to have "de-institutionalized":

–Dwight Eisenhower created the position of The Assistant to the President, the post from which Sherman Adams wielded

his influence, not unlike a chief of staff; John Kennedy abolished
it.

–Dwight Eisenhower dramatically increased the role of the
National Security Council, formalised its structure by the creation of the Planning Board (to define the issues which would
be placed before it) and of the Operations Coordinating Board
(to see that the decisions were carried out), and created a new
post of Special Assistant for National Security Affairs; John
Kennedy drastically reduced the role of the National Security
Council, abolished the Planning Board and the Operations
Coordinating Board, but kept the position of Special Assistant
for National Security Affairs, dramatically increasing his prestige and his influence.

–Dwight Eisenhower created the position of Staff Secretary
to filter and efficiently to distribute the mass of papers and
documents which reach the White House; John Kennedy abolished it.

–Dwight Eisenhower created the position of Secretary to the
Cabinet, to enable the Cabinet to serve as a more efficient
advisory body to the President; John Kennedy abolished it,
and significantly reduced the importance of the Cabinet as
an advisory body.

–Dwight Eisenhower created numerous positions with the
title of Special Assistant, to advise him in different areas of
policy; John Kennedy continued the practice, again enhancing
their prestige and their influence.

That is the bare bones of it, and the first flesh to be added
is the suggestion made by Theodore Sorensen amongst others
that John Kennedy abandoned the practice by which the Cabinet and the National Security Council reached corporate decisions as if it were a board of directors. This is something of a

man of straw, for there is no evidence that this was how decisions were reached in the Cabinet during the regime of Dwight Eisenhower. (We will consider the National Security Council later.) Louis Koenig concludes that the Secretary to the Cabinet "recorded the results of Cabinet discussions," and he talks of "the President's decision in Cabinet," not of the Cabinet's decision. Neither phrase suggests that the President's decision had become a corporate decision, unless he wished it to be. Indeed, both of them remind one of the practice in Britain where the Cabinet as such, powerful although it is, makes no decisions: no votes are called, the Prime Minister merely "collects the voices" of his colleagues and, even if all of them are united in support of a policy, the Prime Minister can still reject their views; his decision is then binding on each and all of them, under the convention of collective responsibility, unless they choose to resign.

Dwight Eisenhower seems to have done no more than "collect the voices" of his Cabinet, so we may forget the man of straw. The real change wrought by John Kennedy was that he held meetings of the Cabinet only irregularly, and then only because "I suppose we should—it's been several weeks since we had the last one." He in fact gave his reasons for reducing the importance of the Cabinet as a corporate body in his own words:

> . . . All these problems Cabinet officers deal with are very specialized. I see all the Cabinet officers every week, but we don't have a general meeting. There really isn't much use spending a morning talking about the Post Office budget and tying up Secretary Freeman who has agricultural responsibilities. . . . If we have a problem involving labor-management . . . it is much better for me to meet with Secretary Hodges from Commerce and Secretary Goldberg from Labor. . . . I think we will find the Cabinet per-

haps more important than it has ever been, but the Cabinet meetings not as important.

In short, he was not much concerned with the views of
Cabinet members on matters beyond the jurisdiction of their
departments.

It adds up to a revealing picture. It gives us a man—a
President—who regarded political problems as "very specialized,"
and the political heads of departments as specialists; who firmly
believed that a problem involving labor and management requires the advice and the attention only of the departments
which are directly interested; who in particular was determined
to remove foreign affairs (as Theodore Sorensen emphasises)
from the interference or commentary of a general body; and
who was more at ease in personal contact than in a general
meeting. We have a picture of a President who was dangerously
inclined to restrict the amount and the character of the advice
which he received; who does not seem to have understood how
much may be learned from an interchange which cannot be
elicited by direct questioning; to whom there were only political
problems, and no political problem.

As a corporate body, and not just as a sum of its members,
the Cabinet is an awkward institution in the American system
of government. It is not the efficient link between the executive
and the legislature which Walter Bagehot noticed in *The English Constitution*, for the obvious fact, known to every schoolboy, that in Britain the members of the Cabinet are also, and
must be, members of Parliament, whereas in the United States
they are not, and cannot be, members of Congress. It has been
used by some Presidents more than by others, by some willingly
and by others grudgingly; but in neither case to much visible
effect. One does not deny that it is something of a red herring.
But, oh! the value of red herrings! They are beyond price! One

suspects that Franklin Roosevelt kept a barrel of them pickled at Hyde Park, as Henry VIII no doubt kept a salthouse filled with them at Hampton Court. The more red herrings that are introduced into the discourse of politics, the less likely that some important factor will be overlooked. The true politician will listen to everything that is said to him, and he will encourage his colleagues to say all that is on their minds. The apparent irrelevance may hold the truth which he needs to know.

The criticism is not so much of John Kennedy's unwillingness to use the Cabinet but of the reasons he gave for not using it. He does not appear to have understood the qualities which are even more valuable than intelligence and competence: that political judgement—at its highest, political wisdom—is often to be found where one would least be inclined to look for it, in men who digress, or who are slow, or who have no ready point to make, but who are feeling their way to an unformed doubt in their minds. Above all, he appears to have been trapped by his belief that he needed the advice only of those who were directly concerned with the problem. But those who are handling a problem, however much they may differ, have to establish very early a frame of reference within which they can contain their differences, and that frame of reference then becomes fixed, and those acting within it find it hard to escape. It is those who are outside it who are likely to question it, and to say something simple like: "Are we sure we are not getting ourselves up a gum tree in Vietnam?"

Moreover, if a President needs to be protected by his White House staff against the departments, he also needs to be kept on guard by the departments against his White House staff, who may all too easily begin to think that only they know the purposes and the needs and the mind of their President,

until *he* becomes *their* creature and believes that his interests
are safe with them. We are told, for example, that, when he
did hold a meeting of the Cabinet to review domestic progress,
John Kennedy took with him Theodore Sorensen and Lawrence O'Brien, Walter Heller and Kermit Gordon, two from
the White House, two from the Executive Office—all of them
the President's men. But he should have been meeting his
Cabinet without his palace guard. At the cabinet meeting on
15 June 1961, Luther Hodges, the Secretary of Commerce,
had placed on the agenda a request for "A candid discussion
with the President on relationships with the White House
staff." John Kennedy ignored the request. But, however dis-
gruntled Luther Hodges may have been at his personal relations with the White House, he was raising a general point
of some significance which deserved to be aired.

Again, when Abraham Ribicoff resigned in July 1962, *Time*
reported, clearly having interviewed him: "Ribicoff found himself outside the President's inner circle of confidants. It was
the technicians of the Cabinet . . . who had the President's
ear, but they seldom saw fit to question his political judgment."
Luther Hodges and Abraham Ribicoff were both politicians—
elective politicians—whose political judgement was exactly what
John Kennedy required to balance the unpolitical judgement
of the technicians such as Douglas Dillon and Robert
McNamara; but they were not given a hearing. "The prince
often gets to hear what he wants to hear," Paul Samuelson
had said of the influence of Presidential advisers, and this is
one of the besetting weaknesses of any system of personal
rule. The atmosphere ceases to be strictly political, and becomes that of a court, call it Camelot or not.

As far as John Kennedy and his personal staff were concerned, the departments should be responsive to the President's

will, and to very little else. "By and large what is wrong," said McGeorge Bundy in the Godkin Lectures which he gave at Harvard University in March 1968, and then published under the title *The Strength of Government*, "is that the Cabinet office is still not understood, at all levels, and by all hands, as truly Presidential in its character and power"; and he added that the role of the Cabinet "is political, but only in the President's interest. It is managerial, but only on the President's terms." Why have departments at all, one wonders? Why give them secretaries? Why not just have a White House staff, and run the departments from there?

The ignorance and impatience with which the people of the traditional democracies today regard their political institutions is nowhere more clear than in their general misunderstanding of, and easy contempt for, the accumulations of departments and agencies which we collectively—and, more often than not, pejoratively—call a bureaucracy. Of course a bureaucracy has sometimes to be pulled and pushed in order to get it to move in a direction to which it is unaccustomed. But it is a foolish politician and a foolish people who refuse to understand the value of its inertia. The tension between the politician who wishes to act and the bureaucracy whose instinct is to warn against action is one of the more important of the conversations, if one may so put it, which should be continuous within the life of politics. One must believe that the bureaucracy—the departments—know something which is not known elsewhere in the political process; because they do. They have been there a long time, they will be there longer still; and, unless one believes that experience confers no wisdom, it is sensible to heed their lore.

In his review of Leopold von Ranke's history of the popes, Thomas Babington Macaulay—himself brought up in a non-

conformist circle—has a famous passage about the survival of
the Church of Rome:

> No other institution is left standing which carries the mind back
> to the times when the smoke of sacrifice rose from the Pantheon,
> and when camelopards and tigers abounded in the Flavian am-
> phitheatre. . . . And she may still exist in undiminished vigour
> when some traveller from New Zealand shall, in the midst of a vast
> solitude, take his stand on a broken arch of London Bridge and
> sketch the ruins of St. Paul's.

Since he wrote, the arches of London Bridge have indeed
been broken, and rebuilt some five thousand miles away in
a desert of the United States where the course of a river had
to be changed so that it might flow beneath them. But, after
all the onslaughts which it has sustained, the Church of Rome
still commands an allegiance and an influence which have no
parallel, either in their extent or in their duration. Even its
quarrels have a vigour about them which is both timely and
timeless; and those of us who are not of its body can only
wonder at its reach across the centuries. If one puts aside
questions of faith, we will find no more convincing explanation of its survival than the continuity and strength and intelligence of the bureaucracy in the Vatican. From time to
time, the Church may require a John XXIII; but it is the
bureaucracy which then settles down, both to absorb the truth
which he may have showed, and to remake the mould to
contain it.

In much the same way, if one were to look for the reasons
why the rulers of the Russian Empire have taken so patient
a view, over so many centuries, of their country's long-term
interests, one would find at least a part of the explanation
in the continuity of its bureaucracy, however inefficient and
ludicrous it may seem in the stories of Nikolai Gogol. The

age-old Vatican and the age-old Kremlin: these are absolutisms, it may be said. But one reason why France has survived both its politicians and its frequent lack of them—it is never clear which is the worse calamity—has been the existence of a bureaucracy of high prestige and unusual brilliance; and it was the civil servants, as the politicians of the Fourth Republic reeled and stumbled, who laid the foundations of the prosperity on which Charles de Gaulle then reared his edifice, just as it is they who are now putting together a new mould within which France can pursue her long-term interests after the distractions of personal rule. In a different way, and within a different political tradition, the civil service in Britain has contributed more than can easily be measured to the continuity and stability of its national life.

The political tradition and the political system in the United States are more different from all of these than they are from each other. But the country has, by now, a bureaucratic tradition of great worth. There is no evidence that Harold Ickes or Stewart Udall or Walter Hickel found the Department of the Interior unresponsive to their wishes. Arthur Goldberg appears to have been able to use the experience and the resources of the Department of Labor to his own—and the administration's—and the President's—needs and objectives. But a department exists, not only to do the bidding of its temporary master, but to warn, and to hesitate, and to demur. Its methods can be irritating. It will fudge, it will obscure, it will delay; it will lose some papers, it will find others; it will go home early, it will refuse to work on Saturdays; dormant and cunning, at such moments, it will even dissemble.

But there is a purpose in it all. Somewhere in the Quai d'Orsay in Paris, for example, or in the Foreign Office in London, or in the Department of State in Washington, there

are Arabists, experts in the affairs of the Arab world. For
a quarter of a century, their countries may commit themselves
to policies favourable to Israel; but the Arabists remain, and
are accused of sabotaging—or of attempting to sabotage—the
policies of their governments. But their governments, as like
as not, will one day be persuaded that they must establish
better relations with the Arab countries, and they need the
advice of Arab experts. Where are they to be found? Lo and
behold! they discover that there are fully equipped desks in
the Quai d'Orsay, in the Foreign Office, in the Department
of State, staffed by dedicated men who for a score of years
have resisted the nagging of their wives: "Why can't you get
transferred to the Soviet desk like Harold?" Suddenly their
wives purr: "Of course, he has known all along that we would
need the Arabs." It is of such that great bureaucracies are made.

They contain many things. The unutterable ignorance of
Joseph McCarthy could not understand this, and he ripped
apart the Department of State, in general, and its Far Eastern
desks, in particular. If one were to adopt his method, and
accuse any member of the Congress of the United States of
treason during this century, the charge would lie against him.
But the warning which men such as he can give is against
our own levels of ignorance; and there is no doubt that, on
a level far above that of Joseph McCarthy, the general attitude
of the Kennedy administration to the bureaucracy was one of
disdain, born of a kind of ignorance. McGeorge Bundy tells us
that the "unending contest between the Presidency and much
of the bureaucracy is as real today as ever," as if it would be
a desirable condition if it stopped. Walt Rostow suggested that
the National Security Council "would be much improved if it
had an independent staff of first-rate men, freed of ties to
particular bureaucracies, paid to think in terms of the totality

of our policy problems, empowered to lay proposals on the table." These statements are rash.

But the temper of the men, in spite of the coolness of which they boasted, was often rash. They had an obsession with activity and brevity and quickness of response, and an impatience with the bureaucracy which questioned the need for them. "Speed is not always the pace of prudence," warned Charles Burton Marshall in the *New Republic* of 25 December 1961. "Blocking a mistake or correcting a superior's misconception may often be more valuable than merely being submissively agreeable." There was a danger, he suggested, that the administration would regard the bureaucracy in foreign affairs as no more than a messenger and a servitor, that it would demand of it only compliance and consider it remiss if it took its time and aired its doubts, that it would cease to respect it as a source of admonitory wisdom. All of this was indeed to happen, as the Presidency was armed to secure the prompt execution of a single Presidential will, uninterrupted by advice or by admonition, so far as was possible, from any other source within the political process.

It is also said that the National Security Council had previously been acting as a board of directors, and that John Kennedy abolished such nonsense. But it was at these earlier meetings that Robert Cutler put his unanswerable question: "What exactly do you mean by preserving democracy in South Korea?"; and it is hard not to avoid the impression from the memoirs that Dwight Eisenhower carried this question with him as he left for the golf course. It is an irritating and a boring question to those who wish to act; but the administration of John Kennedy had far too little capacity for boredom, although occasional boredom, as Edward Weintal and Charles Bartlett say, "is not too high a price to pay for an apparatus which is capable of performing effectively as a safety net under the high-wire act." The high-wire act, in the administration of John Kennedy, was to be performed by McGeorge Bundy.

In announcing his appointment on 1 January 1961, John Kennedy said: "I intend to consolidate under Mr. Bundy's direction the present National Security Council secretariat, the staff and functions of the Operations Control [sic] Board, and the continuing functions of a number of special projects within the White House. . . . It is my hope to use the National Security Council and its machinery more flexibly than in the past." It quickly became clear what this meant. McGeorge Bundy tore apart most of the elaborate structure of committees and formed instead a small personal staff: "he was shaping," writes Arthur Schlesinger, "a supple instrument to meet the new President's needs," and John Kennedy was to refer to the National Security Council as a "little State Department" within the White House.

But, if one is going to concentrate so much of the direction of foreign policy within the White House, one had better make sure that it *is* a "little State Department," that it is organised in some depth, that it has continuing committees, that it knows the uses of paperwork, that it provides its own buffers against impetuous action. This is what has been done by Richard Nixon and Henry Kissinger, under whom the permanent staff of the National Security Council has produced a vast number of studies, these being initially prepared by one of the six interdepartmental groups, all of which are chaired by the appropriate Assistant Secretary of the Department of State; and between these groups and Henry Kissinger and his personal staff there is an elaborate system of committees and boards. No informed observer seems to doubt that this more rigorous method has helped to produce a more coherent approach to the problems of foreign policy, and a less distracted attention to the long-term interests of the United States.

Taking office with a profound suspicion of the informal system which John Kennedy had established—and which was then continued by Lyndon Johnson, in many cases with the same men—the formal system of Richard Nixon and Henry Kissinger has been designed to avoid the "catch-as-catch-can talk*fests*" on which they had relied. It was precisely these which were so much praised at the time, and which are praised in the memoirs. John Kennedy called huddles—the descriptive word used by Theodore Sorensen—believing that they would be flexible and hard-hitting if the number of officials attending them was limited. This was the myth: that to gather together those whom he chose to consult, and to listen to their disagreements, would mean that he was receiving advice which was "hard-hitting." But it was hard-hitting only within a frame of agreement, which itself limited the advice which he would receive. What he needed was the counsel of men who argued from established positions, not necessarily like his own, and represented entrenched interests; and who met regularly and not only when he or his Special Assistant for National Security Affairs decided that their presence was necessary.

In arming his office, John Kennedy had organised it to a simple purpose, the prompt determination of the Presidential will which was then to be promptly executed. He had chosen the right man for the task. McGeorge Bundy once described the center of concern of the man who takes an active part in government as "the taking and using of power itself." He insisted that "executive energy always depends for its effective-

ness on a most intensive *process* of consultation and consensus," and Joseph Kraft once knowingly described him as
the "philosopher of process." He would process the Presidential
will, whatever it might be, as efficiently and as promptly as
he could, because the "heart of the matter . . . is to be found
in power and purpose." This was an extraordinarily limiting
view, not only of politics, but of his own role. His not to
reason why. His background had formed his perspective. An
"instinctive commitment to the Establishment, of which he
was so superb a product," as Arthur Schlesinger puts it, had
tempered and disciplined him not to question too deeply any
current orthodoxy. Indeed, when has any Bundy ever rebelled,
apart from his mother, who resigned from the Daughters of
the American Revolution when it had the insolence to ask
from her a fee of twenty-five dollars to authenticate her geneal-
ogy?

There were three consequences of the Presidency as it was
organised by John Kennedy. The belief that it enabled him
to receive uninhibited advice from a variety of sources was a
myth. In fact, it confined the advice within a single, self-chosen,
pattern from which escape was difficult, not least because the
men whom he had chosen had, to a large extent, enjoyed
the same experiences, received the same education, been trained
in the same method, and were moved by the same purposes.
Between men as important in the field of foreign affairs as
McGeorge Bundy and Carl Kaysen and Abram Chayes, the
intelligence of each not to be doubted, there was no separation: their minds were of the same bent, and their tempers
were of the same discipline. Wherever one looks, the advice
which John Kennedy invited was, for this reason, dismayingly
thin.

Relying on his personal advisers and their informal advice,

John Kennedy determined to bypass the bureaucracy, when it obstructed his will, instead of trying to take hold of it. This was not the method of Franklin Roosevelt, who not only gathered strong men of different experiences, of different minds, and of different tempers, but had a habit of giving them departments or agencies from which they fought each other and even fought him; he gave them territory which they then defended, and he went out of his way to build their territory into the structure of government. If his Presidency was personal, his government was not, and the evidence is to be found in the long life—in some cases, the permanence —of many of the new agencies which he created, not least during his own first "thousand days." In contrast, when one looks round Washington ten years after the administration of John Kennedy, it is hard to find a trace of any method of government which he established which has survived.

But the most important consequence was that the popular expectations of the Presidency—of the office and of the man —were again heightened. The ordinary processes of politics could be bypassed at least, transcended at most, by an exceptional man, served by exceptional men, engaged in an exceptional venture. There would always be action—a prompt execution of the Presidential will; the action would be unusual—in its intention as in its method; and it would not be balked—since the traditional political institutions were to be surpassed by the energy of the Presidency. The people did indeed stand on tiptoe for three years, never considering that the administration which had been formed was dangerously lacking in breadth and depth; or that, in his reliance on the popular leadership to which they responded, the President had armed his office in such a way as to limit severely the opportunities for political leadership.

CHAPTER EIGHT

Guerilla Warfare
and Guerilla Government

IT IS SOMETIMES hard to avoid the impression that the
Kennedy brothers, and those whom they gathered to their
service, thought that something was amiss if they were able
to enjoy an unbroken night's sleep. Even as early as 1956,
Arthur Schlesinger tells us, John Kennedy and Theodore
Sorensen "labored until dawn" on the speech to nominate
Adlai Stevenson—one can be sure that *he* was asleep—and,
on 21 December 1960, the programme of the future administration was characteristically reviewed in a protracted all-day
and late-night session. Anyone who is familiar with the literature
is familiar also with such descriptions. We find the President
awake at 2 A.M. during the fiasco at the Bay of Pigs, walking
on the South Lawn of the White House as he meditated
alone, and he was still up at 5 A.M. during the violence in
Mississippi in 1962, when he telephoned his wife in Newport.
As for Theodore Sorensen, he seems almost to have resented
the possibility that sleep might carry him into the Land of Nod,
oblivious to the cares of the world, and his duty to assuage
them, and we are given repeated glimpses of him as he worked
through the night on the draft of a speech.

One is not denying that such hours are sometimes necessary. What is significant is the emphasis which the men themselves place on them, as if they are proof of their dedication and alertness. If they wish to praise each other, they will say, as Roger Hilsman does of Dean Rusk, that he "worked long hours, more days a week than any other Secretary in history. He is supposed to have taken only four days off in four years"; if to praise themselves, that each of them "responded with an excitement and enthusiasm that had them working long hours," which is Roger Hilsman's description of his own bureau. Bernard Brodie tells us of Robert McNamara that "senior members of his staff hurrying to the Pentagon on Sunday mornings would feel the hood of the Secretary's car to determine by its temperature how long he had been at work. Usually they found the metal distressingly chilled." But the curious fact about these long days and sleepless nights is that the men seem, nevertheless, to have been in a constant hurry, taking last-minute decisions at last-minute meetings, making last-minute corrections to last-minute statements, as if they were always trying to catch up with events, or with each other, or even each with himself.

In an interview which was used by *Newsweek* in its issue of 8 May 1961, John Kennedy reviewed his first hundred days in office, and said that "he was satisfied that at least one goal he had set himself in that period had been fulfilled: to stamp his administration as activist, with a pace and tempo commensurate with the magnitude of the problems." It could hardly be denied that the pace and tempo were there. "Washington is crackling, rocking, jumping!" exclaimed T.R.B. in the *New Republic* of 27 March 1961, and felicitously added, "It is a kite zigging in a breeze." A week later, in the same journal, James MacGregor Burns gave a quotation from McGeorge Bundy: "At this point, we are like the Harlem Globetrotters, passing forward, behind,

sidewise, and underneath. But nobody has made a basket yet."
It was in this mood, at this point in the life of the administration, that the President finally authorised the invasion of Cuba; and it was in response to the fiasco of that adventure that his obsession with guerilla warfare was in part to grow.

After the event, Louis Halle wrote in the *New Republic*: "One of our national characteristics is admiration for the doers, respect for action . . . , contempt for passivity. It doesn't matter that, in international relations, as in love, knowing how to wait may be as important as knowing how to act." It must not be forgotten that in John Kennedy we are talking of a man—and of the men around him—who was—as they also were—a doer: who found it easier to be active than to be passive; indeed, who found passivity all but intolerable. "At all times he was in motion, smoothing his hair, adjusting his tie, fiddling with his belt, clicking a pen against his teeth, slipping his hands in and out of his pockets." This description by Joseph Kraft is difficult to reconcile with the picture in the myth: we are being shown the opposite of a cool man. Arthur Schlesinger attempts a reconciliation: ". . . he radiated a contained energy, electric in its intensity. Occasionally it would break out, especially during long and wandering meetings. His fingers gave the clue to his impatience. They would suddenly be in constant action, drumming the table, tapping his teeth, slashing impatient pencil lines on a pad, jabbing the air to underscore a point. Sometimes the constraint of four walls seemed too much." The energy is barely contained; it is again not a picture of a cool man.

If there was poise, as there certainly was, it was the poise of a hummingbird: a thousand barely perceptible wingbeats as it hovers suspended in the air for a second, before it darts here and there and everywhere. He was personally, by his own temper, committed to activity, and inactivity seems to have been beyond his reach. In the speech which Dean Rusk gave to the senior staff of the Department of State on 20 February 1961, he said of the policy-making officer, "if he waits, he has already made a decision, sometimes the right one," and it is hard to forgive him for not pressing this wisdom on a President who was too little inclined to wait, who seemed to require the simplifications of action, and to smother his anxieties in its consolations. George Ball, in his unusual volume of reflections and memoirs, *The Discipline of Power,* criticises the administrations of Dwight Eisenhower and of John Kennedy because on the same issue—assisting the British government to maintain the unreal posture of a nuclear power—they both acted when all which they needed to do was not to act: "had we done nothing," he says of the first occasion; "simply by doing nothing," he repeats of the second, folly would have been avoided. But the idea of doing nothing, during those long days and sleepless nights, was not within the range of John Kennedy or of most of those who served him.

Let us turn again to the novels of John Buchan for illumination. In *The Half-Hearted,* Tommy Wratislaw proclaims: "The great things of the world are done by men who didn't stop to reflect on them. If a man comes to a halt and analyses and distrusts the value of the thing he strives for, then the odds are that his halt is final. You strive to strive, not to attain." It is uncannily close to the attitudes that one is attempting to describe. In its issue of 14 December 1962, *Time* shrewdly observed of the men around John Kennedy that they were a "group that sees conversation as a necessary delay between acts"; and anyone who has ever dined with any of them, in particular with a number of them together, will know that they do not seem to appreciate the fact that conversation is composed as much of silence as of loquacity, that pause and hesitation and demur are part of its measure and of its purpose. Brevity and alacrity were the watchwords of the administration and, following the example of the two brothers, it became the fashion to take "correspondence courses in quick reading," as the *Manchester Guardian* observed in the summer of 1961; and, in its issue of 7 June 1963, *Time* could still comment that "speed-reading is the rage." John Kennedy could read twelve hundred words a minute, or we have been authoritatively told. It is an achievement, no doubt; but not promising an increase of wisdom.

Roger Hilsman tells that his bureau in the Department of State was able to produce "exactly the right kind of crisp, taut, to-the-point, analyses that were needed" by the White House; but, as Louis Koenig remarks, there was also a feeling among some people that "Kennedy's emphasis on swiftness—terse statement, quick strides from one problem to the next—resulted at times in inadequate consideration of alternatives." This was much the comment made by *Le Figaro* after the fiasco at the Bay of Pigs, that John Kennedy was "stronger in dynamism than in wisdom and experience"; and Hugh Sidey remarked of the episode that "It was a bold plan, the kind that appealed to the Kennedy spirit. This kind of action, the Kennedy brothers felt, fitted the New Frontier. It was full of chance, certainly, but it was audacious, glamorous, and new. It was irresistible." A year later, the *Reporter* observed that the men of the New Frontier were "over-active and playful," and sighed that "one must still have confidence that some day they will learn how to move more sedately, how to stop running around all the time"; but this did not happen.

In *Sick Heart River*, another of John Buchan's novels, Eric Ravelston says of Francis Galliard, "I thought there was something pathological about his marvellous vitality," and Alan Sandison comments that "we are aware of having, at one time

or another, come to a similar conclusion about most of the Ar-
buthnot-Hannay-Roylance set [in the stories], as they sweep
the earth in their romantic and tireless conquest of space." A
little later, he elaborates: "Action [in Buchan] is of a familiar
duality. There is Puritan activism, holding idleness a sin before
God and work an ethical duty, and there is what might be
called 'existential' activism, practised in order to externalize and
identify the self and to fortify moral integrity." The clue that
we began to follow in observing that John Kennedy's favourite
book was the autobiography of John Buchan has been rewarding, for the marvellous vitality of the brothers, and of some of
those around them, cannot be neglected. It was exceptional; and
it expressed itself, not only in touch football, but in their political conduct.

The stories of the vitality are so familiar that we need not
catalogue them. On 3 August 1963, *Time* gave a typical account: "Reckless physical bravery is often expected of the Kennedy guests. . . . A near-sighted guest, narrowly missing a
partly submerged rock while on water skis a few weeks ago,
piled up a lot of Kennedy credit for his pluck. As an alternative
to reckless bravery, brute stamina is acceptable. A lawyer friend
visiting the Robert Kennedys gained favorable attention by participating in five events before breakfast." This spirit was carried into the public life of the country early in 1963, when the
President and the Attorney General of the United States urged
the members of the administration and the people of the country to discipline themselves, as the Marines are disciplined in
their training, by taking fifty-mile hikes. The example was set
by Robert Kennedy, striding fifty miles along the towpath of the
Chesapeake and Ohio Canal, and so many people followed it
that individual doctors and doctors' organisations issued warnings
that, to those who were unused to it, such strenuous exercise

might be fatal. The reaction of James Reston to this spectacle was to invite the National Security Council, including the President and the Attorney General, to a fifty-minute think instead.

"He held up standards for us," as John Kennedy said of his father, "and he was very tough when we failed to meet those standards. The toughness was important." Personal experience infects political attitudes, and "toughness" was one of the most prominent words in the vocabulary of the New Frontier; perhaps no other quality was so highly regarded. He required in his administration, says Arthur Schlesinger, "a tough, nonchalant acceptance of the harsh present," which is another of the themes in the novels of John Buchan. The criteria by which a man would be judged fit to serve in the government were "judgment, integrity, ability to work with others, industry, devotion to the principles of the President-elect, and toughness"; and Arthur Schlesinger, whose intelligence and candour frequently get in the way of his hero worship, frankly admits that this last "provoked considerable jocularity in the press." In the administration of John Kennedy, activity was mistaken for action, which is often a slow gathering of decision, and the rest of the vocabulary followed, reinforcing the confusion. Toughness was mistaken for strength, articulacy was mistaken for clarity, self-confidence was mistaken for character.

Much attention is given today to John Kennedy's—and Robert Kennedy's, it should be added—obsession with guerilla warfare; and rightly so. It was an infatuation which was as revealing as it was dangerous. He had emphasised the need for counterinsurgency—paramilitary operations—in the message to Congress which accompanied his special defence budget on 28 March 1961, and his words must be noted: "In most areas of the world, the main burden of local defense against overt attack, subversion and guerrilla warfare must rest on local populations and forces. But given the likelihood and seriousness of this threat, we must be prepared to make a substantial contribution in the form of strong, highly mobile forces trained in this type of warfare, some of which must be deployed in forward areas, with a substantial airlift and sealift capacity and pre-stocked overseas bases." In an official message, the President of the United States was advocating a policy by which the country would not only give military advice and material assistance to governments engaged in combating internal subversion but actually create its own counterinsurgency forces and deploy them in forward areas.

Immediately after the disaster at the Bay of Pigs, Chalmers Roberts in the Washington *Post* of 23 April 1961 reported that John Kennedy's reaction was "a determination to meet the Communist para-military tactics of guerrilla warfare, infiltration, sabotage, and so on." Three weeks later, in the *Wall Street Journal* of 16 May, a report on the administration's plans for "undercover warfare" concluded with the pointed remark: "Without going into secret details, indications can be reported that at least one such maneuver is being blue-printed at this moment for execution in a vital nation far distant from Cuba." It did not need much ingenuity, as was shown by some, to pick up these words and add the name: South Vietnam. The obsession of the President was infectious. It was fashionable to read, and to quote even if one did not read, the works of Mao Tse-tung or Che Guevara or Vo Nguyen Giap; the Assistant Chief of Staff for Intelligence at the Department of State circulated among senior officers the leading "ideological" works of the French colonels, although their own counterinsurgency against the Algerian rebels had hardly been successful; and the New

York *Times* actually printed a primer of guerilla warfare, taken from Mao Tse-tung.

This was the first occasion on which the personal ascendancy of John Kennedy enabled him to dictate at least the passing mood of almost the entire nation, including most of the press. We may fairly take it as an example of his personal leadership and of its impact on a whole people. On the one hand, we must recognise that it was in the character of John Kennedy and of many of those closest to him that the guerilla method should appeal to them; it was a reflection of their own method. Its style was an echo of their style; its tempo was in tune with their temper. It was not just a peccadillo—a small sin—it was an original sin. But we must also recognise that there was something in the temper of the time, and especially of the American people at the time, which was ready to respond to the guerilla mystique, especially when it found expression in the words and the deeds of so young and so vigorous a President. It was as if they expected from the method a satisfaction which was not otherwise to be enjoyed.

It is sometimes difficult to take the mystique of the guerilla with much sobriety, and one is inclined to applaud Richard B. Russell's suggestion that they should have been called Rangers or even Boy Scouts. Early in 1961, as the Chairman of the Armed Services Committee of the Senate, he told Elvis Stahr, the Secretary of the Army, that it would be a pity if the Special Forces were known as guerillas: "I rather associate guerrillas and bushwackers to be on the side of the bad folks on television, and the Rangers and the Boy Scouts on the side of purity and justice." The humour may have been homely, but there was a sense of proportion in it. The trouble with the guerilla is that he too easily becomes an existential hero, as he in fact is to Jean-Paul Sartre and to Simone de Beauvoir; and that is exactly the mystique which is not required in politics. No one who has read the *Seven Pillars of Wisdom* can doubt the power of this mystique. As one of the earliest and the most brilliant of guerilla leaders, T. E. Lawrence was indeed an existential hero, eventually killing himself on a motorcycle, and the line runs true—perhaps one should say, out of true—in an Orde Wingate or in a Che Guevara; and only now does it seem to be at least temporarily ended.

"Guerrilla fighting," said F. O. Mischke in the January 1962 issue of the *Marine Corps Gazette*, "can only be efficient if it is backed by a fanatical aggressive psychology." Even closer to the truth is the comment of W. E. D. Allen, a guerilla fighter himself, in his unforgettable book, *Guerilla Warfare in Abyssinia*, a description of the irregular campaign in which Orde Wingate and his men ousted the Italians from Eritrea and Abyssinia early in the Second World War. He talks of "the unstable psychology which is generally characteristic of guerillas," and describes them as "undisciplined . . . easily excited . . . difficult to restrain." With a manner which avoids any glamourising of himself, of his leader, or of his comrades, he says that three types usually sent in their names when notices were posted in a regiment asking for volunteers for a guerilla force: "the young and keen; the stale and restless; the old lags. The efficient soldier, good at his job, generally ignored the notices. Some of us regularly entered our names for anything from ski-ing to pearl diving. Commanding officers were inclined to regard the notices as an opportunity for a minor purge." He then adds: "Later, I heard Colonel Wingate complain in an expansive moment"—they must have been few—"that he had been given nothing but 'sick camels and the scum of the cavalry division.'"

W. E. D. Allen then describes three of the men who volunteered with him from the Household Cavalry. There was "Tex"

Mills who "had been a Squadron Sergeant-Major in Strathcona's Horse during the last war. After a spell in the East Indies and service in the Canadian Mounted Police, he had made good money trading down the coast of Mexico." There was Bill Strachan, "an inspector of gas meters in peace time—which seemed an odd job to have. But, when you come to think of it, there must be a lot of people inspecting gas meters in peace time." There was Preedy, "a butcher's assistant before the war. A butcher can be an asset in Central Africa, when it comes to slaughtering, skinning, and cutting up, cattle and game." He concludes: "half a dozen Lawrences were soon to be let loose in the Ethiopian uplands: spectacled old Sandford, the flitting prophet of revolt; lean, snarling Wingate; Boustead and Thesiger and Johnson; Wyberg and Ringrose"; and, in a throwaway line of considerable insight, he announces that the British Empire "is an empire of irregulars"; which it indeed, in its accumulation, to a large extent was.

In the atmosphere of the administration of John Kennedy, the guerilla experience was never defined in this manner, loose and understated, leaning heavily on the fact that the guerilla is likely to be eccentric, if not of unstable psychology. The writings of Che Guevara—whose achievements were smaller than the legend of them—were read by the President and by those around him as if they were the prophetic utterances of a new Carl von Clausewitz, depicting the war of the future, without any reference to their author's certainly unstable psychology, without any question whether such a man could give any sensible advice which could be made to conform to the undriven manners of a democracy. When we are told by his mother that "We would listen to him," when he was a young boy, "gasping, studying, studying on the floor to ease his breathing, but he never complained," we should put aside the works of Che

Guevara as a guide to the practices a democracy should pursue. He may be interesting in other respects—as a representative of those characters, in the words of Kenneth Minogue, who are "dominated by a single passion in whose service they overcome the obstacles of the world until the time comes to die"—but the alienation from the world which is felt by most people is seldom at that pitch, and they are not likely to be found proclaiming with José Marti, the nineteenth-century Cuban patriot, that "my one desire would be to stand beside the last tree, the last fighter, and die in silence"; and the leaders of a free people ought not to encourage them otherwise.

Yet something of this spirit had been excited by John Kennedy in his rhetoric, as he had asked from the American people a personal dedication and a personal sacrifice to a cause greater than themselves; as he had called on them to transcend themselves in the pursuit of an elevated sense of national purpose, even as Walt Rostow had looked for a meaning and purpose in American society which would transcend the nation. The mystique of the guerilla, alone or in a band, defying the great forces of the world, and defining himself in action, reflected this mood. The world appeared to have become impersonal; and military power, in particular, seemed to have become a matter of rockets and megatons, and not of men. Part of the remarkable popular appeal of John Kennedy, part of his astonishing gift for popular leadership, was that he seemed to make personal again the impersonal world of power. To this end, his example of personal rule and the mystique of the guerilla were joined. Each could change the world or, failing, at least defy it; he would at least have striven.

The guerilla experience on which men such as Roger Hilsman drew in the 1960s was once more closely associated with the Office for Strategic Services; and we must consider it again, because it is almost impossible to turn a corner in the literature of the Kennedy administration without bumping into it. It was improvised and led—with equal brilliance—by the legendary William—even "Wild Bill"—Donovan, for the duration of the American involvement in the Second World War. He is described in a volume, *Assessment of Men: Selection of Personnel for the Office of Strategic Services,* which was written in 1948 by the OSS Assessment Staff: "General Donovan himself was a mobile unit of the first magnitude. Space was no barrier to him—the Sahara Desert was a little stretch of sand, the Himalayas were a bank of snow, the Pacific was a mere ditch. And, what is more, time was no problem. No one was at all surprised if he left one morning and returned the previous afternoon." One must notice immediately that, given the peculiar simplifications which exist in a world war, there may be a need for someone to whom the Sahara Desert is a little stretch of sand and the Pacific Ocean a mere ditch; but these are disastrous simplifications when the conditions of peace have returned; and Harry Truman wisely killed the OSS as soon as the war was over.

Perhaps even more interesting is that this excited picture of their leader is given by a staff of considerable intellectual expertise. In their volume, they describe the method by which they selected recruits for the OSS as "the first attempt in America to design and carry out selection procedures in conformity with so-called organismic (gestalt) principles"; and one must admit that one immediately feels more at ease with the regimental notices which W. E. D. Allen describes, and the scum of the cavalry who responded; not to mention the sick camels. Potential recruits for the OSS were taken incognito to an estate in Virginia, where their anonymity was preserved by dressing them alike in army fatigues. (Oh! Kafka!) As the Assessment Staff records, this method "deprived the staff of some of the cues that are commonly used in judging character: the material, cut, and condition of a man's clothing, the color-pattern of his tie, the folds and creases of his hat and the angle at which he wears it, how he carries his handkerchief, with or without a monogram, and so forth. . . ." Organismic (gestalt) principles notwithstanding, this is a pack of nonsense. Not only will the scum of the cavalry division do just as well, but it will be less solemn.

But the solemnity was part of the legacy of the OSS, as we have already observed that the catalogue of the Library of Congress mutely testifies. "Half cops and robbers, half faculty meeting," as McGeorge Bundy said, and the association was a calamity: not at the time, for in the peculiar simplifications of war, especially of total war, "anything goes," but in the continuation of the mystique. In their book, *Sub Rosa: The OSS and American Espionage,* which Stewart Alsop and Thomas Braden first published in 1946, they say that the OSS, after the attack on Pearl Harbor, was "the last refuge of the well-connected," and it is a penetrating remark. Being well-connected, they carried their experience into high places after 1945, into the government and the universities, as we have seen; and they carried, in particular, their exaggerated belief in the efficacy of the intelligence services, if these were well organised. Indeed, the Central Intelligence Agency, especially after the war, and to a lesser but still impressive extent today, is an expert body, acute and unillusioned, which has again and again been accurate in its estimates, many more times than it has been at fault, and which is too often made the fall guy for the mistakes of the politicians. The fault does not lie in the business of intelligence, nor in the professional men, by and large, who conduct it; but in the primacy which was given to it in the administration of John Kennedy.

Stewart Alsop and Thomas Braden published a second edition of their book in 1964, and added a postscript. In the course of it, they remarked that "Kennedy had an almost obsessive interest in intelligence," and they continued: "The quintessential end product of the intelligence industry is a little book, put together in the early hours of the morning by the CIA. . . . While President Kennedy was alive, the nameless editors of the book made an effort to find small items which might interest and amuse the President." This is not a reassuring picture; it is too reminiscent of *Our Man in Havana,* and the methods by which he satisfied his masters. The amusement of John Kennedy was merely the reverse side of his bemusement, and the two reinforced each other. The extent of his obsession is beyond doubt, and it had a part of its origin in the perpetuation of the cult of intelligence-gathering which, in the words of Roger Hilsman, had come to rely "on scholarly research as much as on cloak-and-dagger operations." The business was supposed to have become a science.

Unless a rigorous political judgement, neither amused nor bemused, is brought to bear on the reports and the estimates of the intelligence services, they will nourish three unfortunate attitudes in government: a tendency to see policy in terms of operational problems; a tendency to seek solutions of these problems in covert action; a tendency to act when there is no necessity to do so. It is not the fault of the intelligence services if these attitudes are allowed to dominate. As Roger Hilsman again says: "It was the policy-makers who were fundamentally responsible for making covert action a fad." The advice of an intelligence agency, like that of a military service, and like that of a bureaucracy, is conditional: if you want to do this, then we must do that. The determination of that "if" is the responsibility of the politician; it is at that point that his judgement, and not that of the secret agent or the general or the bureaucrat, must operate. It will not operate if he has already abdicated it.

Immediately after the invasion of Cuba, so Roger Hilsman tells us, John Kennedy exclaimed: "It's a hell of a way to learn things, but I have learned one thing from this business—that is, that we will have to deal with the CIA." In that case, he had learned the wrong lesson. It was not faulty intelligence that was to blame; it was the failure to bring to the intelligence, faulty or not, a political judgement such as enabled William Fulbright and Chester Bowles and Arthur Schlesinger to question the project, and a political review such as *The Nation*, as early as 19 November 1960, when it first had an inkling of the scheme, to denounce it as "hare-brained," and to continue to denounce it during the next five months, until it all happened as it had foretold. Again and again, in the literature of the administration, a mistake is explained by the inadequacy of the intelligence available to the President; but such a reliance on intelligence was the clearest indication that political judgement had been reduced to the level of an operational decision.

The positivism of the American mind sets great store by the gathering of information; no country has accumulated so much information about its problems, to the point, it sometimes seems, of paralysing its will to cope with them. The emphasis on intelligence that persisted after the Second World War was characteristically American, as was the belief that intelligence had become a function of scholarly research. This was again a part of the atmosphere of expectation. An administration whose members belonged to this century would use the instruments of this century: on the basis of intelligence which was rationally gathered, policy would be rationally determined, by men who were rationally disposed. It was a high promise, and the sails of the administration were indeed filled by each breath of the intelligence which it gathered, impelling it forward to yet another operation. What it lacked was an anchor.

One of the first of John Kennedy's reactions to the failure of the invasion of Cuba was to decide that he needed a personal military adviser. He chose Maxwell Taylor, who was recommended to him by Robert Kennedy as a "tough, incisive, well-organized, articulate, taciturn, self-confident expert"; and of whom he was himself later to say that he had "a definitive, tough mind." One can only puzzle over these familiar recommendations, because there is nothing in the record of advice which Maxwell Taylor gave to two Presidents on the conduct of the war in South Vietnam which justifies such language. In its issue of 23 February 1961, *Time* recounted how Maxwell Taylor had recently listened to the estimates of a "body-count" which were being given by the retiring commander of the American forces in South Vietnam, and had then exclaimed: "Why don't you kill 'em instead of counting 'em?" One is ready to admit that his question was tough, incisive, well-organised, articulate, taciturn to boot, self-confident, and definitive; it simply happened to be the wrong question.

Maxwell Taylor did not really leap into the public eye as an out-of-the-ordinary figure until he resigned from the post of Chief of Staff of the Army, and published a book to explain his reasons, under the title *The Uncertain Trumpet*. It appeared in 1960, and it fitted neatly into the time, as John Kennedy took his campaign to the people. It criticised the limits that Dwight Eisenhower had placed on defence expenditure: "We are faced with declining military strength at a time of increasing political tensions." It rejected the reliance on nuclear weapons, especially as it was expressed in the doctrine of "massive retaliation," and pleaded instead for a posture of "flexible response": for "a capability to react across the entire spectrum of possible challenge," not least to "deter or win quickly a limited war." It made much of the "missile gap" that was supposed to exist, but proclaimed that it would be closed "if heroic measures are taken now." In language which would be recalled in the inaugural address a year later, it called for "the sure notes of a certain trumpet, giving to friend and foe alike a clear expression of our purpose and our motives."

But in the context of this chapter our main concern is with his criticism of the Joint Chiefs of Staff, from which he had resigned: ". . . the JCS system has proved ineffective and needs a fundamental overhaul. . . . The JCS, as a body, exercise no command, but have purely staff and advisory functions . . . the JCS have all the faults of a committee in settling important controversial matters. They must consider and accommodate many divergent views before action can be taken." We confront here the attitude of mind which was behind what we may call the guerilla government of John Kennedy: an impatience with established methods of procedure, combined with a reluctance to "accommodate many divergent views before action can be taken." In one of the important speeches given by a member of the administration, defining the new emphasis on guerilla warfare, Roger Hilsman in August 1961 described the tactics which had been employed when he was a guerilla leader in Burma: "constant patrols, good communication facilities, rapid mobility, and a capacity for rapid concentration." It would be hard to give a more succinct summary of the technique that John Kennedy most characteristically used, as if he were at ease with no other, in the conduct of his administration.

The descriptions of the method are many and various. "The criticism is heard," said the *New Republic* on 3 July 1961, "that, while a first-rate collection of people have been brought

into government service these past three months, we do not yet
have an administration." But this was not a temporary condition, as the government settled to work together. It was the
method. John Kennedy's preference of a small staff that was
personal rather than institutional was not confined to the White
House. On the contrary, as Edward Weintal and Charles Bartlett remark, it was one of the functions of the White House staff
"to establish an informal network of responsive officials throughout the government," and one fears that "responsive" could all
too easily have been translated as "accommodating." Instead of
being a goad, an additional pressure which the President could
bring to bear on the established institutions of government,
they became a substitute for those institutions. Instead of using
his government, John Kennedy tried to circumvent it.

"To force action," says Roger Hilsman, "the President began
to appoint inter-departmental task forces," and again one must
emphasise that the method was not temporary. If there was
not such a flurry of new task forces after 1961, it was because
the method had by then been established: "Bringing together
working representatives of every agency concerned with the
matter," as Arthur Schlesinger puts it, "and giving one man the
job of producing recommendations," in a way that would
"greatly improve the speed and co-ordination with which policy
was made." But, if speed is not always the pace of prudence, so
co-ordination at too early a stage may stifle dissenting judgements.

Commenting on the method in the *New Leader* in June
1961, Hans Morgenthau said that "The successive presenta-
tion of views and recommendations" by individuals "is no substitute for the dialectic confrontation of such views in groups";
and those groups, if they are both to entertain and sustain the
dialectic, must have some depth to their own existence, and not

be called together for *ad hoc* purposes. As even Henry Jackson commented in one of the reports of his Senate Subcommittee on National Policy Machinery in 1961, such methods "try to do at the Presidential level things which can better be done by the departments and agencies; they violate sound administrative practice by tending to interpose officials between the President and his Cabinet officials." But more important is the fact that they violate sound political practice. "When the President's man says something," a departmental official remarked of the task forces, "you don't know whether he is speaking for himself or for his boss. The effect can be, and often is, to cut off discussion too soon." Again and again, one finds this deep complaint against the method of guerilla government.

If one looks at its purpose, there is a perhaps even more profound objection. In the *Saturday Evening Post* of 31 March 1962, Stewart Alsop quoted a man who knew John Kennedy well as saying that "he hates to be tied down"; and one of the ways in which he would try to avoid being tied down, as he had promised during his election campaign, was "to exercise the fullest power of his office—all that are specified and some that are not." He was, as *Time* commented on 3 February 1961, "convinced that there are plenty of unused executive powers lying around." But part of the function of established institutions is to prevent the exercise of unspecified—that is, arbitrary—executive power; in part, that is the meaning of their precedents, and the explanation of their inertia. The method of guerilla government employed by John Kennedy was intended to bypass this, as well as other forms, of control, and the American people were inclined to applaud the method. The display of personal energy, however superficial, excited their imaginations, and aroused their expectations, once again, that there were political shortcuts. The most obvious examples are in the conduct of his foreign policy, but it is perhaps better to provide an illustration in the domestic field. In the sharpness of the engagement, in the variety of the methods used, in the legally obscure grounds on which they were justified, in his willingness to use to the full the authority and prestige of his office, it illustrates equally the strength of the method, its weakness and its dangers.

On 10 April 1962, Roger Blough, the chairman of the United States Steel Corporation, sought an unexpected interview with the President. At 5:45 P.M., in a meeting which has many times been described, he entered the President's office. He immediately handed to John Kennedy a mimeographed copy of the announcement which United States Steel was at that moment making to the press that it was increasing the price of steel by six dollars a ton. The rights and wrongs of the increase need not concern us here; it is enough to say that all the major steel companies followed the lead of United States Steel, and the President regarded their action as a challenge to his policies, as a threat to the interests of the country, and as an affront to the dignity of his office. "I think you have made a terrible mistake," he said to Roger Blough, and he summoned Arthur Goldberg to his office, in his capacity as the Secretary of Labor. There followed an acrimonious exchange, and, when the miscreant industrialist had left, the two of them decided that "this is war"; and as such, in the next few days, it was waged.

John Kennedy immediately summoned a "crisis council": Walter Heller and Theodore Sorensen, Robert Kennedy and Richard Goodwin, Kenneth O'Donnell and McGeorge Bundy; and others were called during the evening. By 8:50 A.M. on 12 April, it included: the President; the Secretary of Defense; the Under Secretary of the Treasury; the Attorney General; the Secretary of Labor; the Secretary of Commerce; the Chairman of the Council of Economic Advisers; the Chairman of the Federal Trade Commission; the Special Counsel to the President; the Special Assistant to the President for Congressional Relations; and several sub-Cabinet members of the administration. This was a remarkable assembly: not merely a "crisis council," but a "council of war," to resolve a domestic issue.

The methods used were as follows:

—the President denounced the steel companies, in a televised press conference at 3:30 P.M. on 11 April, as selfish and unpatriotic, reminding his audience that "we are confronted with grave crises in Berlin and Southeast Asia," that "we are asking reservists to leave their homes and their families for months on end and servicemen to risk their lives," and that "four were killed in the last two days in South Vietnam." He concluded: "I asked each American to ask what he would do for his country and I asked the steel companies. . . . we have had their answer";

—the Department of Justice, led by the President's brother, announced that it had begun an investigation into the possibility that the steel companies were guilty of criminal price-fixing;

—the Department of Justice announced that a grand jury had been convened to investigate the same possibility, and that subpoenas had already been served on officials of some of the companies;

—the Department of Justice, in the words of Hobart Rowen, "dug deep, even into the personal expense accounts reported by some" of the corporations' officials, but the President here restrained his brother;

—agents of the Federal Bureau of Investigation, ordered to assist in the inquiries of the Department of Justice, telephoned a

reporter of the Associated Press at 3:00 A.M. on 12 April, and
two of them arrived at his home at 4:00 A.M. to question him.
Another reporter, John Lawrence of the *Wall Street Journal,*
was awakened at 5:00 A.M., and at 6:30 A.M., when James L.
Parks, Jr., of the Wilmington *Evening Journal,* arrived at his
office, to commence his day's work, two further agents were
waiting for him;

   –the Federal Trade Commission began its own investigation
of the commercial practices of the steel companies, with an implied threat of action;

   –committees of both the Senate and the House of Representatives were encouraged to commence their own investigations, and William Bundy and George Ball testified before the
Foreign Relations Committee of the Senate—no less!—on the
magnitude of the crisis;

   –the Department of Defense announced that it would deny
contracts to the offending steel corporations, and awarded a five-
million-dollar contract for armor plate to Lukens Steel Company, one of the smaller corporations which had not raised
their prices;

   –an intensive telephone campaign was waged to keep the
smaller companies from raising their prices; it was organised by
Edward C. Gudeman, the Under Secretary of Commerce, who
himself telephoned P. D. Block, a vice-president of Inland Steel,
who in turn telephoned Joseph L. Block, the chairman of the
company, who was in Japan, while Arthur Goldberg telephoned
Leigh B. Block, its vice-president for purchasing, and Henry
Fowler, the Under Secretary of the Treasury, telephoned John
F. Smith, Jr., its president; John Kennedy himself telephoned
Edgar Kaiser, the president of the Kaiser Steel Company; and
Robert McNamara, at the Department of Defense and George

Ball, at the Department of State, each with influential acquaint-
ances in commerce and industry, also made telephone calls;

—throughout the few days of the crisis, there was an intensive
process of leaking to the press vague threats of intended actions
which the administration was considering, to break up the
United States Steel Corporation into smaller units; to seek more
stringent anti-trust legislation; to regulate steel prices by law;
and to manipulate tax concessions of the industry.

Even this account gives only an inadequate impression of the
feverish activity of the administration. It was at its happiest:
a group from the Bureau of Labor Statistics was kept at a meeting until 2:45 A.M. on 11 April, and then dispatched to prepare
a "white paper" showing that the proposed price increases were
unjustified; Walter Heller and James Tobin and Kermit Gordon,
the entire membership of the Council of Economic Advisers,
met until 4 A.M. on the same day, the first two of them going
home for a few hours of sleep, while Kermit Gordon bunked
down on a couch in his office; the President himself made a
call late that night to Archibald Cox, the Solicitor General, who
was in Tucson, Arizona, asking him for suggestions, to which
he pluckily responded by staying up all night, "thinking and
making notes." Under this extreme pressure, the offending corporations surrendered.

It was a famous victory: the immediate objective was gained,
and this is the strength of the method: the powers of the President exercised to the full in a guerilla operation of "incom-
parable dash," as Arthur Schlesinger at one point describes the
style of the administration. But the weakness and the dangers
are equally obvious, and they were vividly illustrated in this instance. Estes Kefauver, a consistent foe of the steel companies,
commented after the crisis: "There is no gainsaying the fact

that the treatment of the steel industry was episodic and lacking in standards. The need is very real for a systematic and regularized approach." Louis Koenig has argued that, "although sensational in appearance," the pressures applied by the President, if they had been continued, would have been superficial in their effect: the threat of anti-trust legislation had "the force of a pop-gun"; investigation by the Senate was "an old experience" to the steel industry; the manipulation of defence contracts was a "highly limited expedient." As it was, when the steel companies announced a selective price increase in April 1963, and then further increases in October 1963, John Kennedy was "hampered . . . by the fact that he had reacted so vigorously in 1962." He could not extend himself—or the country—in another display of spectacular personal leadership on the same issue.

He said himself, after the price increases in April 1963, that "There is no sense in raising hell and then not being successful"; but it was he who had put himself, by his earlier conduct, in the position where the only course of action open to him was to "raise hell." In fact, he had quickly retreated from his struggle with Roger Blough, since his long-term objective was the support of big business. During the fall of 1962, the committee led by Estes Kefauver continued its inquiry into the conduct of the steel companies and, impressed by the fact that the export prices of the American corporations were thirty per cent higher than those of their European rivals, it struggled to force them to disclose their costs. In this effort, it received no support from the White House, even though the inquiry had been undertaken at the request of John Kennedy during the crisis in the spring. In the speech which has already been quoted, Roger Hilsman described the methods of the guerilla as he had em-

ployed them in Burma: "we ambushed; we hit; we ran." This
was the method which John Kennedy used in the steel crisis;
as a substitute for policy, guerilla government must always be
inadequate.

The more profound objection to the method was that the
exercise of executive power was arbitrary. With some passion,
as one would expect, the *Wall Street Journal* described the conduct of the President as an effort to use "the pressure of fear—
by naked power, by threat, by agents of the state security police." A more interesting indictment was delivered in the *New
Republic* of 30 April 1962, by a young lawyer, none other
than Charles A. Reich, the yet-to-be author of *The Greening
of America.* He began by saying that, in as little as three days
after the surrender of the steel corporations, the administration
had decided to "demobilize the pressures against the steel industry," and asked: "Can acts or conditions that are criminal
on Tuesday become less criminal by the following Monday? Are
crimes by steel and other industries permitted so long as the
criminals 'co-operate' with the administration?" He was object-
ing to the arbitrary exercise of great power:

> Such use of power, whether its objectives are good or bad, is
> dangerous. Income tax investigations are legitimate, but should they
> be undertaken specifically . . . to frighten someone who opposes
> the administration's policies . . . ?
> The very immensity of government power demands . . . that
> it be used in a disinterested manner, and only for the exact pur-
> poses intended. It was dangerously wrong for an angry President
> to loose his terrible arsenal of power for the purposes of intimidation
> and coercing private companies and citizens. . . . Congress has
> given the President no power to fix the price of steel.

Charles Reich still fears the immensity of government power;
but one must confess to some regret that he has exchanged the

precise address of his lawyer's words for the fuzziness of beads
and bell-bottoms.

When he returned to the subject three weeks later, he
complained in particular against the impropriety of using the
Chairman of the Federal Trade Commission, "a supposedly independent quasi-judicial agency," to serve the ends of the administration. In the same way, when Robert Kennedy tried to
enforce the observance of civil rights in the South by guerilla
methods—a deliberate policy—he also brought pressure to bear
on an independent regulatory agency, the Interstate Commerce
Commission, to reinforce his actions. Victor S. Navasky, in
Kennedy Justice, describes this intervention as "an extraordinary
proceeding"; and the commission at first balked but then abdicated. "It had taken persuasion," as Helen Fuller wrote at the
time. There are good reasons why the regulatory agencies are
intended to be autonomous, and their autonomy in America is
frail enough as it is, without the effort of incumbent politicians
to force them to act as a political arm of the executive.

"Law is the custodian of generalized conduct," said Dean
Rusk to the American Political Science Association on 7 September 1965. "Our legal adviser [in the Department of State] is
responsible for putting to us the question: What happens if
everyone else acts as we are proposing to do?" It is a question
which ought to have been asked, during the administration of
John Kennedy, as much of guerilla government at home as of
guerilla warfare abroad. Both were attempts to transcend the
limits of generalised conduct, of which law, civil or international, is the custodian. One of the attractions of guerilla warfare is that it can be secret and undeclared; this was also one of
the temptations of guerilla government. The two were locked
together, reflections of a system of personal rule which acknowl-

edged no limits but the possible, and which inclined, as it always will, to an arbitrary exercise of executive power.

A surprisingly varied number of people questioned the concept of counterinsurgency even as John Kennedy proposed it. In the issue of *Newsweek* of 8 May 1961, Kenneth Crawford wrote: "The American people who want their games won cleanly and right away, . . . won't like what they are permitted to know about para-military operations"; and, a month later in the *New Republic*, T.R.B. commented that, "Paramilitary warfare is dirty warfare. Should the United States go in for it? It is a very important issue indeed . . . is the United States really cut out for this sort of thing? It means lying to the public. . . . It means undercutting democracy. It violates the treaty obligations of the United States. Again and again, Kennedy comes back to it; it is being accepted without debate. . . . It is a trap in which the United States might well lose its good name"; and so it was to be.

In a special issue of January 1962, the *Marine Corps Gazette*, which was generally sceptical of the whole idea, published a warning from Peter Paret and John W. Shy: ". . . there is reason to suspect that our ability to conceal from others and from our own population what we are doing is not very great. It has been argued that the adoption of guerrilla subversion as American policy would lead to fundamental changes in both our internal structure and our international objectives. To many Americans, such changes are unacceptable, in that they seem to erode the very basis of our national existence. . . . If such a break with what we like to think of as traditional policy also ruptures the general American consensus on national purpose, then we may have weakened ourselves internally more than any international gain may be worth." Five years later all that they had said had come true: the American people had found the method unacceptable; it had imposed an intolerable strain on the national structure; it had confused the country's international objectives; and it had subverted the faith of the American people in their traditional ways.

But at the time the American people were as engrossed by the call to guerilla warfare as they were by the summons to a fifty-mile hike as they were by the success of guerilla government in forcing the steel corporations at least temporarily to their knees. Some people questioned, but they could do so only in an atmosphere which submerged all questioning. As a whole, the American people had been persuaded that personal rule could confer benefits which the traditional processes of their politics were unable to bestow. By the proclamation of a Presidential will, communicated directly to the people by television as an elevated sense of national purpose, the people then rallying to its support as individuals, a war could be fought without in fact going to war, and inflation could be conquered merely by postponing temporarily the rise in price of a single commodity. Government had become a series of dramatic episodes.

Anyone who has returned to the story of the administration of John Kennedy must come away with the impression that he has been watching a film in which the narrative has been cut to a succession of barely related events. As the frames jump, he is jolted from episode to episode, in which the same heroic figure is always engaged in the same spectacular displays of the same uninhibited personal leadership. There was no time to question the behaviour in one episode before the action had jumped to another, the audience left too breathless in anticipation to do anything but applaud. In becoming a series of episodes, politics had also become theatre, and it was the idea of politics as theatre—not least on the streets—which most vividly entered the social imagination of the American people during the decade that was to follow: a magnified expectation of the meaning of personal gesture. The guerilla was theatre; the fifty-mile hike was theatre; the crisis councils were theatre; the confrontation with the steel corporations was theatre; and the American people imagined that they were real.

CHAPTER NINE

Images of Excellence

WHEN HE WAS resting at Santa Monica in the late summer of 1962, John Kennedy left the house where he was staying, one afternoon, to take a swim from the public beach. He was immediately surrounded by well-wishers, many of whom followed him into the sea, including one fully clothed woman. He had been elected only by a hair's-breadth majority, if by any at all; yet the aura of royalty—an invisible emanation—appeared to go with him always, powerful enough to make a fully dressed woman follow him into the waves; and she would have followed him, no doubt, if he had swum strongly and far enough, until they had closed over her head, and carried her to a grave which was watery but blissful. As early as 22 May 1961, in *Newsweek,* Kenneth Crawford had contributed an article under the title, "Royalty USA," in which he said: "We don't like to have our symbols making mistakes, so we don't acknowledge that they make them. These attractive Kennedys . . . enlist our empathy. We want them to be all that they seem to be." Two years later, in his newsletter of 24 June 1963, I. F. Stone said that "the atmosphere of Washington . . . is like that of a reigning monarch's court." Immediately after the assassination, in the *New Republic* of 7 December 1963, Murray Kempton and James Ridgeway quoted a man whom they overheard at the Senate:

"You know, I wish it was a dynasty, and the kid was taking over, and she was the regent." When they exist in a republic, such attitudes of subjection need to be explained.

"A family on the throne is an interesting idea," said Walter Bagehot of the British monarchy. "It brings down the pride of sovereignty to the level of petty life." There was, for a thousand days, a family in the White House; a family with special properties. It was young; it was extensive; it was united; it was political; and such a combination is likely to nourish the feeling that the Presidency has been occupied, not for one term, or even two, but for as long as the family seems to carry within itself the secret of its own appointment to majesty. By the end of 1962, the eldest surviving brother was the President; the second was the Attorney General; the third was a senator; and one brother-in-law, Sargent Shriver, was in charge of the Peace Corps, thus identifying the family with the evangelism of the administration. In these circumstances, the fear could easily grow that, with the death of the king, there would die also the king's justice: a fear which in the Middle Ages assisted in elevating the hereditary, above the elective, principle of succession.

In 1962, when Edward Kennedy, within a period of six months following his thirtieth birthday, first announced that he would seek the Democratic nomination in Massachusetts for election to the Senate, then crushed the opposition of Edward J. McCormack, Jr., the son of the Speaker of the House of Representatives, and was finally elected after a campaign which was an exact replica of the earlier campaign of his brother, people began seriously to calculate that, if the three brothers took the Presidency in succession, it would carry the country to 1984—when it would have become accustomed, no doubt, to

listening to Big Brother and Middle Brother and Little Brother
—and that the succession could then begin to pass to the sons.
But the family—glamorous and young and vigorous—was an asset; the projection of it was relentless, and there is no sense in
pretending that it was not in part their doing.

The young President, whose wife was expecting a child, did
not disdain to tell a gathering of the wives of senators and representatives in spring of 1963 that she was "engaged in increasing the gross national product in her own special way." In spite
of their protestations that they would protect their daughter
from publicity, *Newsweek* was able to carry a cover story on
15 May 1961 under the title, "Caroline in the White House,"
adding to the intimate family photographs, which could have
been secured only with their co-operation, a posy of verses:

> *Sometimes he calls her "Buttons"*
> *And sometimes she calls him "Jack."*
> *She comes for a kiss in the morning,*
> *And then she gives it back.*
>
> *Some people run for office,*
> *Others purely for glee.*
> *Want to know why Caroline runs?*
> *That's simple—she's three.*
>
> *What's all this talk of recessions and such,*
> *Of missiles and atoms to scare you?*
> *When Caroline's mother is sitting right there,*
> *The world is an undepressed area.*

If the adulation of monarchy is to be fostered, it is perhaps best
to retain the language of ritual, or even of the courtier; whatever
else may be required, servility cannot afford to be banal.

The projection of the family, so various in its pursuits, assisted in the purpose which was noticed at the beginning: the

desire, not merely to govern, but to rule the manners of a society, its taste and its fashion, its science and its arts. The consequences of the contrived publicity were noticed by Mary Paul in *The Nation* of 17 August 1962: "the amassing by the President of personal power; and—most insidious of all—the irrational world-wide identification of him with the country as a whole." She said that "Mr. Kennedy has become synonymous with the United States; his victories are American victories; his health, American health; his smile, his family, his hobbies, his likes and dislikes, become symbolic of the country." She concluded that "we are beginning to respond to the Chief of State as we have responded to movie stars." But this exaltation of the office, and of the man in the office, was intended by John Kennedy: at no level of their lives were the American people to escape the connection between power and excellence which was being made; to reject the power would be to reject the images of excellence in which it was arrayed; each put the other beyond question.

The publicity which John Kennedy both contrived and attracted far exceeded that of any of his predecessors or of his two immediate successors. The regular televised press conferences were a most dangerous innovation in a free society; the reporters at them generally played the role of supplicants; and he handled them, as he handled the occasion, with a personal mastery which few politicians could have rivalled. His preparation for them was intensive and elaborate. One of the purposes of the weekly meetings of the press officers of the executive branch was "to prepare a briefing for the President for his press conferences. . . . For questions in sensitive areas, we would prepare the text of an answer and an up-to-the-minute

background briefing." These meetings were on Tuesday after-
noons, and Pierre Salinger continues:

> I would give the material to the President early in the evening
> and he would study it before going to bed. The next morning, with
> his top advisers present, we would go through a dry run at break-
> fast. The regulars were Vice-President Johnson, Secretaries Rusk
> and McNamara, Dr. Walter Heller . . . , and Sorensen, O'Brien,
> Bundy, and Deputy Special Counsel Myer Feldman from the staff.
> I would sit directly across the table from JFK and fire the ques-
> tions at him (between forkfuls of ham and eggs) in the language
> I thought the press would use.

The tension then mounted:

> There were usually six or eight questions for which he required
> more facts, and I would start digging them up, immediately
> after breakfast. The President always took a nap after lunch to in-
> crease his alertness for the press conference, which most often
> took place at 4 P.M. Bundy, Sorensen, and I would wake him
> around three and run over the new information with him as he
> was dressing. The President and I would arrive at the State Depart-
> ment ten minutes before four. Rusk, Under Secretary George Ball,
> and State press officer Manning would be waiting for me in a small
> room off the auditorium, with the latest information off the State
> Department teletype. There was also a direct telephone line to the
> White House, in case of a major, last-minute news break there.

One has to ask whether, week after week, the time and the
energy of so many people, many of them bearing the heaviest
of responsibilities, should have been conscripted to such a purpose.

"Exactly at four, the President would stride onto the stage,"
and a stage it was; scarcely an egg was thrown by the attendant
reporters, and he left it, week by week, unspattered. The reporter whom Pierre Salinger praises is Edward Folliard of the
Washington *Post*, "who often came into my office on his own.

'Here's a question I'm going to ask your man today,' he would say. 'You had better have him ready for it.' Folliard was one of the old-timers who recognized the press conference for what it was—an opportunity to give his readers the most direct possible access to the President's thinking." But, if the political journalist perceives his role in these limited terms, he becomes no more than an equerry of the President.

No one who today reads the transcripts of the press conferences will find much substance in them; but the manner was beyond criticism. "He either overwhelmed you with decimal points," says James Reston, "or disarmed you with a smile and a wisecrack." His alertness to the point in a question on which he could fix to his advantage, his recapitulation of statistics, whether they were relevant or not, his contrived emphasis on words of no particular significance, giving his utterance an air of conviction—all were brilliantly caught by Vaughn Meader on the record, *The First Family*, which he issued in the fall of 1962. Asked by "the First Lady" why he had not touched his salad, "the President replied":

> Well, let me say this about *that*. Now number *one* in my opinion the uh fault does not lie as much with the *salad* as it does with the uh *dressing* being used on the *salad*. Now let me say I have nothing against the dairy industry. However, I would prefer that uh in the future we stuck to *coleslaw*.

Even more accurately, "the President" was represented as settling an argument between his children about their toys in the bath tub:

> Yes, well let me make a judgment about that. Now, the uh following toys have been appropriated for tub *use*: eighteen PT boats, three uh Yogi bear uh beach balls, two Howdy Doody plastic uh bouncing clowns, a ball of uh Silly Putty, and a rubber *swan*. Now, let me make a judgment on the disposal of these items:

nine of the PT boats, two of the yogi bear uh beach balls, the uh ball of Silly Putty belong to Caroline; *nine* of the PT boats, *one* of the Yogi bear uh beach balls, and the uh *two* Howdy Doody plastic bouncing clowns are Baby John's. . . . The rubber swan is mine.

It was not unfair. Although given facts and statistics and judgements, the reporters for three years barely extracted from the President one significant statement about the American involvement in South Vietnam.

The purpose of the press conferences was to appeal directly to the people; and, by the command of his presence, which could not be denied, to win their support. He used them most theatrically at times of crisis when, in an opening statement which had been solicitously prepared, with maps behind him and charts at his side, he recharged the will of the people to further sacrifice. At such moments, he would appear as exalted as an emperor of Byzantium at a public ceremony, receiving the acclamations of the subject people, then to turn towards heaven "to forward the people's wishes and prayers to divinity itself": not only the vicar of the Pantokrator—the omnipotent ruler of the universe—but also the Autokrator on earth—the autonomous ruler—and the Kosmokrator—the ruler of the known (at least, the free) world.

Such comparisons are barely exaggerated, for what was nourished in the direct relationship between the President and the people which it was the purpose of John Kennedy to magnify was the feeling that he would intercede on their behalf, if not with a divinity, at least with the forces which governed their lives. The expectation that he aroused by his personal leadership cannot be understood except in these terms. The substance of the press conferences may have been thin, but their importance was that they were a "strictly regulated liturgical ceremonial," enacted in the homes of the people, instead of in the hall of the throne at Constantinople; and the people attended, week by week, in anticipation of hope or admonition or exhortation. Command was there in the presence; excellence was there in the performance; power was there at their disposal, with all of which all might be accomplished.

"A news management policy not only exists," wrote Arthur Krock during the third year of the administration, "but in the form of *direct and deliberate* actions has been enforced more cynically and more boldly than by any other previous administration. . . . One principal form that it takes is social flattery of Washington reporters and commentators—many more than ever got this treatment in the past—by the President and his high-level supporters." Arthur Krock had a grouch, no doubt, since he was not among those who were being flattered, but that does not invalidate the force of what he was saying, from his long experience. The personal friendship of John Kennedy with some journalists—Benjamin Bradlee and Charles Bartlett, for example, Joseph Alsop and Rowland Evans—was more important as a symbol than for the corruption which it involved of the relationship between power and the press. James Reston, before the administration took office, suggested to Pierre Salinger that the President-elect should forthwith stop seeing these journalists socially. But the suggestion was refused, and at one of his press conferences while he was in office John Kennedy even emphasised his friendship with some journalists.

Arriving in Washington for the first time in 1965, an English journalist could not help being surprised that it was a common practice for American political journalists to break bread with American politicians in each other's homes. They seemed to be too unseparate, and it was puzzling to know how the political journalist could, in these circumstances, maintain his posture as a critic. After all, the breaking of bread in another's, or in one's own, home is a ceremony; and, having accepted the hospitality of a politician, or extended his own, the political journalist is not in a strong position to go to his typewriter the next morning and write that the man is a liar.

But the problem is more complex. On the occasions, in one's own journalistic career, when one has formed too close a relationship with a politician, one has "understood" him and his problems too well, and one has even been in danger of liking him. One has been with him when he has relaxed, and listened to him as he has unwound; one has savoured his anecdotes; and it is always fascinating, because his materials are not just the wood of the carpenter under his lathe, or the iron of the blacksmith under his hammer, but human nature itself, individually and in the aggregate, intangible and unmalleable, under the impact of his own nature, his temper and his skills. It is necessary that the political journalist should understand the materials and the skills of the politician, but he must not "understand" them so well that he begins to talk the politician's language, and even to make the politician's own excuses for him. It is not only that there can be no truce between them, but that none should be sought.

The personal aloofness of the political journalist from the world which is his subject is, of course, easier to maintain in a capital such as London, which has many worlds, than in Washington, which has only one world. The politician in Washington is adorned and adored because he has no competitor. Night after night, power is wreathed and hymned because there is no other brow to decorate, no other ear to please. Under the high blossoms of the magnolias, in bowers of lushness and of fragrance where one would expect Aphrodite to be worshipped, only the name of power is sung. Nowhere but in Washington would a hostess be grateful to have a Secretary of Defense at her dinner table; nowhere else would nymphs garland him with myrtle, and coax the very doves of Aphrodite to coo about his brow. One can well understand how, in the impoverished intellectual and cultural life of Washington, it was taken to be a marvel that a politician could quote some lines of W. B. Yeats, or pronounce the name of Aristotle. There may not have been books on the New Frontier, but there were books of quotations.

It was in such a city, in which power already had no challenger, that John Kennedy could make it seem becoming. "He had that special grace . . . ," Benjamin Bradlee, in every other respect an unillusioned observer of the world, wrote in *Newsweek* after the assassination, ". . . that special grace of intellect which is known as taste." Foreseeing that the time would come when the historian would inquire as rigorously into the performance of John Kennedy as into that of any other politician, Benjamin Bradlee then observed that "historians are far removed from love." It is an astonishing remark, and outrageous from a journalist, who should feel closer to the historian than to any politician. But the question which one must ask is why Benjamin Bradlee, an unusually equipped journalist, should have fallen flat on his face before this one politician, and before no other. One cannot put the entire blame on John Kennedy; one must put some of it on Benjamin Bradlee, and the others who were similarly tempted.

John Kennedy presumed on his relationships with individual journalists, and the journalists tolerated the presumption. But the use of friends who happen to be newspapermen, and their willingness as newspapermen to be used as friends, is not the heart of the matter. What must be explained is the radiance of approval—and, if not of approval, at least of anticipation—with which the press in general clothed the acts of John Kennedy and his administration. He personally took great trouble with the press; it was he, for example, who conceived the idea of inviting the leading publishers of the country to lunch on a state-by-state basis; and the lists of guests for the twenty-five such lunches which were held were carefully compiled. "This gave the President a good cross-section of the state's press," observes Pierre Salinger; it in fact gave him a good cross-section of unusually gullible listeners.

"I will never be able to write another glib editorial attacking the President," one of them wrote to Pierre Salinger, "without thinking of that lunch and the great burdens of the American President." But he should not, as a publisher, be thinking in these terms; he should represent other concerns, and he should not be persuaded by a single lunch in a throne room that his expression of them is glib. The effect of this flattery—not only on local publishers, but on Washington reporters—was that the participants emerged, in the words of Arthur Krock, "in a state of protracted enchantment evoked by the President's charm and the awesome aura of his office." This was the atmosphere in the informal television interview which he gave on 17 December 1962 to three reporters who co-operated with him in his purpose. At great length, he spoke of the nature of his office: ". . . the problems are more difficult than I had imagined they were. . . . The responsibilities placed on the United States are greater than I imagined them to be. . . . If you take the wrong course, and on occasion I have, the President bears the burden of the responsibility quite rightly." All of this was put in a more down-to-earth manner by Harry Truman when he said that if a man could not stand the heat of the kitchen, he should get out of it, and journalists should not assist a President in making his office seem awesome.

But even as careful a reporter as Hugh Sidey, when he interviewed John Kennedy in 1963, could write of "an awesome presence in that Oval Chamber which was then quiet, cool, sunlit," just as he said of the televised press conferences that they showed "the worried face of a young man with an amusing accent trying desperately to do a job which anybody could tell you was impossible, beyond the bounds of human capacity." It will appear to be beyond the bounds of human capacity only if one expects of politics, not the modest arrangements which are their proper concern, but a superhuman achievement, an inhuman fulfilment; and it was this expectation which was being unwisely stimulated. If a Richard Nixon in the White House is still the Richard Nixon who clambered his way there, not suddenly transformed from a politician into a monarch, so was John Kennedy still only a politician, and his actions should have been reported as such by the press, so that they might be regarded as such by the people. Instead, for three years, they exalted the man and the office, and the people joined in the liturgy.

During his election campaign, as we saw, John Kennedy had called for "the pursuit of excellence in all phases of our national life," and added, "I think the President can do a good deal in setting that tone." We have been told that he was a happy President, and the significance of what might otherwise seem a peculiarly irrelevant observation lies in his belief that the Presidency provided him with the opportunity to use his faculties to the full in the pursuit of excellence: a concern so persistent in him, and in John Buchan, that it has the character of an obsession. Yet again, in an article, "The Arts in America," which he contributed while he was the President to the issue of *Look* of 18 December 1962, he said that the increasing recognition of "the essentiality of artistic achievement" was part of "a nation-wide movement toward excellence." Whether or not he in fact pursued excellence, he adorned his Presidency with images of it.

He gave a dinner to the Nobel prize winners of the Western hemisphere, and another of dazzling elegance, ten days later, to Andre Malraux; he invited Pablo Casals to the White House for the first time since he had played to Theodore Roosevelt, and Igor Stravinsky; learning that the President of the Sudan had a fondness for Shakespeare, he invited Ralph Richardson to be a guest at the state dinner, and summoned the American Shakespeare Festival Theatre from Stratford in Connecticut to present excerpts from its repertory. He "made of culture a form of patronage," says Joseph Kraft; and much the same was done in the world of the intellect. The result was as intended as it was inevitable: learning and the arts were not just in style; they were the style that rippled from the White House. That was the image, certainly, but the intention and the consequences were more serious. His "desire to bring the world of power and the world of ideas together in alliance," as Arthur Schlesinger puts it, confused the ends of both of them.

It may be that, as David Bevington says in *Tudor Drama and Politics,* we are today inclined to overemphasise the separation of politics and art; but if we do so, he continues, it is "partly because of our distrust of ever-increasing state power over the minds of men." Mass society—the totalitarian vice—total war: it is with these, in the modern age, that the artist can make no terms. In this condition, the poet and the artist will try to make a footing in "the deserts of the heart." John

Kennedy sought to prize him from this insecure hold, and to bring him into the palace. "I was desirous of according a recognition to his trade," he said on 26 February 1961 of his invitation to Robert Frost to take part in the inauguration; and, commenting on the prominence which he was then accorded by his countrymen, Robert Frost said in March of 1962: "It's been a new world for me. President Kennedy gave me a kind of status that nobody ever had before. People come up to me in dining rooms. Of course, I think it's a little presumptuous to come across a dining room floor with a menu card to ask for an autograph, but the people do it kindly." The picture is not reassuring; the poet had been made into a celebrity and, as such, it was he in turn who gave the President a status which he had not enjoyed before.

Robert Frost was a complex man. We know more about his personal life since he died, and it was not lived at ease. His poetry is less straightforward than it might seem from the more popular poems in the anthologies. But his name and his poetry were continually used by John Kennedy to a simple purpose. In a speech on 26 October 1963, the President said that he was "impressed, as I know all you were who knew him, by a good many qualities, but also by his toughness." (Even the poets on the New Frontier had to be tough.) "He gives the lie, as a good many other poets have, to the fact that poets are rather sensitive creatures who live in the dark of the garret." (Robert Frost was an acutely sensitive man, and the dark in which he lived much of his life was deeper than that of any garret.) "He once said that America is the country you leave only when you go out and lick another country." (It was a silly remark, which had little to do with either his life or his poetry, and only a politician would have thought to recall it.) "He was not particularly belligerent in his relations, his human relations, but he felt very strongly that the United States should be a country of power, of force, to use that power and force wisely." (The poet is thus made the spokesman of a foreign policy.) This was the manner, and it was always the manner, in which John Kennedy used the images of excellence to adorn his Presidency, and to sustain his policies.

In one of the last speeches of his life, on 18 November 1963, he offered another quotation from Robert Frost: "Nothing is true except a man or men adhere to it—to live for it, to spend themselves on it, to die for it." To this he added himself: "We need this spirit even more than money or institutions or agreements." But it is these which must normally be the concern of the politician; and this was particularly true of the subject to which the President was at that moment addressing himself: the Alliance for Progress. The last thing Latin America needed was a truth to which to adhere, on which to spend itself, for which to die; and, if it should ever need such a truth, it will be unlikely to find it in the United States or in a politician. Robert Frost may have been saying something which is valuable about the soul of man; but politicians should leave the soul of man alone, and not tamper with it.

When he returned from his tour of the world in the spring of 1962, Robert Kennedy talked of "the misunderstanding and misinformation" in other countries about the United States, and he exhorted "our artists, our poets, our musicians, our writers, to go across into those countries and give lectures, . . . and stand up there and answer questions." They should explain, he said, "that we believe that the state exists for the individual, that this is what capitalism is about, and this is what we are fighting for." The mind boggles: Robert Lowell and Allen Ginsberg, say, Louis Simpson and William Stafford, travelling the globe to explain "what capitalism is about"; to proclaim that "we believe that the state exists for the individual," even while they were doing the bidding of the state. The apotheosis of the attempt to make a connection between power and excellence was achieved in the succeeding administration, when a festival of the arts was arranged at the White House. To put it mildly, it was an implausible occasion, given the presiding figure of Lyndon Johnson; but the implausibility was, in truth, considerably more healthy than the plausibility conferred earlier by the magnetic figure of John Kennedy.

In the October 1965 issue of *Commentary,* at the end of a visit to the United States, I observed as an outsider the unfortunate consequences of the excitable connection that John Kennedy had made beween the world of politics and the world of the intellect; and it may help if a few sentences from this earlier description are recalled:

> The dearly bought, and even more dearly maintained, privacy of the intellectual life is something for which American intellectuals have scant regard. . . .
>
> Removed from his own discipline, no one is more vain than the intellectual. Precisely because his mind is able to handle ideas with ease and excitement, it is all too easily turned when he is invited to discourse outside his own field. Inside his own field, the intellectual would never lay claim to omniscience, and not often to authority. Outside it, his claim to both is breathtaking. . . .
>
> . . . the American intellectual . . . was raped by President Kennedy. . . .
>
> Power is un-intellectual: President Kennedy was allowed to give it intellectual excitement. Power is safe only if it is exercised without enchantment, without claim to reason, and without pretence to virtue: President Kennedy was allowed to endow it with all three. Power is, no doubt, necessary: President Kennedy was allowed to make it seem desirable. . . .

At the time, these sentences provoked considerable indignation. Seven years later, it is hard to find anyone in the world of the intellect who is not inclined to agree with their import, even if not with every emphasis.

The connection which was being made between power and the intellect was recognised, as it was advertised, from the beginning. Richard Rovere, writing in *The New Yorker* immediately after the inauguration, observed the intellectual attainments of many members of the administration, especially at the level immediately below the Cabinet, and commented on the danger: "The great majority of them are new to power, and their education has included little in the way of training in the uses of power. It is a most radical experiment"; and he had previously described the experiment as "a preference for intellectuals—professional, amateur, *manqué*." Arthur Schlesinger, who was one of them, was later to talk of a "summons to the scholar-statesman"; and Joseph Kraft, who knew them, said that they "dazzled the nation by intellectual brilliance and social swank," and he later summarised the meaning of it all when he said that there had taken place "a palpable transfer of ideas from the world of system-thinking to the world of folk-thinking."

Richard Hofstadter, writing in 1963 in *Anti-Intellectualism in American Life*, made the important distinction between intelligence, which is "manipulative, adjustive, and practical," and the intellect, which is "critical, creative, and contemplative." By these standards, John Kennedy was intelligent, but he was not an intellectual; and we may rid ourselves of the need for further definition by acknowledging that he was a non-intellectual with a good mind. This is in no way a criticism, far from it; for the best of reasons, a politician should not be an intellectual, inhabiting a world of nominal abstractions, of systems and models. But he had to be announced as an intellectual: that was another of the images of excellence. Theodore Sorensen describes him as an intellectual; he proceeds immediately to define his intelligence as practical, his interest in action. In fact, the intelligence which is being described was once well expressed by Vince Lombardi, when he was the coach of the Green Bay Packers: "I think we excel at area blocking because we have a very intelligent line. By intelligence, I mean a linesman's ability to improvise and adjust simultaneously." This is indeed the intelligence which is required in a politician, but it is not intellectual.

Having asserted that John Kennedy was, "as politicians go, an intellectual," Arthur Schlesinger then seriously discusses him, on the basis of *Why England Slept* and *Profiles in Courage*, as an historian. "The historical mind can be analytical, or it can be romantic," he says. "The best historians are both, Kennedy among them." That a man whose father was an historian—and a stimulating teacher of history—and who was himself trained as an historian and set out to be one, should place John Kennedy among "the best historians"—apparently of all time—would be unbelievable if the statement were not there in cold print, and expanded for the length of three pages. To place him in the company of Thucydides and Herodotus or, in our own time, of Pieter Geyl and Marc Bloch, of Henri Pirenne and F. M. Stenton, of Richard Hofstadter and Lacey Baldwin Smith, was to lose all sense of reality, of the fitness of things. But this was the manner in which he was regarded.

The concern was with the images of excellence, both to influence the verdict of history and to attract support in the present. "If the emphasis on brains was genuine," writes Joseph Kraft, "it also had a political purpose. . . . It was aimed . . . at the egghead liberals within the Democratic Party." In particular, it had begun as an attempt to win these liberals away from their allegiance to Adlai Stevenson, and it continued as an attempt to prevent them from transferring their allegiance to a new prophet. "He was interested in ideas and theories, but not for their own sake," says Roger Hilsman. "His interest was aroused only when the ideas had some practical consequences." This is the opposite of the attitude of the intellectual, and it is not surprising when we are told that intellectuals were not typically among his close friends, even though this may make a McGeorge Bundy or a John Kenneth Galbraith wonder at his placing.

"Where is the meaningful relation of intellectuals to power?" asked Alfred Kazin and, at the end of February 1961, William V. Shannon gave the only answer: "An intellectual's basic posture is that of critic. He has no right to be enamored of power." But this was not the prevailing attitude. More characteristic was the observation which was later made by James Reston: "We are just beginning to develop a new class of public servants who move about in the triangle of daily or periodic journalism, the university or foundation, and government service. These roving writers and officials are a growing and hopeful breed . . . but much more of such cross-fertilization could be done." Of course, the universities are today engaged in the difficult task of trying to extricate themselves from the close connection with government which John Kennedy had fostered.

In the *Harvard Alumni Bulletin* in July of 1962, Nathan Pusey, the president of Harvard University, warned against the connection. He said that, in the distribution of research funds, the government agencies were showing "an increasing desire to say how things are to be done, and who may or may not appear in them. . . . We feel that, at some future time, our new associate may begin to make demands upon us inconsistent with the character of an independent university." A month later, *Time* examined the way in which many universities were rapidly becoming "contract research factories," and it paid especial attention to what it called "the convenient device" of "the great research centers, mostly war-bred and usually off campus, which universities run under contract to federal agencies," such as the Los Alamos and Livermore and Lawrence Radiation Laboratories at the University of California, the Lincoln and Servomechanisms laboratories of the Massachusetts Institute of Technology, and the Jet Propulsion laboratory at the California Institute of Technology; and the list could, of course, be extended.

The devices for concealing the enslavement into which the intellectual community was drifting were many. Early in 1961, the New York *Times* described the role of the Institute for Defense Analyses, of which several of the great universities were members. It "operates in a gray area between the government and the campus, at times paying the salaries of scientists who are working in government offices. In short, it makes it possible for the government to get the services of experts who might be reluctant to leave the academic atmosphere for full-time government employment." In this way, "it is institutionalizing the role of the university scientists who divide their time between secret government projects and their campuses." Thus, as a member of the Institute, the Pennsylvania State University assumed responsibility for the management of an anti-submarine warfare research centre at La Spezia in Italy, in conjunction with the North Atlantic Treaty Organization; and, during 1961, both Stanford University and Michigan State University had advisory groups in South Vietnam, the first of which, at least, reported to the President, while a member of the second, Frank C. Child, significantly argued that, in so far as he saw any hope in the situation, it lay only in a military coup against Ngo Dinh Diem.

Once again we find ourselves in the atmosphere of "half cops and robbers, half faculty meeting"; the atmosphere was dangerous, and the intellectuals should have striven to hold aloof from it. Joseph Kraft, in a memorable description of the RAND Corporation, said that it bore "the dual impress of the gladiator and the philosopher." This was indeed one of the images of excellence—the "gladiator-philosopher" as well as the "scholar-statesman"—in which John Kennedy arrayed himself and his administration and his purpose. What was needed from the intellectual community was something of the disdain of Reinhold Niebuhr, who refused to attend the dinner for the Nobel prize winners with the comment: "I'm too old at my age to travel that far to eat with strangers." Unhappily, almost everyone else was ready to make the journey; and the people, as they watched their poets and their artists and their scholars and their thinkers in a throng about the seat of power could be forgiven for looking to politics with an expectation which was beyond the possibility of fulfilment.

Julius Caesar was impatient of the omens by which he was supposed to guide his own fortunes and those of the state. The augurs might offer their sacrifices, and report to him their ominous findings—the maculation of the heart of a goose, or the displaced liver of a cock—but he set no store by them. "I have inherited this burden of superstition and nonsense," Thornton Wilder makes him say in *The Ides of March*. "I govern innumerable men but must acknowledge that I am governed by birds and thunderclaps." But he understood that the people and his soldiers believed the omens; and, when he was in a difficult position, he was quick to make use of them, or to manufacture them, and then to interpret them to his advantage. The stories are numerous, each a tribute to his presence of mind and to his unillusioned appraisal of the realities of his power.

Suetonius tells us that, when he reached the Rubicon, "an apparition of superhuman size and beauty was seen sitting on the river bank playing a reed pipe. A party of shepherds gathered around him to listen and, when some of Caesar's men broke ranks to do the same, the apparition snatched a trumpet from one of them, ran down to the river, blew a thunderous blast, and crossed over. Caesar exclaimed: 'Let us accept this as a sign from the Gods, and follow where they beckon, in vengeance on our double-dealing enemies. The die is cast'"; and his soldiers followed him to the farther bank. On another occasion, he slipped and fell as he led his men ashore on the coast of Africa, but he "turned an unfavourable omen into a favourable one by clasping the ground and shouting: 'Africa, I have tight hold of you!'"; and his soldiers followed him once more. We are unwise if we smirk; even in a godless age, we attend to omens, elevate the high priests who interpret them, and follow the politician who has the quick wit to read them to his advantage. In much the same manner as Julius Caesar, and to much the same end, John Kennedy formed his association with the priesthood of our time, the artists and the intellectuals, and carried their oracles, interpreted to his own purposes, to the multitude beyond the palace gates.

Through them he would extend his sway; through the scientists, and through the astronauts; through fashion, and through taste. It was all brought together by *Time* in a cover story in its issue of 27 July 1962, in which it described what it called the "New Society," which most of us can remember, but which has already faded. "It is an open-ended one, energetic, and international-minded. Its members jet to Gstaad for ski-ing, Venice for the film festival, Paris for the spring collections . . . a different and more stimulating social stream of people with more education and more to talk about, who want their friends to be intelligent, active, and amusing [one of their favourite words]. . . . It is a society to which the Kennedys have given considerable impetus. . . . As one hostess summarized it: 'You can either be very rich, very aristocratic, or very famous.' To this the Kennedys, with their glittering evenings for Nobel laureates and French cultural arbiters, have added another significant category—'powerful.'"

"Kennedy is slavishly followed—and more than slightly feared," wrote *Time* again in its issue of 7 June 1963. "In today's Washington, no one really attacks President Kennedy personally. Respect plays a large part in this reticence. So does fear. The word is around that the Kennedys will exert their vast influence against all those who buck them." It noted that "Cigar sales have soared. . . . Hat sales have fallen. . . . Button-down shirts [are avoided]. . . . His ideas about physical fitness have put all official Washington into sweat socks." On one level it might seem not to matter; but on another it mattered greatly. Only ten years later did the American people appear to be recovering their sense that their President is a politician, to be judged as such, and not a warrior and priest, philosopher and king, from whom all good things will flow.

In his debate with Arthur Schlesinger, which has been mentioned earlier, Alfred de Grazia said that, in the United States today, "We have an officer called the President, who, considering that our age is not religious, nevertheless begins to satisfy the divine aspects of the Roman Imperator," and he continued to make his point with considerable force:

> The President is believed to represent the people, not in any ordinary sense, but in the most remarkable of ways, involving psychic waves, psychological projections, even the statistical proofs of scientoid professors who feel themselves immune from vulgar obsessions. With the expansion of the Presidential constituency to include the world there is no possibility of a competitor short of the Universal Pope or Stalin or Mao Tse-tung.

He concluded by scorning the "vulgar magic of one-man rule"; and it was the appeal to this magic that not only persuaded a fully clothed woman to follow the President into the sea but encouraged the state of mind in which John Kennedy could remark to Chalmers Roberts during the crisis in Laos in 1961 that "he had no doubt that," in spite of a popular antipathy to the use of force, "the nation would follow the President if he ordered men into combat," and on this conviction he relied.

If its power and prestige are exalted, the American Presidency can be a dangerous office, exciting a false relationship with the people. Thus, when Abraham Lincoln was assassinated, Walt Whitman chanted:

> For you they call, the swaying mass,
> their eager faces turning,
> Here Captain! Here Father!

When Franklin Roosevelt died, it was a common observation of doctors that the dreams of their patients were "suffused with the characters of their fathers." So it was to be after the assassination of John Kennedy. During the days which followed, sociologists and psychologists across the United States made their observations, and some of them are collected in a volume, *Children and the Death of a President*, edited by Martha

Wolfenstein and Gilbert Kliman. To a reader from a demure constitutional monarchy, the essays are as disturbing as they are astonishing.

Roberta S. Sigel reports her observations in Michigan, listing the observable reactions in adults and children:

Symptom	Adults	Children
Didn't feel like eating	43%	37%
Had headaches	25	22
Had upset stomach	22	18
Cried	53	39
Insomnia	48	45

Schoolchildren who were inclined to support the Democratic Party "reported more trouble sleeping, more loss of appetite." Martha Wolfenstein reported from her observations that "children were exposed to the unaccustomed sight of their parents, teachers, and other adults, openly weeping. This emotional breakdown of the grown-ups was probably quite alarming to children."

In an article entitled "Oedipal Themes in Children's Reactions to the Assassination," Gilbert Kliman reported that "various forms of castration dreads appeared, presumably because of fears that the unconsciously wished for parricide would be revenged. Oedipal and latency-age children sometimes expected the President's ghost to appear. Girls as well as boys found themselves responding with oedipal themes." A student at Yale University, a full twenty-one years old, said that "five times since Friday I have broken down and cried unashamedly." There were some unsympathetic reactions. Martha Wolfenstein reports the belligerent comment of one schoolboy. "Someone should have shot him sooner, then we wouldn't have had to have all this physical fitness"; but she points out that he was a clumsy child, and obese. His comment is interesting, neverthe-

less, since it emphasises how widely and deeply the example
of the President had intruded into the personal lives of even
boys and girls at school.

"Anxiety and apprehension of other bad things happening
were widespread," say the editors of the volume in their conclusion. One would think that one was reading about the death
of a pharaoh in ancient Egypt, when people did indeed think
that the sun would be darkened forever, that the moon would
leave its course, that the very stars would be affrighted, at his
passing. One would not think that one was reading about the
death of a politician in a republic, with a pragmatic temper
and a positivist tradition, in the middle of the twentieth century.
Even when every allowance has been made for the human un-
kindnesses of the tragedy—the violence of the death, the relative
youth of the victim—one must still say that the popular reaction
was unhealthy: that the office had been exalted, and the man
in it, to a degree which had distorted the people's attitudes
to politics in the previous three years, and which would continue
to do so during the painful years which were then to follow.

CHAPTER TEN

The Illusions of Consensus and the Temptations of Pragmatism

THE "CONSENSUS POLITICS" which John Kennedy and, following him, Lyndon Johnson, sought to practise during the 1960s was a child of the "consensus theories" with which American sociologists became fascinated during the 1950s. A model which was useful in the intellectual world was transferred to the actual world, and wrought havoc with the American political system. Only now are the American people recovering from the illusion that there should be a consensus in support of particular policies and of individual politicians; only now are they growing accustomed once more to the fact that there will rarely be any unity of national feeling except on matters which are not generally spoken; only now are they learning to live again on their raft, with their feet always in the water. This recovery could always be predicted; one had only to wait. A people with a political tradition and a political system which are as active and as instructive as those of the United States do not for long delude themselves.

Once again, we must make the effort to place John Kennedy in his time. It was not an accident that American sociologists became absorbed by the idea of "consensus" during the years after 1945. (Some of them, of course, challenged the idea, and the debate still continues.) They were trying to explain the stability of societies which do not depend, for their coherence, primarily on coercion; and, in its most general definition, the idea of "consensus" was used to explore the fabric of beliefs and attitudes and prejudices about which a society is fundamentally and voluntarily agreed. In a traditional society, of course, the fabric of "consensus" is taken for granted, but the United States is not a traditional society, and the foundations of the traditional societies of the Old World have been shaken in the past two hundred years, and especially since 1914. What is it, then, which holds contemporary democratic and liberal societies together?

The obvious answer would seem to be that history does; and by history one means narrative. It is the essence of all human life, social and individual, that it is narrative. Animals cannot make up stories about their heroes or their ancestors, any more than they can imagine stories about their futures or the futures of their children; they are confined to the present. But human beings roam, with their stories, far into the past and deep into the future; and men hold together in societies because they have common stories to tell. Their music, their literature, their history, their folklore, their habits, their speech: they are all stories, and it would be lonely without them. The story may be no longer than a greeting such as "Hi!" or it may be as complicated and fearful as the history of slavery;

but it will bind. But suppose that one is a member of a society which is not historical—in the deepest sense, because the avowed reason for its existence is that it repudiated history, and created a New World—how does one then account for the fact that men hold voluntarily together in their societies? This was the problem which faced the American sociologists in the situation, peculiar to their country, which existed after 1945.

By 1945, their country had a history, a remarkable history; it had arrived, so to speak; there was the accomplishment of a narrative, for all the world to see, which began in 1492 or in 1620 or in 1776, whichever date one chooses. The facts which they sought to explain were real, for no country in the history of the world had achieved so much, with so little parallel, in so short a space of time. How could it be measured? By 1945:

—the continental expansion of the United States had been completed two generations earlier, and the fact of it had been absorbed;

—the mass immigration of the last quarter of the nineteenth, and the first quarter of the twentieth, centuries appeared to have been absorbed, as was indicated in such a work as *Beyond the Melting Pot,* by Nathan Glazer and Daniel P. Moynihan;

—apart from the mass immigration, there had been an astonishing intellectual immigration, largely as a result of Hitler's conquest of Europe, and these often brilliant minds found themselves at home in America;

—after the collapse of France in 1940, New York had become the "art capital" of the world, to yield almost immediately its own school of painters, dictating to the Western world, and retaining this position even when Europe had been liberated;

—the extraordinary industrial expansion of the United States which began after 1865 had been completed and absorbed, and was now being followed by a technological revolution of equal significance;

–the energy of the New Deal, one of the genuinely creative political accomplishments of this century, had worked its way into every corner of American society, endowing it with new values and new institutions;

–twice in less than thirty years, the United States had stepped forth, as Winston Churchill put it, to redress the balance of the Old World, and its society had taken the strain of the experience.

In particular, the American intellectual could not help being affected by the question put by Daniel Bell in *The End of Ideology,* one of the most significant works of the 1950s: ". . . though large-scale unemployment during the depression was more prolonged and more severe here than in any country in Western Europe, the Communist movement never gained a real foothold in the United States, nor has any fascist movement on a European model arisen. How does one explain this?" But the American sociologists could not just tell a story about it, and find the answer in the narrative of their country; not least because they have, as Richard Hofstadter said of American intellectuals in general, "a lamentably thin sense of history." So they wrote a cookery book, instead; they concocted a recipe, and they called it "consensus"; at least some of them did, for others of their number retorted that "conflict" is the basis of a stable society. The reader who follows the argument of this book will understand that it leans to the second of these ideas; but there is no need to enter the debate.

All that concerns us is that at the end of the 1950s, as John Kennedy prepared to take office, the idea that there is a "consensus" in a free society was the conventional wisdom in the

United States, given convincing expression in different ways from different angles by powerful minds. The complexity of the idea—of which no hint has been provided here—did not prevent it from being simplified and vulgarized as it was carried directly into the actual world of politics. From the belief that there was a "consensus" which makes society possible, it was only a step to the belief that a "consensus" could be created in support of particular measures. This was the meaning of the "consensus politics" of the 1960s which, by smothering the intense conflicts which are always generated by large issues, could lead only, on the one hand, to the delusion of magnified expectations and, on the other, to the bitterness of unarticulated opposition.

As we have seen in an earlier chapter, it was one of the convictions of the administration of John Kennedy that the domestic problems of the United States had been largely solved: that "a national consensus on them exists," as Walt Rostow said, "within which we are clearly moving forward as a country." The liberalism of the New Deal, said Arthur Schlesinger in the New York *Times Magazine* of 4 August 1957, "has successfully established its principles—a balance of forces, countervailing power, the mixed economy." In 1962, in an introduction to the second edition of *The Vital Center*, he affirmed that "The problems of the New Deal were essentially quantitative problems—problems of meeting stark human needs for food, clothing, shelter, and employment. Most of these needs are now effectively met for most Americans." Only a year later, Michael Harrington was to publish *The Other America*, an exposure of a society in which poverty is not only widespread but deep, and in which the quantitative problems of bad housing, of hunger, of ill health, and of unemployment, have not been solved for a substantial proportion of the population.

Given the belief, to quote Arthur Schlesinger once more, that "the major problems of economic structure have been solved," John Kennedy was easily persuaded that he could attract the support of big business to build the "consensus" which he desired. As early as 13 February 1961, in addressing a luncheon of the National Industrial Conference Board, he had talked the language of "consensus" to the business community: "In short, there is no inevitable clash between the public and the private sectors—or between investment and consumption— nor, as I have said, between government and business. All elements in our national economic growth are interdependent." He then gave a pledge: "On behalf of my associates in the Cabinet, I want to be very precise: we will not discriminate for or against any segment of our society, or any segment of the business community"; and he continued to explain that "We know that your success and ours are intertwined—that you have facts and know-how that we need. Whatever past differences have existed, we seek more than an attitude of truce, more than a treaty—we seek the spirit of a full-fledged alliance." Some other Cabinet members spoke on the same occasion, and *Time* commented in its issue of 24 February 1961 that they "tossed in some plums of their own in an outburst of pro-business sentiment that would have stunned an old New Dealer." The course had been set.

On 21 May 1962, immediately after his confrontation with the steel companies, John Kennedy personally addressed a White House Conference on National Economic Issues, and carried his argument forward:

> I would like to say a word about the difference between myth and reality. Most of us are conditioned for many years to have a

political viewpoint, Republican or Democratic—liberal, conservative, moderate. The fact is that most of the problems, or at least many of them, that we now face are technical problems, are administrative problems. They are very sophisticated judgments which do not lend themselves to the great sort of "passionate movements" which have stirred this country so often in the past.

Three weeks later, in the commencement address that he gave at Yale University, he elaborated his theme. Even as he questioned some of the myths most popular with the business community—especially about the role of the government in the economy—he insisted that, "in the wider national interest, we need not partisan wrangling but common concentration on common problems." The problems of the 1960s presented "subtle challenges, for which technical answers, not political answers, must be provided"; the United States must be "prepared to face technical problems without ideological preconceptions," finding their solution in "the most sophisticated and technical judgment." In short, politics were to be transcended.

"He never took ideology very seriously," says Arthur Schlesinger, who also records that, when he was making the appointments to his administration, he observed: "Now, on these key jobs, I don't care whether a man is a Democrat or an Igorot. I want the best fellow I can get for the particular job." In all of this, he represented the views, not only of his administration, but of his time. Writing in *Newsweek*, in its issue of 15 May 1963, Walter Lippmann noted that in the United States as in Europe there were signs of "a suction toward the center . . . a notable tendency to turn away from the dogmas and slogans of the class struggle," and he added: "President Kennedy, we must remember, is himself a man of the center. He is far removed from the social struggles of the New Deal, and by any serious measure, in any other modern country, he would be called an enlightened conservative." He had himself said that he would prefer to be called, not a conservative, but a realist.

He and other members of the administration certainly thought of themselves as pragmatists. We grow used, in the memoirs, to the claim that its members were pragmatic rather than dogmatic; and James Tobin, when he was appointed to the Council of Economic Advisers, declared: "We are all pragmatists." John Kennedy was "pragmatic in the sense that he tested the meaning of a proposition by its consequences," writes Arthur Schlesinger; "he was also pragmatic in the sense of being free from metaphysics." The administration, said *Life* in its issue of 6 January 1961, was characterized by a "singular immunity from prior doctrinaire commitment"; and, a little later, the *Reporter* observed that "they are dogmatic; but their dogmatism is relieved by the absence of dogmas." In this way, believing that their policies were exempt from the judgement of political values—a less treacherous word than dogma or ideology—and that they would be supported by an unpolitical "consensus," the administration of John Kennedy had in fact freed themselves to act as they wished.

It was not an accident that, as Samuel Huntington observes in *The Soldier and the State*, Theodore Roosevelt had become "the intellectual godfather" of the pragmatic liberals. Action without direction, purpose without belief, energy without thoroughness, activity without consequence: the story of Theodore Roosevelt should not, perhaps, be given to small boys or to grown liberals. It overheats the blood. Here, as in the attraction to John Buchan, one finds another illuminating comparison. We can learn from the fact that, whether in the speeches of John Kennedy or in the writings of Arthur Schlesinger, this un-ideological activist was elevated in their pantheon. It was not only that Theodore Roosevelt exalted the Presidency—"I declined to adopt the view," he wrote in his autobiography, "that what was imperatively necessary for the Nation could not be done by the President unless he could find some specific authorization to do it"—but that he exalted it as a personal office, unrestrained as far as possible, not only by prior doctrinaire commitment, but by any political values exterior to it.

"He stood above the contending classes," Richard Hofstadter wrote in his essay on Theodore Roosevelt, "an impartial arbiter devoted to the national good, and a custodian of the stern virtues without which the United States could not play its destined role of mastery in the world theater"; and these were exactly the roles, for himself and for the country, which John Kennedy assumed and proclaimed. "Psychologically he identified himself with the authority of the State, and jealously projected his pressing desire for 'mastery' into the trust problem"; and in this way John Kennedy responded to the action of the steel corporations as a challenge to his own mastery, a response in which there was no more political conviction and no more conceptual strategy than there was behind Theodore Roosevelt's spasmodic attacks on the trusts. "What Roosevelt stood for, as a counterpoise to the fat materialism of the wealthy and the lurking menace of the masses, were the aggressive, masterful, fighting virtues of the soldier"; and this was both the temper of John Kennedy himself and the temper which he strove to inspire in the country. " 'Manly' and 'masterful,' two of the most common words in Roosevelt's prose"; but they were no more common than "tough" and "tough-minded" in the vocabulary of the New Frontier. "As his most discerning biographer, Henry Pringle, points out, he was a perennial volunteer"; and it is hard to think of a more suitable phrase to describe the camaraderie, overactive and playful, of the administration that took office in 1961.

The kind of leadership that is being described will always take two forms: the ceaseless urge to activity; and the attempt to convert the Presidency into a vehicle for moral exhortation. This second was another legacy of Theodore Roosevelt. "The role in which Theodore Roosevelt fancied himself was that of moralist"; and no phrase of his making occurs more frequently in the language of the New Frontier than his assertion that the Presidency should be used as a "bully pulpit." It is a discomfiting phrase, as if America were not already subjected to too much preaching, to too insistent a moralising, to too frequent "Great Awakenings." But the combination of moralism and activity is one to which the American people, from time to time, are peculiarly eager to respond, as if they hope, by such a shortcut, to transcend the limits of politics. What is more, the "bully pulpit," on the one hand, and "a burst of hectic action," on the other, are the substitutes for the political values which he has disdained to which the pragmatic liberal is most likely to reach: fostering within the unpolitical "consensus" which he strives to maintain a too high expectation of the man and the office, of the President and of the Presidency, and what they alone may achieve.

No one can question the brilliance with which John Kennedy practised the "consensus politics" which suited his temper and his ambitions. He not only occupied the entire centre in American politics; he enlarged it even as he occupied it. Less than two weeks after the inauguration, Walter Lippmann offered one of those panoramic views of American political history in which he makes it seem, not without some justification, that it has in fact coincided with his own life:

The center in American political life is an enormous majority
of the people, and the party which controls the center is virtually
unbeatable. The Republicans controlled it most of the time from
the Civil War to the Taft-Roosevelt schism of 1912. The Democrats controlled it from the Great Depression to the Korean War.
Eisenhower had a chance to take command of it, and to inaugurate
a new Republican era. But he did not know how to go about it.
But this young man Kennedy understands perfectly the meaning
of the center. He intends to lead it, and he knows how to go about
doing it.

We are at this point, with John Kennedy, in the presence of
a commanding instinct for popular leadership, which is hard
to explain in so young a man of so little experience, but which
had borne him to power and which sustained his popularity
while he exercised it. At this level, he possessed a skill that
can be appreciated both as his greatest strength and as his
greatest weakness.

In a phrase of exceptional insight, Joseph Kraft wrote of
him: "His motto might have been: no enemies to the right."
The basic political strategy was explained by Carey McWilliams
in *The Nation* of 26 May 1962: "If 100 represents the outer-
most limit of the right, and 0 the boundary of the left, then
the Kennedy administration might be said to hold almost un-
disputed possession of the territory from 0 to 80. . . . In the
absence of a left, President Kennedy only had to move a few
steps to the right (usually by protecting his foreign policy
against right-wing criticism) in order to occupy virtually the
entire spectrum." This was a matter of grave concern to the
independent liberals and the disorganised left outside the administration. "The politics of our country," wrote I. F. Stone
in his newsletter of 22 January 1962, "have grown dangerously lop-sided. There is a vocal extreme right. There is a
center, which Mr. Kennedy has pre-empted. There is no longer

a liberal opposition." In this situation, fearing only enemies to the right, it was inevitable that the instinct of John Kennedy should carry him to the right; and it is one of the illusions of "consensus politics" that the practice of them exempts the politician from such pressures; they were merely not recognised.

There was not at the time, and there never can be, a centre as extensive as that which he appeared to occupy. If he held the territory "from o to 80," it was because the left was disorganised and demoralised (in part, by him), and because he had moved his own position in order to capture an important part of the right. There could be only one result: as he moved towards the right, the ground to his left would begin to grow, and others would occupy it. In short, a "new left" would come into existence, and it was already growing during his last year in office.

The general incomprehension of what was happening in the United States—and especially on its campuses—continued throughout most of the life of the administration, in part concealed by the success of the "consensus politics" which was being practised. What mattered—and could be observed—at the time, was that two attitudes to American society and to American politics, which might have been expected to contradict each other, were in fact coalescing. As was noticed by Robert Martinson in *The Nation* of 19 May 1962, "Alienation from the big society and an active desire for meaningful commitment are inextricably mixed"; and it was indeed this curious, tormenting, and self-defeating combination of attitudes that was to be the mark of the decade: a felt alienation from society and an active desire for participation within it. "I feel about me an ambient insanity," the editor of the student newspaper at the University of Michigan had written, "a social malaise which must be opposed." The students were beginning to follow the admonition of C. Wright Mills before his death, "to follow the example of their fellows abroad by acting as a self-conscious 'elite' with a mission to transform the nation"; and the evidence was everywhere to be found.

There were the sit-ins and the Freedom Riders; there were demonstrations for peace; there were the sudden growth of youth organisations on a national scale and the first national conference of campus political parties; and there was the new phenomenon of the graduate student, whose numbers had dramatically increased since 1945, as an active force on the campus and beyond it. An editorial in the student newspaper of the University of North Carolina had described "what is becoming a familiar feature of graduate life": a "loosely organized discussion group," calling itself "The New Left Club," whose "socio-economic and political views fall somewhere in the vast area left of Kennedy." In fact, "To be on the same side as Kennedy, even for a moment," observed Robert Martinson, "is considered to be bad form in some circles." In its issue of 22 November 1963, the day of the assassination, *Time* reviewed the state of campus opinion, and concluded that "Campus disenchantment with President Kennedy now spreads far and wide."

Even if there had been no dramatic escalation of the American involvement in the war in Vietnam, there can be little doubt that, during the second half of the 1960s, the left in the United States would have become more combative than in the previous two decades. It had been given no choice but to try to disrupt the suffocating atmosphere of "consensus" that prevailed, in the world of the intellect as well as in the world of politics. "American political thought in the post-war world," wrote Stephen Rousseas and James Farganis in *The Nation* of 23 March 1963, "has been leeched of all its passion of

meaningful social reform and has degenerated into the apotheosis of a non-committed scientism. . . . It is convinced that
democracy today has solved all the major problems of industrial
society, and that those which do remain are of a second-order
magnitude involving merely technical adjustments within a now
prevailing *consensus gentium.*" This was the depth of the protest which was growing, even as John Kennedy himself called
for "technical answers, not political answers" to the problems of
the country.

We can have no certain idea how John Kennedy would
have reacted to this movement if he had lived; for it would
have questioned the very foundation of his political strategy.
As the area to his left began to grow, and to be occupied by
vocal groups and active leaders, they would have challenged
his foreign policy: even his most legendary achievement.
(Shortly before the assassination, Edward D. Eddy, Jr., the
president of Chatham College in Pittsburgh, had already
traced "youth's decreasing identification" with the President
to the "shock and terror" which they felt during the Cuba
missile crisis.) But it was by his foreign policy that John
Kennedy hoped to keep the right within the "consensus" on
which his popular leadership was built; and it is doubtful
whether even he, once the left had become vociferous, could
have straddled such a distance. "Woodrow Wilson once said,"
he proclaimed when he was on the stump again four days before
his assassination, "that a political party is of no use unless
it is serving a great national purpose." But it was the idea of
a single national purpose—and of the "consensus" which supported it—that was at last being challenged.

On 3 February 1961, the Leadership Conference on Civil
Rights, in the persons of Roy Wilkins, its chairman, and Arnold

Aronson, its secretary, submitted to the new President a memorandum, in which they described the actions which they believed were necessary in that field. At a meeting at the White House three days later, they were told by Theodore Sorensen that the President would neither introduce nor support any civil rights legislation, that he would rely instead on executive action, using the powers which were available to him. Late in March, the National Association for the Advancement of Colored People met in Washington in a stormy mood, and they were addressed by Harris Wofford, previously an active worker in the cause of civil rights, and by then one of John Kennedy's principal advisers. His speech was uncomfortable: "I do not mean that the new avenue of executive action will be easy. This course has plenty of contradictions, and it will not . . . resolve the built-in political contradictions." But it was these political contradictions, of course, which "consensus politics" was intended to bypass; and executive action, designed to avoid both public controversy and a struggle in Congress, was a part of the method.

During the campaign, when he was seeking the support of the liberals, John Kennedy had asked Joseph Clark, in the Senate, and Emanuel Celler, in the House of Representatives, to put the civil rights programme of the Democratic Party into legislative form; and, by the beginning of May 1961, they had introduced six bills, designed to implement the party's election pledges. The principal bill would have sought to hasten the desegregation of public schools by requiring every school board which was still operating a racially segregated school to adopt a desegregation plan within six months. Although they had already observed John Kennedy's determination to placate the Southern bloc in Congress, the sponsors hoped at least for his benevolent neutrality. Instead, on the day after they were introduced, Pierre Salinger publicly dissociated the President from them, saying that in his view legislation was at that time not necessary.

A year later, in *The Nation* of 3 March 1962, Martin Luther King said what he thought of this approach: "As the year unfolded, executive initiative became increasingly feeble, and the chilling prospect emerged of a general administration retreat." He argued that the "basic strategic goals" of the administration had been narrowed, and accused it of "aggressively driving towards the limited goal of token integration." He described its strategy and its tactics in this way:

> The administration brought forth a plan to substitute executive order for legislative programs. The most challenging order, to end discrimination in federal housing, while no adequate substitute for the many legislative acts promised in the campaign platforms and speeches, nevertheless was alluring, and pressure abated for Congressional action. The year passed, and the President fumbled. By the close of the year, a new concept was adopted; the President now wished to "move ahead in a way which will maintain a consensus."

Yet, as Martin Luther King had pointed out earlier in his article, the conditions of "consensus" on this issue were no longer attainable. During 1961, "despite tormenting handicaps, Negroes moved from sporadic, limited actions to broadscale activities different in kind and degree from anything done in the past." The sit-ins and the Freedom Rides and the boycotts all carried the same message.

But even in the execution of his own moderate policy, John Kennedy still procrastinated. During his election campaign, for example, he had several times scoffed at Dwight Eisenhower for failing to order the desegregation of public housing. It could be done by executive action alone, he said;

it required no more than "a stroke of the pen." But, in office himself, he delayed. Throughout 1961, he delayed, and throughout 1962, until an "Ink for Jack" campaign spread across the country, and bottles of ink began to arrive at the White House so that he might make the stroke of the pen that was needed. At last, immediately after the election of 1962, he signed a qualified executive order. It rejected the recommendations which had been made to him in 1961 by the majority of the Civil Rights Commission, and instead reflected the lowest common denominator of agreement which all its members, who included three Southerners, had been able to reach. It was no wonder, in these circumstances, that Martin Luther King, again appraising the year's progress, said in *The Nation* of 30 March 1963 that "If tokenism were our goal, the administration moves us adroitly toward it."

Martin Luther King was voicing the injury which the moderate leaders of the black population were beginning to feel. Wishing to co-operate with a President who was new and young, and who professed to support their cause, they were beginning to understand that they were being used: that they were being "moved adroitly" into a position in which they appeared to be willing to accept "tokenism." At a time when John Kennedy should have been anxious not to destroy the credit of the moderate leaders among their increasingly impatient followers, he recklessly did so. He neither gave them what they needed, nor allowed them to stand apart from him, able to criticise the slowness and the inadequacy of his actions. He required them in the "consensus" which he sought to maintain.

Neither he nor his administration—including his brother who, as Attorney General, was in a strategic position—understood the magnitude of the movement which had begun. Loreen Miller, the publisher of the *California Eagle,* an old Negro newspaper, tried to make it clear in an article, specifically addressed to white liberals, which was published in *The Nation* of 20 October 1962. She recalled the recent statement of James Baldwin that Negroes "twenty years younger than I don't believe in liberals at all," and said that the liberals who were shocked or surprised by it "haven't been doing their homework. Discontent with the liberal position in the area of race relations has been building up for the past several years." She concluded by bidding to liberals "a fond farewell with thanks for services rendered, until you are ready to re-enlist as foot soldiers and subordinates in a Negro-led, Negro-officered, army under the banner of Freedom Now." It is interesting to notice how early this statement was made.

The incomprehension was displayed again at the famous meeting which took place on 24 May 1963 between Robert Kennedy and two of his senior officers at the Department of Justice, on the one hand, and James Baldwin and several of his friends, on the other. When one of the blacks, Jerome Smith, remarked that, if the United States went to war with Cuba, he would not fight in it, Robert Kennedy was shocked, at which another of the blacks, Kenneth C. Clark, afterwards commented: "We were shocked that he was shocked, and that he seemed unable to understand what Smith was trying to say." Arthur Schlesinger reports that Robert Kennedy told him later: "They didn't know anything. They don't know what the laws are—they don't know what we've been doing or what we're trying to do. . . . It was all emotion, hysteria. They stood up and orated. They cursed. Some of them wept and walked out of the room." But one of the things which Jerome Smith had been trying to tell him was that he felt "nauseous" to have to beg for protection when he was only fighting for his constitutional rights.

As the protests became more violent throughout 1962 and the early months of 1963, their meaning began to penetrate the consciousness of the white liberal. In its issue of 8 May 1963, *Newsweek* carried a story in which it gave prominence to a remark of James Farmer: "I like the word 'black.' I like to use it. It's an attempt to have some identity." It noticed the "increasingly restless and militant mood" of the Negro, saying that it was "freighted with dynamite." It ended by quoting Whitney Young: "We're liable to get some real violence: in Chicago, in Detroit, in New York." But the administration was still inclined to see only separate incidents, whether in Mississippi or in Alabama, and only separate villains, whether Ross Barnett or Eugene T. "Bull" Connor. As I. F. Stone remarked on 24 June 1963, "the shot that killed Medgar Evers . . . was not simply the act of barbarity which the White House termed it. It was part of the system the South has used for a century to keep the Negro in his place." The problem was larger than that, since the problem had already moved to the North; but the administration was still refusing to face the question put by Walter Lippmann at the time: "Is the rising discontent which is showing itself among the twenty million Negroes going to change in important ways the shape and pace of American politics?"

John Kennedy may have seemed to face it on the television address which he gave on 11 June 1963. It did indeed represent a commitment on the part of the federal government to fight against discrimination, and he sought a "consensus" in support of it: "We face, therefore, a moral crisis as a country and as a people." But, even if such a "consensus" was possible, he was not in a strong position to call for it. He had himself moved on the issue only when the Negro had already moved out of the courts into the streets. At the beginning of the administration, Robert Kennedy had said of the demand for civil rights: "There has got to be—and there is going to be—leadership from the White House. That is going to make the difference." For two and a half years, this leadership had been absent, and the form in which it was now offered was predictable.

Once again, there was to be a spectacular display of personal leadership: an appeal for a national commitment which would obviate the necessity for a bitter political struggle. A moral "consensus" of a kind did indeed seem to have been created, in this atmosphere, during the march on Washington in the fall of 1963, which ended in the rally at which Martin Luther King proclaimed: "I have a dream." It is remembered by many white liberals today with a nostalgia which is as sweet as it is bitter. But the mood was false: at a crucial moment in a profound social and political upheaval, reliance was to be placed on professions of good will. The attitude of John Kennedy was characteristic. "When the Negro leaders announced the march," Bayard Rustin observed at the time, "the President asked them to call it off. When they thumbed —when they told him they wouldn't—he almost smothered us. We had to keep raising our demands . . . to keep him from getting ahead of us." In one mocking phrase, Murray Kempton declared: "When the President finally mentioned the march in public, he issued something as close as possible to a social invitation."

Many of the accounts at the time as well as many of the memories in retrospect indicate how the march and the rally were indeed transformed into an almost festive occasion. It was characteristic that John Lewis of the Student Nonviolent

Coordinating Committee was forced by the organisers of the rally to soften his words, in which he had proposed to challenge the white liberal leadership which the belated actions of John Kennedy had once again placed at the head of the civil rights movement. When the President welcomed the leaders of the march at the White House, he used the greeting, "I have a dream." In much the same way, when Lyndon Johnson addressed a joint meeting of the two houses of Congress nineteen months later, he used the slogan, "We shall overcome." This manner of political leadership is false. It not only has little to do with the real political struggle which lies ahead; it in fact makes that struggle more difficult to win. It distracts the energies which should be given to developing the kind of political strategy which, thirty years earlier, had carried the New Deal, deeply and irresistibly, into the heart of the political process of the country, and of the political attitudes of the people.

Significant political and social movements can be expected to engender conflict, since the claim of one group to a right which it has been denied must usually mean the surrender by another group of a privilege which it has enjoyed. It is false to try to manufacture a "consensus" in such a situation; and it was false in the 1960s to try to do so in the cause of civil rights. It could only be a distraction, certain in the end to provoke the frustration as much of the advocates of the cause, whose expectations had been aroused, as of its opponents, who felt with some justice that the political processes of the country had been bypassed. The attempt from 1954 onwards to deal with the problem of racial discrimination in the courts was similarly an attempt to achieve by a "consensus," that of the law, what the political processes of the country were failing to achieve.

If an attempt is made to ignore or to transcend the political processes of the country, these processes remain to be used, and the "populist movements" of opinion, as they have been designated, which have been evident in the electoral politics of the United States in recent years have at least one element in common: a desire on the part of a considerable number of people, who feel that they have been ignored, to use in their own interests the political processes of their country, which they also feel have been ignored. There clearly exists among them an impression that they have in recent years been governed by an elite, self-chosen and self-perpetuating; and one of the main criticisms put forward by some sociologists against the "consensus" view of society is that, if a "consensus" exists at all, it is an "elite consensus," formed by the persons and the organisations which are entrenched in the controlling positions in the existing society. There can be no question that the "consensus politics" which were practised by John Kennedy and his administration were an attempt to impose an "elite consensus" on the American people; and it was done with such conviction that they eagerly responded. At home or abroad, it seemed, they had only to submit to a national commitment to which they had been called by their President, and good would prevail. It is never so easy.

The pragmatic realist, acting within a "consensus" that he seeks both to foster and to manipulate, frees himself from political values, only to find that he has bound himself to react pragmatically to events as they occur, able to judge only their urgency, and not their importance. The point is made with considerable acuteness by George Ball, who from the beginning opposed the commitment of the prestige of the

United States to the war in Vietnam, in this passage from *The Discipline of Power:*

> . . . there has been a recent tendency to scoff at the utility of conceptual thinking in foreign policy in favor of a pragmatism that masquerades as a commendable hospitality to fresh ideas. Without doubt, rigidity as such can be a serious fault. But a foreign policy conducted without some well-developed conceptions as to desirable structures of power is not a foreign policy at all but simply a series of unrelated improvisations. It is because of my feelings on this point that I have been dismayed over the years at the extent to which many—but by no means all—of my academic friends, inspired no doubt by the yeasty air of the Potomac, have been so seduced by the challenges of operational problems as to renounce any attempt at conceptual thinking as "theological," and, in aid of their own abstractions, have erected a specious dichotomy between "theologians" and "pragmatists."

He quotes the comment made to him by a European that, "If America ever dies, it will be from a surfeit of pragmatism"; and in a speech to the American Society of International Law, in April of 1966, he emphasised that "It is easy and tempting to become absorbed in the operational aspects of foreign relations and to ignore the long-range implications of policy." In all of which there is wisdom.

"That word 'options,'" exclaimed Bernard Brodie in the July 1965 issue of *World Politics,* "one now recognizes as a favorite word of Mr. McNamara's." It was a favourite word of the administration. Problems would be submitted to a rational process of examination, which would yield the options from which the President would make his decision, which in turn would be executed by a further exercise of rational process. The word expressed the naïve idea that the more options which were available to the President, the less probable it was that he would make a wrong decision; but it is at least as likely

to be true that the more options which are available for decision, the more probable that they will include some which
are mischievous. After all, in any situation, there are not all
that number of courses of action which are likely to be wise,
and there should be some a priori political judgement which
can be brought to bear in order to reduce the options: indeed,
to suggest that the only sensible option may be to do nothing.
Faced by any new situation, Dean Rusk told the senior officers
of the Department of State, they should always ask before
acting: What difference does it make?

It may make none. But the temptation of the pragmatic
realist is to imagine that each new situation presents a new
problem demanding a new response. In an illuminating phrase
in the December 1963 issue of the *American Political Science
Review*—and it was intended as a favourable judgement—Richard Neustadt described the political method of John Kennedy as
one of "emergencies in policy with politics as usual." But it is
illuminating only in so far as it goes, for the limits of "politics
as usual" could always be transcended by an appeal to the "consensus" which the emergencies, actual or artificial, themselves
helped to foster. By and large, the pragmatist is best equipped to
improvise in policy, and he is therefore tempted to interpret any
event as an emergency, to which improvisation is an appropriate
response; rallying to the emergency when it is proclaimed, the
people are persuaded to form a "consensus" in support of the administration, and its improvisations are then endowed with the
appearance of high policy. It was by this method that the American people were, for three years, kept in a state of anxious expectation of the perils which beset them, on the one hand, and of
stupefied admiration of the brilliance of the administration
which rescued them, on the other: always at the edge of danger,
always in time brought back from it.

On 17 August 1960, George Kennan had written to John Kennedy an eight-page letter, in which he suggested that two courses should be followed by the United States in the following years: first, to reduce the number and the extent of American commitments overseas; secondly, to work by diplomatic means to heighten the divisions in the Communist bloc. He called for "a succession of carefully calculated steps timed in such a way as not only to throw the adversary off balance but to keep him off." Instead of heeding the counsel, "Kennedy's tenure in office," as Edward Weintal and Charles Bartlett put it in *Facing the Brink,* "was marked by a series of reactions to Communist initiatives"; his foreign policy was "pragmatic and operational, more in the nature of a fire-fighting exercise than a careful and long-range campaign for fire-prevention." But this was only one reflection of a consistent method.

In domestic policy, the same criticism was made by Hobart Rowen in the same words. Instead of trying to improve the machinery for the arbitration of labour disputes, "the administration depended on Goldberg's willingness and ability . . . to spend more time putting out fires than running the Labor Department"; and he added that these *ad hoc* efforts were unsettling to both labour and management, who regarded them as meddling. In much the same way, in its issue of 4 November 1963, *Newsweek* observed that in his handling of the issue of civil rights, at least until then, John Kennedy had been satisfied to use "the easy foil of rabble-rousing bigotry"; he would put out a fire. The method did not change. He awaited the occasion to which he could react, which he could seize by a dramatic exhibition of his personal leadership. He was a pragmatic realist who sought to create and to manipulate a "consensus" in his support by waiting until an issue had become an emergency, or could be represented as one: until a fire had started, which he would put out.

"He still sought something that the historians like to term 'national unity,' a condition of general support from the many segments of the population," reported Hugh Sidey in 1963, before the assassination. "He sought this unity openly, despite the fact that history shows that all the great Presidents of the past presided over deeply divided countries, that they were forced to achieve their programs painfully over vigorous and noisy opposition." Except in time of war, political leadership which is to be genuinely creative must be prepared to invite conflict, and to live with it. Franklin Roosevelt may have been a master of the arts and the devices of popular leadership, but he used them, during his first two terms, in situations of conflict, many of which he had provoked, not to try to foster a "consensus" to transcend the divisions, but to attract the support which he needed to sustain him as he fought. If he had sought such a "consensus," he would hardly have introduced the programmes of the New Deal in the form in which he did, and he would never have carried them even if he had done so.

We must remember that John Kennedy had excised any mention of domestic issues from the inaugural address, because they tend to divide; and it was in this manner that he conducted his administration. It was not only on the issue of civil rights that he waited until the conscience of the American people had begun to stir before he determined to lead that conscience. On the issue of Medicare, at a crucial point in the early summer of 1962, he declared, "And this year, I believe, or certainly as inevitably as the tide comes in, next year, this bill is going to pass," hardly the statement of a leader who was boldly taking the initiative against a recalcitrant Congress. On the issue of public education, he never tried to rally popular support for his proposals, as they at first languished in Congress, and were then killed in the course of two successive years. Even on the one domestic issue on which he did seek to use the opportunities of the Presidency for popular leadership, the proposal to reduce taxation to stimulate a laggard economy, he waited in 1962 for popular support to develop; when it did not, he postponed the idea. "He could have tried to mobilize public opinion to support his convictions," wrote Hobart Rowen, "but he decided to duck what could have been a losing battle."

"The only reason for a man to have a popularity rating of 75 per cent," Leon H. Keyserling observed at about that time, "is to bring it down to 72 per cent when he does something he believes in." But that was not a risk which John Kennedy was inclined to take. His method of leadership required the 75 per cent: the "o to 80" on the spectrum of public opinion. But such a "consensus" could not be created on domestic issues, so his remarkable gifts of popular leadership were employed always to excite support for his foreign policy: not only in emergencies, whether in Laos or in Berlin or in Cuba, but to carry the Alliance for Progress in 1961, the foreign trade bill in 1962, and the nuclear test ban treaty in 1963. In these crises and on these issues he could appear, fully arrayed, as the national leader: the eyes of the people were turned outward, where they could feel as one, and not inward, where they would be distracted by the normal divisions of a free society. It was by this method, and in this atmosphere, that he practised the politics of expectation.

CHAPTER ELEVEN

The Idea of
the American Empire

IN THE SAME months of the same year in which John Kennedy announced that he was a candidate for the Presidency of the United States, Harold Macmillan made the journey through Africa during which he announced, in a variety of ways, that the "winds of change" were blowing through the continent, and that the white settlers could no longer sensibly resist them. He was saying, in short, that the people of Britain could no longer support or protect those of their own number who had gone abroad to do the business of empire; and, at the same time, by a series of manoeuvres which only he could have accomplished, Charles de Gaulle was conveying the same message to *les colons* in Algeria. Between 1960 and 1963, twenty-seven countries in Africa or in the Mediterranean were granted their independence, and the same process was being completed in Asia, and had been begun in the West Indies. The movement was novel, and its meaning was not clear.

The expansion by which Western Europe had grown to dominate the entire world seemed to have been reversed. That was how it appeared at the time, and it was no wonder that, during the next ten years, not only the United States, not only the Soviet Union, but even Communist China, gazed on the chaos of these newly independent countries and wondered what could be made of them and what they would make of themselves. Not only John Kennedy, not only Nikita Khrushchev, but even Mao Tse-tung, all believed that they were a battleground. There were to be "many Vietnams" and, for a decade, the air routes of the world were travelled ceaselessly by the agents of America and Russia and China in search of political advantage. In its issue of 14 May 1962, *Newsweek* reported that Dean Acheson had said of the emerging nations: "I don't think they can make any contribution to international politics. I don't much care if they bargain with the Russians and get something out of them. That makes less for us to do." But this was not the approach of John Kennedy, and it was not the attitude of most informed Americans.

John McCloy spoke for him and for them, Democrats and Republicans, when he wrote in *Goals for Americans* in 1960 that the emerging countries "promise to be the principal battle ground in which the forces of freedom and Communism compete"; and the basic thesis had once more been put forward by Max Millikan and Walt Rostow, that "a much-expanded long-term program of American participation in the development of the underdeveloped world can and should be one of the most important means of furthering the purposes of American foreign policy." The members of the administration talked of the lands of the rising peoples in which the defence and the expansion of freedom would be contested. This is the language of empire, and to an outsider from an older imperial tradition it is familiar.

"The lands of the rising peoples" is no more and no less

than the vocabulary of Rudyard Kipling, whether in *The White Man's Burden* or in *Recessional*. The picture which Arthur Schlesinger provides of Robert Komer patrolling "the gray areas" of North Africa and the Middle East and South Asia recalls many a career spent on the frontiers of the British Empire before the sun had set on them. Indeed, if one wishes to hear the accents of empire today, one must go to the Metropolitan Club in Washington, take a seat at the head of the stairs on the second floor, and listen as the men who are just leaving for, or have just returned from, the outposts of empire greet each other. From time to time, one is ready to admit, this feeling of empire has filled one with nostalgia, and it has been tempting to perceive the United States as the successor nation to the United Kingdom, to imagine a Pax Americana bestowing on the world the boons, which were not trifling, of a Pax Britannica; but the world had ceased to be so simple.

Nevertheless, it was the general mood of the United States until 1965, and it became the all but universal mood, exalted by his speech, during the administration of John Kennedy. If the illusion has now been broken, it is all the more necessary to discuss it with some candour. There were few men who did not share it—the name of Robert Taft springs to mind—and they were not honoured at the time. There was no more characteristic expression of the Pax Americana than the Fulbright scholarships, and their sponsor did as much as anyone to foster the belief that the United States had become the instructor and the benefactor of the world. For twenty years after 1945, with few dissident voices, even fewer of which were regarded, the successive administrations of the United States faced the unsettling consequences of the political collapse of Europe, and determined that they would undertake the responsibilities of world empire.

Even today, the significance of the movement by which the nations of Asia and of Africa gained their independence is generally misunderstood. An historical perspective is needed. Until the expansion of Europe, the civilisations of the world, in Europe and in Asia, in the Middle East and in Central America, lived apart from each other; here and there, now and then, they encroached on each other, and had dealings, but the power of none of them was so great that it could go forth and overwhelm another. After the middle of the fifteenth century, however, the power and the enterprise of Europe began at first to modify, and then to upset, this "fourfold balance of the Old World," as William H. McNeill calls it in *The Rise of the West*. By 1850, it had been decisively altered: Russia had been brought within the Western world by Peter the Great, the settlement of North America had been completed, the subjugation of India had been accomplished, and societies of Europeans were established from Australia to South America to Africa. After 1850, the continent of Africa was partitioned, and "the Far Eastern citadel fell to Western gunboats." Europe dominated the world, the culmination of a phenomenal movement.

But, at the very moment at which the final expansion was achieved, Europe began to retreat. Even as the Chinese Empire finally collapsed in 1912, a direct result of Western intrusion, even as the Western nations completed the division of the Ottoman Empire during the First World War, the clamour of the subject peoples for their independence began, and the colonial powers were in no position to resist it. For here we come to the paradox which is too little recognised. As John

Plamenatz says in his important work *On Alien Rule and Self-Government,* "To the extent that the peoples of Asia and Africa subject to European rule demand independence for the sake of democracy and freedom, they can be said to be claiming against the West the right to imitate the West." The fact is that democracy and freedom are European ideals, and it is European peoples who have invented the institutions and the processes which make possible their realisation. The colonial powers carried the ideals and, to some extent, the institutions and the processes with them; and, when the subject peoples began to adopt the ideals, and to employ the institutions and the processes in their own cause, the West was in no position to deny them their right to imitate it.

But the West also carried with it the evidence of its wealth and its power, and of the science and the technology which are their source. The leaders of the subject peoples, as they have sought the independence of their countries, have aspired to nothing more eagerly than to possess the science and the technology which seem to them to be the keys to wealth and power in the future; once again, they are claiming against the West the right to imitate the West, for there can be no going back for them. "The peoples of Asia and Africa cannot now return to what they used to be before the Europeans forced themselves upon them. For better or for worse, they have adopted many Western methods and values, and are likely to adopt more. . . . By breaking in upon them, the Europeans started among the peoples of Asia and Africa a process of change which these people now no longer wish to stop or reverse, but which they aspire to control; and they cannot control it unless they are self-governing." This is the paradox of their situation, and it will be disconcerting for many years.

But the process of Westernization, "broad and deep though

it has been," as John Plamenatz says, "has also been disruptive and incomplete. It has greatly changed the lives of hundreds of millions of people without making Europeans of them culturally and politically." It was to this problem that Karl Marx was addressing himself when he discussed the "destructive" and "regenerative" aspects of British rule in India. Writing in the New York *Daily News* in 1853, he denounced Indian society as it had existed before the British conquest with all the polemical vigour of which he was capable. It was "the solid foundation of oriental despotism"; it "restrained the human mind within the smallest possible compass, making it the unresisting tool of superstition"; it supported a "stagnatory, undignified and vegetative life . . . concentrating on some miserable patch of land"; it was "contaminated by distinctions of caste and slavery." No matter that England, he went on, "in causing a social revolution in Hindoostan, was actuated only by the vilest interests, and was stupid in her manner of enforcing them . . . , whatever may have been the crimes of England, she was the unconscious tool of history in bringing about that revolution. . . . The work of regeneration hardly transpires through a heap of ruins"; but it had been started.

Noticing this passage, John Strachey, who was a socialist member of the government which gave independence to India, observed: "The real criticism which must be made of the British record in India is that it did *not* effectively break up the stagnation of Asiatic society: that rural India remains to this day largely untouched: that even what Marx here calls 'the material premises' for development were not laid down on a sufficient scale." We are less confident today that Western civilisation will automatically confer such benefits, but we should not allow our doubts to alter our perception that the thing has happened, for better or for worse, that the West has intruded in a way from which there is no going back. It is this forbidding fact which statesmanship must confront. The "destructive" work has been done, how can the "regenerative" work proceed? The answers—for it will not be only one—have yet to be found.

For a time, one of the attractions of Russia and then of China to the emerging nations was that their examples seemed to suggest that Communism could offer a shortcut to the science and the technology by which the work of regeneration could be accomplished. But here was another paradox: the Communism itself was a Western ideology. For a time, some were persuaded that Communist China could provide a non-Western ideology, and a non-Western road to, or escape from, the inaccessible treasures of science and technology. It would rally, it proclaimed, the "countryside" of the world against its "cities," and on this promise a thousand illusions have flowered in the past decade: the myth of the guerilla, and the even more remarkable myth that the privileged students in Western societies were in the same predicament as, and could identify themselves with, the peasants of Asia and Africa and Latin America. But the leaders of Communist China do not govern one of the oldest empires in the world, and have not inherited one of the strongest bureaucratic traditions in history, in order to make fools of themselves, and their ancestors, for long. They have clearly begun to transform their country into one of the "cities" of the world; and the process, as elsewhere, cannot be stopped, and will not be reversed.

But it is not difficult to understand the perplexity of the emerging peoples when, having been conquered by one civilisation, and then claimed against it the right to imitate it, they found that it had split into two parts. "It is largely because they now have two standards, 'Western' and 'Communist,'" as John Plamenatz says, "that the non-European peoples are greatly bewildered." But the "Western" and "Communist" worlds were, during the 1960s, equally bewildered. They did not perceive that, in spite of their different forms of political organisation, they were both inheritors of the Western political tradition, any more than they perceived that the claim for independence which the new nations were making against the West was itself a part of their continuing Westernization. They thus imagined a "third world" when there was none; they believed that its allegiance was at stake and must be contested between them; they made of it a battleground when there was no battle to be fought. They cannot be condemned for this too facilely: the meaning of great events as they occur is usually obscure.

What is more, radical critics in the United States, and elsewhere, were guilty of the same misinterpretations. Taking their cues from men as politically illiterate as Frantz Fanon, they too imagined a "third world" of "the wretched of the earth," who were participating in the common experience of "decolonization," and even establishing a common identity by the use of violence as a common method of action. Their perceptions were "global" in exactly the same manner as those of John Kennedy and his administration. By all and sundry, left and right, what was happening in Algeria was thought to be the same in every respect as what was happening in Indochina; what had been managed by a few guerillas in Cuba could be repeated by them in the immense spaces of South America. Laos was Malaysia was Egypt was Tanganyika was the Congo was Tunisia was the Dominican Republic was Cuba: only the Lord of Creation, when he exercised his considerable powers for six days in an unparalleled explosion of political creativity, had been so presumptuous, and determined to make all men in the same image. One had only to speak of the world, and the world was astounded. But the fact that the world knew itself as one, and could be seen as one, was only the end of the movement by which the West had grown to dominate it.

Whether one calls it a continent or a sub-continent, South America is a vast area; its landscape as diverse as its peoples; many of its countries with long histories, distinctive even during the days of colonial rule, and with political traditions which may seem to us to be fanciful, but which are vital. In 1492, Elio Antonio de Nebrija, the historiographer royal at the court of Castile, completed a Castilian grammar, the first grammar of a modern European language. When it was presented to Isabella, her admirable practical sense prompted her to inquire: "What is it for?" At this, the Bishop of Avila stepped forward with the subtle plea, "Your majesty, language is the perfect instrument of empire"; and she immediately accepted the work. One cannot recall this story, and then look south to the empire of language which exists today in Latin America, without understanding that, however else one may respond to such a remarkable historical creation, immense and varied, one does not idly tamper with it.

The loftiness of purpose with which the Alliance for Progress was launched was itself a form of tampering. Attention was distracted from the individual problems of separate nations by its "global" pretensions and its "regional" approach: it was, said Dean Rusk, "a concrete part of an indivisible whole . . . it rests on the concept that this hemisphere is part of the Western civilization which we are pledged to defend." Whether in distributing the billions of dollars which were allocated, or in reacting to political developments in the various countries, or in trying to persuade them to adopt a uniform approach to

Fidel Castro, the administration consistently thwarted its good
intentions by the inability, which was revealed time afer time
in the conduct of its foreign policy, to act patiently on any
level below that of yet another "grand design" for yet another
region of the planet.

It is difficult to make a majestic oration about the problems
of Peru; even the Peruvians, acquainted with the mundane
character of their problems, are unlikely to listen. But it is
easy to speak the exalted language with which John Kennedy
inaugurated the Alliance for Progress on 13 March 1961: "If
we are to meet a problem so staggering in its dimensions, our
approach must itself be equally bold, an approach consistent
with the majestic conception of Operation Pan America. Therefore I have called on all the people of the hemisphere to join
in a new Alliance for Progress—*Alianza para Progreso*—a vast
co-operative effort, unparalleled in magnitude and nobility of
purpose. . . ." On and on the periods rolled, the work for
the most part of Richard Goodwin: "a historic decade of
democratic progress. . . . an example to all the world that
liberty and progress walk hand in hand. . . . the rule of
courage and freedom and hope for the future of man." The
inspiration was high.

The promises of rhetoric were given an aëry substance by
the promises of money. These were indeed impressive when
they were made at the meeting of the Inter-American Economic
and Social Council which was held at Punta del Este five
months after John Kennedy had delivered his oration. But,
when the same council met in October of 1962 to review the
achievements of the first year, the mood was one of pessimism;
a year later, it had not changed. In terms of the failure of any
actual programme of development, there were many explanations. But the real fault was that the internal contradictions of

the whole concept were never resolved: neither the conflicts of interest between the individual countries of Latin America, nor those between these countries, individually and collectively, and the United States. Words and money—a customary North American prescription—were to be enough. In this way, the inspiration confounded the intention. The concept withered, as Abraham Lowenthal put it in the April 1970 issue of *Foreign Affairs,* because it had been characterized by "slogans without much substance and programs without clear purpose."

The literature on the failure of the Alliance for Progress is by now voluminous, but we need be concerned with only two of its aspects, which illustrate the nature of the imperial pretensions which governed John Kennedy and his administration. Even before he took office, a task force had met at the Faculty Club of Harvard University on 19 December 1960, and given their assent to a paper entitled, "Alliance for Progress —a Program of Inter-American Partnership," in which they declared: "It is indispensable that the initiative come from the United States." It was in this spirit that John Kennedy acted in office. It was he who called the ambassadors of the Latin American countries to the White House to launch the concept; it was he who called on the people of the hemisphere to join in the vast co-operative effort; it was he who said that he would "shortly request a ministerial meeting of the Inter-American Economic and Social Council." No one could doubt from his manner that the Alliance for Progress, originally a Latin American concept, had been transformed into an instrument of the imperial mission of the United States, if not, even more directly, of its foreign policy.

In this mood, the pretence was cultivated that the United States was in a position, morally and politically, to determine which governments in Latin America had come to power by "constitutional" means and might be considered "democratic" in their natures; to which was added the rider that, by making such a judgement, the United States could then decide whether to grant or to withhold its recognition and, of course, its assistance. John Kennedy was confronted by the consequences of this pretension on two occasions in 1962, when the military authorities in Argentina, in March, and in Peru, in July, refused to accept the outcomes of the elections which had been held, and deposed the Presidents of the two republics. After successive displays of indignation by the United States, including the suspension of diplomatic relations with Peru, the administration eventually recognised both the new regimes.

Arthur Schlesinger describes John Kennedy's calculations on both these occasions. Of the overthrow of Arturo Frondizi in Argentina in March:

> Kennedy, despite his distaste for military coups, had a realist's concern not to place himself in positions from which he could neither advance nor retreat. Since Frondizi's overthrow had been greeted with vast apathy by the Argentine people, the prudent policy seemed to be to accept the constitutional argument, however tenuous. This in due course he did.

Of the overthrow of Manuel Prado in Peru in July:

> But, he [John Kennedy] added, neither the Latin American governments, most of whom were now preparing to recognize the junta (the Chilean foreign minister had already warned the United States against being more royalist than the king), nor the Peruvian people themselves, as was shown by the collapse of the general strike, had given us the support for which we hoped. His concern, he said, was that we might have staked our prestige on reversing a situation which could not be reversed, and that, when we accepted the situation, as eventually we must, we might seem to be suffering a defeat. The problem now, he said, was to demonstrate

that our condemnation had caused the junta to make enough changes in its policy to render the resumption of relations possible.

Arthur Schlesinger makes this claim.

We must first notice the presumption. The views, not only of other Latin American governments, but even of the peoples of the countries in which the *coups d'état* had occurred, were taken into account only reluctantly and secondarily; they were factors influencing the decisions of the United States, not factors which were considered to have their own priority. They "had not given *us* the support for which *we* hoped," as if the United States were one of the actors in a domestic situation in another country. The administration of John Kennedy was presuming that it had the right to dictate to the nations with which it formed alliances the characters of their internal arrangements. "For a time he even mused about the possibility of a 'club' of democratic Presidents . . . which might meet regularly in Palm Beach or Puerto Rico," records Arthur Schlesinger, "hoping that this might be an incentive for other chiefs of state to commit themselves to the struggle for democracy." What an incentive! At this point, the presumptuousness touches the level of banality.

Did he really think that it would be of assistance to the leaders of these countries, in which nationalist feeling was increasingly strong, it be invited regularly to the soil of the United States as if to a club? Similarly, what did he expect the reactions of these countries to be to the withdrawal of recognition or assistance by the United States? The two examples which have been given, says Arthur Schlesinger, "suggested the limitations of American power"; but from where had he gathered the notion that those limitations did not exist, or could be transcended? In both cases, he had to retreat from expectations which he himself had aroused; it was his own actions which had placed him in situations from which either advance or withdrawal might be difficult to contrive; and this was, throughout the thousand days, frequently the result of his conduct of his foreign policy.

Indeed, in the case of Argentina, he and his administration were at least partially responsible for the situation as it had arisen. At the Eighth Meeting of Consultation of the Organization of American States, which was held at Punta del Este in January of 1962, the government of Arturo Frondizi opposed the resolution to exclude Cuba from the Inter-American System; but, the resolution having been passed, he then broke diplomatic relations with the government of Fidel Castro. It was, as the *New Republic* observed on 2 April 1962, "a politically disastrous example of trucking to the unpopular generals" in Argentina, who supported the actions against Cuba, and to the equally unpopular Yanqui. The consequence was unavoidable. At the elections in Argentina which immediately followed, the party of Arturo Frondizi lost its congressional majority, the Peronist candidates winning more than a half of the seats which were at stake, as well as ten of the nineteen provincial governorships. At this point, the military authorities acted, and overthrew the unfortunate President whose position had been so exposed.

Moreover, that position had not been improved by the inept announcement, shortly before the elections, of a loan of $150 million under the Alliance for Progress, which merely confirmed the impression that the United States was intervening in domestic politics. Arthur Schlesinger gives no hint that the fall of Arturo Frondizi might have been, at least in part, the result of the actions of the United States, which had forced him into the open. He was recognised at the time as the most pro-American politician who had held power in Argentina in this century; but Arthur Schlesinger calls him "the artful dodger," because his government, "after originally floating the idea of excluding Castro from the OAS, had mysteriously glided away from its own formula and finally voted against it." But, if he was dodging, it was for the reasons which compel most politicians to dodge as a difficult election approaches. He was maintaining, in terms of the politics of his own country, a position which was remarkably favourable to the United States; he needed to blur that position; but the administration of John Kennedy forced his hand, publicly gave him thirty pieces of silver, and then held up its hands in pious horror that a "constitutional government" had fallen.

This was tampering. Instead of paying attention to the individual politics of the separate countries of Latin America, the administration of John Kennedy insisted on seeing the problems as single: the countries as a region, the region as part of the hemisphere, the hemisphere in the world, must combine to the single end of defeating the challenge of the Communist powers, in general, and of Fidel Castro, in particular. This was the second of the attitudes which distorted the intentions of the Alliance for Progress, and revealed the character of the imperial pretensions of the administration. Even as he prepared to take office, the task force which advised him had talked of "the dangerous momentum of the Sino-Soviet drive to engulf the Americas": language of such extravagance that one can only wonder what ocean of ideology or of arms they imagined would engulf a continent which stretches from one pole of the world to another; and the same language was still being used by Dean Rusk when he talked, at the Punta del Este conference in 1962, of Cuba's alignment with "the Sino-Soviet bloc." There was a form of madness here. It infected the time; it infected the administration; it infected the man who led it.

But we should not be satisfied to explain it, as are most commentators, only in terms of the grip which the ideology of the Cold War had on the time, on the administration, on the man. That was important; its strength is certainly not questioned here. But part of the argument of this book is that, even if that ideology had not prevailed, the manner and the method of the politics that were practised by the administration of John Kennedy would have prevented it from thinking and acting in lesser terms than of "grand designs" for regions, for continents, for oceans, for the world, for space. Even as late as 1968, one must recall, Robert Kennedy was talking of the right of the United States to the moral leadership of the planet. This is what one means by the imperial pretensions of the administration; and the existence of the Cold War only provided the occasion.

If the moral leadership was not followed, political leadership would be imposed. No other word describes more accurately the methods which were used by the United States at the conference at Punta del Este in 1962 which, in the words of Arthur Schlesinger, "launched the indispensable supporting policy for the containment of Castro." The conference resolved that the existing government of Cuba was incompatible with the Inter-American System, and determined to expel it from the Organization of American States; and it adopted further resolutions for collective defence and for a partial suspension of trade with Cuba. The two-thirds majority required to exclude Cuba was achieved only after an extraordinary exertion of American diplomatic pressure; and even then it did not include the largest of the Latin American countries, Brazil and Argentina, Chile and Mexico. The delegation of the United

States included two senators and two representatives, whose duty it was to remind the delegations of the Latin American countries that the Congress of the United States could hardly be expected to continue aid under the Alliance for Progress for countries which failed to take an open stand against Fidel Castro. In fact, the required two-thirds majority would not have been achieved if economic pressure—indeed, bribery—had not been used, in particular, to win the support of the government of Haiti, which could hardly be counted as either "constitutional" or "democratic" by the standards of John Kennedy.

Above all, the resolutions against Cuba violated the Charter of the OAS as it had been agreed at Bogotá in 1948. The imposition of an arms embargo and the encouragement of further economic sanctions directly violated Article 16; the declaration that the regime of Fidel Castro was incompatible with the Inter-American System was a flagrant violation of Article 9; and nowhere in the Charter is there an article providing for the exclusion of a member state. All of this is waved aside by Arthur Schlesinger, who says that the speech of Dean Rusk to the meeting, "with its social and economic emphasis, provided a relief, welcome even to the Latin Americans, from the juridical disquisitions standard for such gatherings." What are treaties and charters, one must ask, but pieces of paper which impose juridical obligations; and what "social and economic emphasis" can justify the violation of those obligations, or be allowed to obscure the violation?

When brought to the test, the Alliance for Progress was an unequal alliance; and history can provide a parallel which illuminates its nature. Rome first extended its power through the peninsula of Italy, which stood in much the same physical relationship to it as Latin America does to the United States, with the help of two political concepts: the *foedus aequum*, a treaty between equal partners, and the *foedus iniquum,* a treaty between unequal partners. The main characteristic of the *foedus iniquum* was that one of the contracting parties was subordinate to the other, and that it was bidden, in its subordinate position, *maiestatem populi Romani comiter conservare,* to preserve the majesty of Rome in a friendly way; and it was also bidden to assist Rome in wars in which its own interests were not at stake. This was, to a profound extent, the relationship which John Kennedy sought in the Alliance for Progress: in the world-wide struggle that the United States was waging against Communism, he looked for an alliance with the Latin American countries by which they would be bound to assist him in that war, whether they felt threatened or not, and to uphold the majesty of the United States—its image and its prestige—in a friendly way. One can hardly doubt that a Roman would have understood.

None of the colonial powers of Europe were so infected by the madness of empire as was the United States in these years. The business might have to be done, since the expansion of Europe was a genuine historical movement. But it required few men and little money. The equipment of the first voyage of Christopher Columbus cost less than a ball at court. Exactly four hundred years later, in 1893, when the British rule of India was absolute, the Covenanted Service (who were British) numbered only 898 out of a total Indian Civil Service of 4,849 members, the rest being employed by the Uncovenanted Service (the vast majority of whom were Indians). In other words, a thousand British civil officers, give or take a few, ruled an entire sub-continent; and at their back, to control a population which was teeming, were only (the figures are those for 1885) 73,000 British soldiers, the remaining 154,000 being Indians. The business could be done efficiently and economically, because the countries which the European powers were occupying had not yet been Westernized, and could not use against them the methods and the arguments of the West; when this position had changed, the powers of Europe, refusing the expense of empire, rapidly withdrew.

Not until late in its day, and even then never successfully, did any colonial power attempt to rule its empire with the help of an army or of money which had been conscripted at home. (Taxation is money which is conscripted.) Almost the only certain advantage which Britain reaped from its rule of India was the recruitment of an Indian Army of 150,000 men, which could be rapidly expanded in time of war. "This was a net profit to Britain," as D. K. Fieldhouse observes, "for it was paid for entirely out of Indian revenues"; and it was the existence of this army which "enabled Britain to play a role in world affairs which the British taxpayer would not have been willing to pay for; to take a major part in the partition of East Africa and Southeast Asia, and to conquer much of the Ottoman Empire during the First World War." He might have added that, even as late as the Second World War, in spite of the campaign of civil disobedience in India, the Indian Army played an indispensable role, especially between 1940 and 1942, in securing the survival of Britain and in prolonging its influence in world affairs.

But, by the end of the Second World War, it was clear that the British could not continue to rule India without a larger *British* civil service, a conscripted *British* army, and increased *British* taxation. It was in these circumstances that Archibald Wavell, the Viceroy of India, wrote to George VI, saying that India could be held if the British people wished to hold it, but that he thought that the will at the centre had gone. It was a penetrating observation, and the will at the centre had evaporated, of course, because the British people were at last to be asked to pay for the uncertain rewards of empire by the conscription of their men and their money. One must ask—and is this not one of the lessons to be learned as much from the British abdication in India as from the French evacuation of Algeria as from the American reversal in South Vietnam?—whether a free country within the Western political tradition can maintain dominion over palm and pine—and pampas—with a conscripted army and by conscripted money? Will the people not rebel?

It was this problem which John Kennedy tried to transcend by his appeal to an elevated sense of national purpose, by the exhortation: "ask not what your country can do for you, ask what you can do for your country." The collective energy of the country was to be drafted; and seldom in time of peace has the administration of a free country been able to recite with such conviction the lines of the original "jingo" song: "We have the ships, we have the men, we have the money, too." Robert McNamara had made certain of that, and so had Douglas Dillon; and they were able to make certain of it because the political method of John Kennedy had been able to exalt the power of the state. No serious demand that he made for support for his foreign adventures, whether the conscription of men or the conscription of money, was ever refused. But it was inevitable that the American people would before long turn round and question the cost, not only of their involvement in the war in South Vietnam, but of the entire policy which called them to be the "watchmen on the walls of world freedom," the phrase which John Kennedy had prepared to deliver at the Trade Mart in Dallas on 22 November 1963, if he had not been assassinated a few hours earlier.

Empire on the scale and with the purpose which John Kennedy envisaged and proclaimed must cost a fortune, in men and in money; and it did. One of the ways in which he tried to evade this problem was to give the impression that the thing could be done by only a few men, by displays of the activity and interest which, it was claimed, were brought to the problems of Latin America by a "host of New Frontiersmen," not by armies of soldiers but by guerillas and advisers. It was not only that he sent 25,000 "advisers" to South Vietnam with hardly a question being asked; he scattered them across the globe with an equal profusion, and they were willing to go; not a few hundred of them, but many thousands of them, eager for "war and diplomacy," however these were disguised. The task force on Latin America had said that "Professionally competent young men, with a sympathetic understanding of the revolutionary ferment in Latin America, are needed in our overseas posts." The men were found; they offered themselves; they were posted around the world.

In his intelligent book, *A Diplomat Looks at Aid to Latin America*, William L. Beaulac, the former American ambassador to Argentina and to Cuba, is refreshingly sharp on this point:

> No sooner had our government launched the Alliance for Progress on a sea of oratory than it began to set up small replicas of the Agency for International Development in the various Latin American countries in an effort to make them over. During a trip to Latin America in 1963, I visited ten countries. I found that our AID missions had grown enormously. . . .
>
> It seemed to me . . . that, for every need a Latin American country had, the United States had sent a technician to meet that need. It mattered little that the country might not have asked for the man and might not even want him. It mattered less that the technician, who probably was an earnest worker in the AID vine-

yard, might be ignorant of the language of the country where he was to work, and of the social and political environment to which he must adjust if his work were to be useful; indeed, if it were not to be harmful. . . .

He then describes, not only the activity, but the kind of activity, of Teodoro Moscoso, whom John Kennedy had placed in charge of the Agency for International Development, in terms which summarise much of the political method of the entire administration:

> He flew up and down the continent, holding press conferences without regard to the views of our ambassadors, bestowing praise on governments here, and censure there, and discussing such politically sensitive subjects as tax reform and land reform with fewer inhibitions than he would have had in his native Puerto Rico. He became such an authority on development in Latin America that he gave ratings to the various countries, much as baseball teams are given ratings in our country. When I flew out of Miami for South America, I read in the Florida papers that Columbia was leading the development league. When I flew into Houston from Guatemala City a month later, Peru had taken over first place, and Columbia was in the cellar.

All of which has a ring of truth.

But the sending of the youth of the United States to the outposts of the empire, to exercise the right to the moral leadership of the planet, required an expressive symbol, and it was found. There is no need to add here to the reappraisal of the Peace Corps which has taken place. It was acknowledged from the beginning to be an instrument of American foreign policy. Appearing before the Foreign Affairs Committee of the House of Representatives in March of 1962, George Ball agreed that, "in appraising the usefulness of the Peace Corps as an instrument of our policy, we have to balance the utility against the amount of money we are spending for it," and concluded: "I suppose that we probably are getting more for our money in the Peace Corps than in almost anything we are doing." This is the point on which most of the latter-day criticism has concentrated, but the argument is not weighty. Since the purposes of American foreign policy are many, the Peace Corps as an instrument of that policy is not necessarily to be condemned.

The more important truth is that it was a lamentably frivolous experiment, accurately described by Harris Wofford, when he was its associate director, as holding a place in American mythology "somewhere between the Boy Scouts and motherhood." No one questions that many of the volunteers were good-hearted individuals, making the transition from motherhood to the Boy Scouts with more dedication than is usual. But it was, again, an extraordinary presumption that "a battalion of cheery, crew-cut, kids," as *Time* called them in 1963, "who two years ago hopped off their drugstore stools and hurried around the world to wage peace," could make a serious contribution to the countries to which they momentarily journeyed. Once again, the idea was being fostered that empire was an exciting moral adventure, good for the character: a kind of Outward Bound school for the youth of the United States as it turned outward bound on its course in the world. It was in this mood that the Peace Corps was applauded, and it was suited to the inspiration of the moment.

But, if the business of empire, as John Kennedy envisaged it, is to be done, another method and another manner are required. In direct imitation of the education which **Plato** prescribed for the guardians of the state, the families of the governing class in Britain agreed that their sons should be torn from their parents at the age of eight; immured in boarding schools until they were eighteen, secure from what were then still considered to be the softening influences of the other sex; allowed an idyllic period of belated maturity at the university; and then banished to the far corners of the empire, not to return until the career had been completed, and the life was all but over. Frederick Sleigh Roberts, one of the great commanders-in-chief of the Indian Army at the end of the nineteenth century, whose father had also given his life in its service, vividly described in his memoirs what such a career meant.

A cadet, when he embarked for India, knew that he would be allowed leave only once during the whole of his service, and that "ten years had to be spent in India before that leave could be taken. . . . Ten years is an eternity to the young, and the feeling of loneliness and homesickness was apt to become almost insupportable." Not long after his own arrival in India, he was fortunate enough to be posted to serve in the same regiment as his father: "I had left India an infant, and I had no recollection of him until I was twelve years old, at which time he came home on leave. Even then I saw very little of him, as I was at school during the greater part of his sojourn in England, thus we met at Peshawar almost as strangers." In 1892, at the end of his career, he was asked to remain as commander-in-chief, "an offer I would have gladly accepted . . . if I could have taken a few months' leave to England. But, during a quarter of a century, I had only been able to spend eighteen months out of India. . . . *Under the existing regulations, a commander-in-chief could take no leave.*" [Italics mine] The last words hardly require any emphasis, except that it is hard to believe them, even in the cold print.

To some it will seem to be harrowing; and it was. These men were exiles, the gilded convicts, the chain gangs of the East, who are described by Rudyard Kipling in his stories.

But, if the business of empire is to be done on the scale and with the purpose which John Kennedy envisaged and proclaimed, it is hard to believe that it can be done in any other way; and it is at this point that an outsider may be allowed to observe what many Americans have always known, that the work of empire on this scale and with this purpose is not for them. Even when they are dispatched abroad, for brief tours of duty, the comforts of home must be supplied to them, and Bob Hope sent to them as a den mother. The life on the Northwest Frontier as it is described by Winston Churchill in *The Story of the Malakand Field Force,* was one of limitless boredom, and men such as his commanding officer—with a name, Sir Bindon Blood, which is memorable—exhausted themselves in it. But it was across that frontier that the two empires of Britain and Russia watched each other for a century, keeping the peace between them.

There is an important sense in which John Kennedy and his brothers were subjected to a Platonic upbringing, in which they were nurtured and educated and trained to be the guardians of the state. Certainly, there was something in the atmosphere of the administration which was reminiscent of the gymnasium in ancient Greece, men set apart, endowed in body as well as in mind with the capacity to excel, taking the state as their mistress. But this is not the character of the American people, and John Kennedy attempted to transcend it, as so much else, by summoning the American people to undertake the imperial mission, while concealing its meaning and the cost; to undertake it in the role to which they are accustomed —as tourists. For brief periods, they would travel the world, as advisers, as A.B. generalists in the Peace Corps, as teachers, as doctors, as technicians, as Special Forces; they would shake the hand of the world, and then they would come home. It was in this manner that the American people were persuaded that they could stand on the walls of freedom across the world, enjoying the sensation of empire, exalted by the mission which had fallen to them, but never to bear the pain.

CHAPTER TWELVE

Crisis as
an Instrument of Policy

FROM MIDDAY ON 20 January 1961 until midday on 22 November 1963, the people of the United States lived in an atmosphere of perpetual crisis and of recurring crises, and under this pressure, at one moment, they came near to panic: playful and overactive, it may be, in the manner of the administration, but a reaction in which the element of panic was strong. In his special message to Congress on "Urgent National Needs," which he delivered on 25 May 1961, John Kennedy called for a programme of "identifying present fallout shelter capacity and providing new and existing structures," which would "protect millions of people against the hazards of radioactive fallout in the event of a large-scale nuclear attack." Two months later, in his television address to the American people on the situation in Berlin, he was more specific about what should be done: "To identify and mark space in existing structures—public and private—that could be used for fallout shelters in case of attack; to stock these shelters with food, water, first-aid kits and other minimum essentials for survival; to increase their capacity"; and so on. "The lives of those families which are not hit in a nuclear blast and fire can still be saved—if they can be warned to take shelter, and if that shelter is available." His aim was to arouse a public which he believed to be slumbering, and he succeeded too well.

As an outsider, one has not only read the literature of the time, but has listened to the memories of what then happened. On a campus in 1970, a class of sociology students were invited by their professor to put in writing the reasons why they were joining the student strike after the killings at Kent State University, and several of them in their essays returned to this single experience which they had shared as schoolchildren: how they were compelled week by week to take part in a terrifying drill, kneeling in their fallout shelters, their hands clasped behind their necks, to steady them against the blast. But one has listened also to the memories of those who were young mothers at the time, or who were pregnant, struck with horror at the thought of the imminent catastrophe to which they had borne or were about to bear their children. The memories of others may be less vivid, but the evidence, in print and in recollection, is there.

For at least a year after John Kennedy had drawn attention to the possibility of a nuclear attack, and to the possibility—which he converted almost into a promise—of surviving it if one had only taken adequate precautions, the people of America ceased to compete by buying a new car every year, or a second car, or a swimming pool; they built their own fallout shelters, and they stocked them. In its issue of 25 August 1961, *Time* reported that twelve million American families "have got ready for nuclear attack." Three weeks later, in its issue of 15 September, *Life* published its infamous cover story under the headline: "How You Can Survive Fallout. 97 Out Of 100 People Can Be Saved," a statistic which was so false as to be unforgivable. Yet the story, which was introduced by an approving letter from John Kennedy himself, made the improbable suggestion that an adequate fallout shelter could be constructed within four hours by just two men using only a screwdriver and a wrench to bolt together eighty-four pre-fabricated pieces; for American commerce, ingenious as ever, had already produced and marketed a do-it-yourself fallout shelter kit.

In fact, *Life* showed a picture of a happy American family in its shelter, which it had procured, ready to be assembled, for $700 from the Kelsey-Hayes Company. The group included a girl who was laughing and talking on the telephone, one wonders to whom: it seemed that the Pepsi generation, as it was soon to be advertised, could take even an all-out nuclear attack in its vivacious stride. "The best first-aid for radiation sickness," said *Life*, was to "take hot tea or a solution of baking soda." The folly could hardly be stopped, and, by the end of the year, the Department of Defense had published its own leaflet on fallout protection, the preparation of which it had in the beginning entrusted to a team from Time, Inc., headed by none other than Edward Thompson, the managing editor of *Life*. It was hardly surprising, therefore, that "the tone of the whole booklet," as the Baltimore *Sun* observed on 2 January 1962, "whatever it may say specifically, is to suggest that safety in a nuclear attack is really rather easy and quite natural"; and this was indeed the heart of the matter.

If the appeal of John Kennedy for an adequate civil defence programme "went beyond his own expectations and desires," it was because his administration had already begun to excite the notion that the unthinkable—ultimate thermonuclear war —was thinkable: that the emphasis on a comprehensive shelter programme—which anyhow, Theodore Sorensen admits, the administration did not have—was part of a comprehensive administration policy designed to establish that ultimate thermonuclear war could be "safe," at least for ninety-seven out of one hundred of the American population. When the San Francisco *Chronicle* on 26 December 1961 spoke of the "political dynamism" which "John Kennedy and others . . . have evidently concluded" they might find in the shelter programme, it was making only half of the real point. The political dynamism was being generated to gain support for his foreign policy, and he persistently used crisis to this end.

In spite of all that was said in the previous chapter, there is a sense in which the United States must be regarded as an empire. "Empire" is a word like others; its usefulness is that it helps us to talk of great power in its duration as well as in its extent. It would be misleading, for example, to say that Adolf Hitler created an empire; his conquests were extensive, but they lasted less than a decade. On the other hand, Russia is today clearly an empire, and so is the United States, and so is China, whereas Japan is not, and is unlikely to be, and by no stretch of the imagination is it conceivable that Western Europe, even if united, will again become one. If we refuse to talk of empires, we find ourselves reduced to speaking of superpowers, a term which tells us something of the weight of the power which is possessed, and something of its extent, but nothing of its duration, realised or probable. In this way, George Ball imagines five (or four-and-a-half!) superpowers in the immediate future: Russia and America, China and Japan, and a united Western Europe. But, whatever the energies and the wealth of Japan and Western Europe may accomplish, they will not become the determining influences within the world order which Russia and America and China today are, and will obviously for a long time remain, the stretch of their power still reaching ahead of them.

One of the most telling characteristics of an empire, as Irving Kristol has observed, is that what it does not do is as important as what it does; its decision not to act is in itself an act. When he was asked the meaning of "non-intervention," Talleyrand ineffably replied that it was a word, metaphysical and political, which means the same as intervention; and so, in the case of empires, it does. Since 1965, it has not much mattered whether Britain and France intervened in the Middle East; their imperial power in that area was then surrendered to America and Russia, who significantly acted in unison during the Suez crisis to restrain them; and it is now the intervention or the non-intervention of these two new empires which helps to determine what happens there. An obvious example of the difference between a nation of considerable power and one of imperial power is that, although France is one of the most energetic suppliers of arms to countries in some of the most disturbed regions of the world, it does not thereby become a shaper of events. It is intervening, but its intervention is not political; it may alter the balance of arms, but still not alter the balance of power; its role is that of a salesman, not that of a patron; states may be its clients, but they do not become its client states. But the furnishing of arms to other countries by America or Russia is at once a political act, adjusting the balance of power.

A revealing illustration of what the power of the United States has meant since 1945, and of what it requires, is given by Henry L. Kissinger in his description of the diplomacy of the great powers after 1815, *A World Restored*. The object of their statesmen was to re-create a world order which would be recognised as "legitimate" in the face of the "illegitimate" forces which had been released first by the French Revolution, and then by the daemonic energy of Napoleon Bonaparte. He defines a legitimate world order as "no more than an international agreement about the nature of workable arrangements and about the permissible aims and methods of foreign policy"; it "does not make conflicts impossible, but it limits their scope." Such legitimacy clearly vanishes "whenever there exists a power which considers the international order or the manner of legitimizing it oppressive"; and the distinguishing feature of such a revolutionary power is "not that it feels threatened . . . *but that nothing can reassure it.*" He concludes that "Diplomacy, the art of restraining the exercise of power, cannot function in such an environment." It follows that the task of a legitimate power in such a situation is to seek to restore the legitimacy of the world order, so that the illegitimate powers will find reassurance in it, and in the international agreement which it represents. Almost to the letter, Henry Kissinger in office has followed this historical prescription, so that diplomacy may resume its tasks.

Whatever the revisionist historians of the Cold War may now say, the United States since 1945 has been the upholder of a legitimate world order; and the two revolutionary powers, Russia and China, have gradually been persuaded that, in the absence of "an international agreement about the nature of workable arrangements and about the permissible aims and methods of foreign policy," even their own existence becomes unbearably insecure. The re-establishment of the principle of legitimacy in the international order has been the task of the United States and, without its legitimizing influence, even the revolutionary powers would today have to act in a revolutionary world order in which nothing could reassure them. This has been a part of the meaning of the dispute between Russia and

China: as revolutionary powers, the relations between them were also revolutionary; they could not reassure each other; and it is the United States, since 1969, which has begun the work of providing this reassurance, intervening in their relations, seeking from either or from both of them an acknowledgement that the adjustment of differences through negotiation is possible only in international orders which are accepted as legitimate.

The tragedy of the foreign policy of John Kennedy was that he met the revolutionary power of Russia and of China with his own revolutionary enterprises: to this extent, the revisionist historians are justified in talking of his policy as counter-revolution. He was right—which the revisionists will not acknowledge—in perceiving the actions of Russia and of China at that time as subversive of a legitimate world order; he was wrong—and he was tragically at fault—in meeting them with his own forms of subversion. Faced by the threat of guerilla warfare that was provoked and sustained by an external power, he chose to practise it himself, equally the leader of an external power. At a crucial period in the relations between the great powers, he was guilty of subverting the idea of legitimacy for which the United States had stood since 1945, and he obscured it, as much for Americans as for others.

With an inadequate understanding of the nature of power, he never seemed to appreciate, and this was even more true of Robert Kennedy, that it is a source of patience; that it need not, and usually should not, be a goad to action. He would never let it lie, just to speak for itself, to be seen and not heard. More than the ideology of the Cold War as such, this was the cause of the adventurousness of his foreign policy. It was characteristic of him that, when he discovered in 1961 that the United States, far from being at a disadvantage in the arms race, enjoyed the clear superiority of which Dwight Eisenhower had consistently spoken, he hastened to report this fact to Nikita Khrushchev, who understandably regarded the passing on of the information as a threat, and proceeded in return to make a series of threatening gestures of the power of the Soviet Union. But it is one of the characteristics of empire, of the duration of the great power which it possesses, that it creates the opportunity for patience; and it is this which neither John Kennedy nor the members of his administration appear to have understood about the nature of the power of the United States, of the Soviet Union, or of Communist China.

Early in September 1961, Robert McNamara addressed the Armed Services Committee of the Senate in language which was not exceptional:

> There is no true historical parallel to the drive of Soviet Communist imperialism to colonize the world . . . there is a totality on Soviet aggression which can be matched only by turning to ancient history when warring tribes sought not merely conquest but the total obliteration of the enemy. To this primitive concept of total obliteration, the Communists have brought the resources of modern technology and science.

If this is the kind of history which is learned at the Ford Motor Company, it is not surprising that Henry Ford I said that "History is bunk." At no time, past or present, have the leaders of Russia embarked on so insane a project as to colonise the world; and their record in obliterating the subject peoples whom they could not absorb has hardly been more remarkable than that of the Americans in dealing with the Indians, the Australians with the Aborigines, or the New Zealanders with the Maoris. But there is no mention of *Russia* in the passage, although it was of a historical entity, the Russian Empire, that he was speaking, and whose ambitions had to be calculated.

Whether under the tsars or under their successors, whether

calling itself the Third Rome or the Third International, the fact of the Russian Empire has not changed since the Dukes of Muscovy first set forth to establish their dominion over their immediate neighbours. In his preface to *Imperialism: the Last Stage of Capitalism*, we find V. I. Lenin making an acidulous reference to the conquered peoples who had been incorporated into the Russian Empire by the tsars; but not one of them was granted its independence when he seized power. For five hundred years—even longer, if one carries the story back to Alexander Nevski—the rulers of Russia have displayed a remarkable sense of the permanence of Russian interests. With a stupendous patience, they have expanded when possible and retreated when necessary; and there is no need to tell a European, accustomed for centuries to wondering at the hordes which may come out of the steppes, how closely they must be watched. But their patient pursuit of their long-term interests, whether in advance or in retreat, whether in the east or in the west, has never resembled the description given by Robert McNamara.

The administration of John Kennedy did not contemplate the Russian Empire, only "Soviet Communism"; in the same way, they did not contemplate the Chinese Empire, only "Communist China." It was for this reason that they were so slow to understand the significance of the dispute between the two countries. On 8 November 1962, in a speech in which it was intended that he should speak the mind of the administration on the subject of the dispute, Roger Hilsman declared: "Communist ideology, with its goals of world revolution, still provides an overall basis for unity between Peiping and Moscow." It is true that he also said that "we cannot foresee any genuine reconciliation of the dispute"; but, to the very end, the binding conviction of the administration was that the Communist ideology had a unifying power. Indeed, one of the reasons why the

American people have been so exaggerated in their anti-Communism may be that their historical memory, reaching back only to 1776, does not include the complex story of the church and the papacy: if they had been more familiar with the tendency of Christian doctrine to divide, they might have been less persuaded of the power of Communist ideology to unite.

One has not travelled far towards an understanding of John Kennedy and his administration if all that one can in the end show is that they were Cold Warriors, past the time when the Cold War was a reality, and that he was the chieftain of them. It is true that, in a speech in the House of Representatives on 25 January 1949, after Mao Tse-tung's victory, he said that "The responsibility for the failure of our foreign policy in the Far East rests squarely with the White House and the Department of State," and that he spoke of "our diplomats and their advisers, the Lattimores and the Fairbanks," in language which it was hard to distinguish from that of Joseph McCarthy; and it is also true that in office he was ready to use any means that were available to him to prevent the replacement of Nationalist China by Communist China at the United Nations; all of this is known, and it matters. But it is only the beginning of the inquiry. Sustaining the ideology of the Cold War and its fascination for him was an inadequate understanding of the nature of great power, of the long-term interests which it generates, and of the opportunity which it provides to pursue them patiently. He thought of great power only in terms of the immediate strength which was available; not in terms of its duration.

In the May 1962 issue of the *United States Naval Institute Proceedings*, Charles O. Lerche, Jr., deplored the manner in which the United States appeared to be "resting its security and survival on nothing more substantial than its ability always to improvise an effective response to an external threat." In an article which is as entertaining as it is thoughtful, he suggested that "probably the most basic difference in strategic style between the Soviet Union and the United States is dramatically suggested by the Russian preference for chess as an intellectual pastime in contrast to the American predilection for either poker or contract bridge." The essence of strategy in chess, he suggested, is "its integral unity. The entire plan of attack is tied together from the very first move." In contrast, poker and bridge "both consist of a series of analytically independent strategic confrontations (deals) tied together only loosely by a central strategic purpose. 'Victory' in bridge or poker is achieved by amassing a large enough margin or profit out of an indefinitely prolonged series of separate strategic situations to emerge the winner. Each situation is, furthermore, operationally unique."

The foreign policy of the United States, he said, "moves through time dealing with one foreign policy crisis after another, with top priority assigned in practice to the current or the most recent one. . . . The United States 'wins' if the Soviet Union is balked, and 'loses' if Moscow has its way." Warming to his subject, he suggested that even football, as it is played in America, had an influence on the conduct of its foreign policy: "The national proclivity to conceive policy as a series of direct Soviet-American confrontations, separated by more or less static pauses for practice, affects the planning of American action." But the result, anyhow, was clear: "Each crisis is as important as any other; all are absolutely critical and call into question far-reaching matters of national prestige, survival, and world role. . . . Soviet planners avoid the trap of assigning to each issue the same—necessarily absolute and transcendent—importance."

Theodore Sorensen is not alone in emphasising the international crises which followed the assumption by John Kennedy

of his office, and it is worth summarising those which he cat-
alogues:

–13 February: the threat of a new intervention by the Russians in the Congo after the assassination of Patrice Lumumba;

–9 March: the possibility that forces led by the Communists
would take over all of Laos, requiring the introduction of American troops;

–18 March: the decision of Portugal to send troops to Angola
to repress a nationalist uprising there;

–21 March: the demand of the Russians, in the nuclear test-
ban talks, for a right of veto over any power of inspection;

–12 April: the orbiting by Russia of the first man into space;

–19 April: the defeat by Fidel Castro of the attempted invasion at the Bay of Pigs;

–1 May: the announcement by the Communists in both
North Vietnam and South Vietnam that they were in a position to take over the whole country by the end of the year;

–15 May: the overthrow by a military coup of the government
of South Korea;

–30 May: the assassination in the Dominican Republic of
Rafael Trujillo;

–4 June: the warning of Nikita Khrushchev that a peace
treaty with East Germany would be signed before the end of the
year;

–19 July: an outbreak of fighting between France and Tunisia over the existence of the French base at Bizerte;

–13 August: the construction of the Berlin Wall, and the
accompanying threat to the right of access of the Western powers to the city;

–25 August: the overthrow of Jânio Quadros, the President
of Brazil;

–30 August: the announcement by the Russians that they intended to resume nuclear testing with a series of high-megaton explosions;

–18 September: the death of Dag Hammarskjold in the Congo, and the demand of the Russians in the United Nations that he should be replaced as Secretary General by a troika.

It is a breathless list, indeed, but it is no more. At the very most, one can count only three of these situations as crises to which the United States was bound to respond with urgent action; at the very least, seven of them were situations which required no positive action at all; for the rest, if they needed a response, it should have been delayed and patient and should certainly not have been taken in an atmosphere of crisis. One may even point out that two of the situations—in Cuba and in the Dominican Republic—had been precipitated by actions of the United States, which sponsored and encouraged the invasion at the Bay of Pigs, and which had a hand in the assassination of Rafael Trujillo. But the point which matters is that an administration which imagines every untoward development in the world to be a crisis is confusing the urgent with the important, a valuable distinction, in politics as in the other affairs of men, which Henry Kissinger has consistently suggested that the American people should make.

"Great crises produce great men," John Kennedy wrote in *Profiles in Courage*. It is not a thought which should enter the mind of a statesman, but it appeared to enter his own without resistance. If he did not actually enjoy leading his country to the edge of danger, one could not tell so from his words or from his actions. The remark which he made in 20 October 1962—"Well, we earned our pay this month"—is rightly famous, if not for the reason given by his admirers. It was characteristic of him that he considered that he had done his job only if he had confronted peril, and led the nation to confront it, whether in the Cuba missile crisis or in the violence at the University of Mississippi, the incidents to which he was referring on this occasion. It was no wonder that, as early as 12 August 1961, Jerry Greene wrote in *The Nation* of his military policies: "The President, in many ways, will be walking a finer wire even than Dulles did with his 'brink of war' approach"; and I. F. Stone echoed in his newsletter of 2 January 1962 that "Our foreign policies keep us on the brink of war in a half-dozen places from Vietnam to Berlin." The method could have no other consequence.

Robert McNamara was later to remark that there had been 164 "significant outbreaks of violence between 1958 and 1966," and one can only respond that one lived through those years, had the task of trying to interpret them, and has returned to study them; and that no conceivable definition of "significant" will support his statement. But it was in this condition of heat that these cool men, as they boasted themselves to be and as the country was persuaded to regard them, seemed always to act. What did they think would happen if they ignored—say—ninety per cent of those outbreaks? What fear—or need of fear—compelled John Kennedy to trumpet forth in his first message on the State of the Union in 1961, "Each day we draw nearer to the hour of maximum danger, as weapons spread and hostile forces grow stronger"? What was the temper which could announce, when the country was prosperous and at peace: "The news will be worse before it is better. And while hoping and working for the best, we should prepare ourselves now for the worst"?

Dean Rusk in 1968, to an audience at Yale University, said, "Since I have been Secretary of State, I have lived through sixty *coups d'état* in various countries of the world. These things happen, and in almost every calendar year there will be forty-five or fifty elections or changes of government in one or another country around the world." It was his duty, he had told Eric Goldman in a television interview on 12 January 1964, to take into account "the attitudes of 114 governments with which we do business." Every day, about thirteen hundred cables were received by the Department of State, and about a thousand were sent out; this was the continuing business which was its daily concern. The lesson to be drawn from all this was that "In our foreign relations, we are dealing with a world which we can only influence, we can't control." As he told the American Political Science Association on 7 September 1965, "We can only shape what happens in the world by influencing the views of other nations. . . . Few problems can be solved by the United States alone." It was a voice needed in the administration, and it was a tragedy that Dean Rusk did not raise it firmly enough. From time to time, John Kennedy acknowledged the restrictions on the power of the United States, but this was not the mood in which he acted. He was, says Roger Hilsman, "an activist in foreign policy . . . , and determined to attempt to shape events." In order to transcend the restrictions, he again and again sought to create an atmosphere of crisis in which America must act immediately and alone, and so defeated his object: instead of shaping events, he was able only to react to them.

The methods were always the same: the excitement of public opinion at home; the demand for an increase in the military forces of the country and a strengthening of its armaments; threats to use these forces and gestures to underline the threats; and the actual employment of them in some cases, open and covert. It was an unavoidable result of the method that the complexity of any situation was simplified. When he addressed the nation on television on 23 March 1961, on the question of Laos, he could not explain the background; he could not invite the people to follow the roles of Souvanna Phouma and Souphanouvong and Phoui Sananikone and Phoumi Nosavan, or the manoeuvres of Kong Le; and their names did not occur in his statement. He could only harangue the people, tell them that they faced danger, and excite them to be prepared to meet it; and the same was true of his television address on 25 July 1961, on the situation in Berlin, as it continued to be true in any crisis, imagined or real, in which he appealed directly to the people for their support in meeting an external threat. What he found in the atmosphere of crisis was at least some of the simplifications of war.

At ease with these simplifications, he appeared to wait until a situation had developed to the point at which it could be given the character of a crisis, which in turn gave him the opportunity to act; and what he meant by action was a spectacular display of his power in a situation of maximum peril, *as he defined it*. He authorised the disastrous invasion of Cuba four months after he had been officially informed of the plans, and five months after the first news of the preparations had been printed in the United States. He made his "Television Report to the American People on the Berlin Crisis," as it is called in the official volumes of his public papers, five months after Nikita Khrushchev had revived the question of the status of Berlin in an *aide-mémoire* to Konrad Adenauer; and, a month later still, the Berlin Wall was being built. Similarly at home, in Mississippi and in Alabama, he waited until violence had actually erupted, or was immediately threatened, before he intervened: once again with a spectacular display of his personal leadership.

Even within his own country, the President seemed to be most at ease when he could act as the Commander-in-Chief; in the atmosphere of crisis, he sought military solutions to diplomatic problems abroad. He sought them, not because he was a militarist, which would be an idle accusation, but because they were simplifying, like the atmosphere of crisis itself. Again and again, we find him and his advisers planning the successive stages of a military response. Confronted by the situation in Laos early in 1961, preparations were made to increase military action by seventeen specific steps, including the ultimate use of "all-out force"; and some of the steps were taken. It was exactly this method of stage-by-stage escalation of military pressures that was planned, nineteen months later, in the Cuba missile crisis; and the method was explicit as well as implicit in his response to the increasingly unmanageable situation in South Vietnam. This was the flexibility which he boasted—because he believed —he had given himself; both by the process of decision which he had established in the White House, and by his strengthening and diversification of the armed forces of the country. But it was flexibility in only one direction: the choices available to him were only a progression, "from military advisers to a token unit to all-out force."

This was the military legacy that he passed on to his successor, and it was embedded in the minds of the men who were also passed on, Robert McNamara and McGeorge Bundy, Maxwell Taylor and Walt Rostow, and a score of others, who were all still there in the spring of 1965 to recommend the final escalation of the war in Vietnam. For written into the politics of crisis, and the military solutions that were sought, was the demand for victories, rather than for victory; for visible triumphs in the succeeding emergencies, rather than for the patient accumulations of a long-term policy. It was not in the method of John Kennedy and his advisers to bear in mind the three axioms proposed in May 1962 by Charles Lerche: that "International crises are not independent and self-contained events, capable of being attacked as isolated decisional systems"; that "All crises are not of equal importance, nor is one victory as meaningful as another"; that "No state, no matter how powerful, can realistically hope for an undefeated season every year." This wisdom was disregarded.

It was inevitable that it would be disregarded because, if crisis is made an instrument of policy, the result can only be that policy will become the slave of crisis. Chester V. Clinton, in *Hail to the Chief*, records that John Kennedy, shortly after he took office, had learned "with stunned amazement" that, if he sent ten thousand men to South-east Asia, the United States would have practically no strategic reserves left for other emergencies. (Such a condition will seem to be appalling only if the premises are accepted: that ten thousand men should be sent to South-east Asia, and that there will be other emergencies to be met.) A thousand days later in the last speech of his life, he was able to boast that he had added five combat ready divisions to the Army, and five tactical fighter wings. In fact, the expansion of the conventional forces was larger than that; and early in 1965, in an approving book, *The McNamara Strategy*, William W. Kaufmann said that it gave the Secretary of Defense "a ten division strategic reserve." He went on: "With it he could handle a Korean-sized engagement and still have several divisions left over for another emergency." On how many fronts, one can only ask, was the United States meant to fight simultaneously?

In reviewing this book in the July 1965 issue of *World Politics*, Bernard Brodie seized on the phrase, "a Korean-sized engagement," and let fly: "The American people considered it a war, and a nasty, unduly prolonged, and unsatisfactorily concluded, one at that. They are not eager to enter another such—as their present attitudes towards Vietnam confirm." He was writing in the spring of 1965! "What are the occasions," he asked, "when the United States failed to respond because of lack of conventional weapons?" It was impossible to think of one. Robert McNamara himself had said that, even in the Cuba missile crisis, the success of the United States had been due to the exercise of its full military capacity, including its nuclear capability. The increase in the conventional forces, concluded Bernard Brodie, had meant "a sizable net increase in our own already high military budget, as well as a continuation of the draft, and this at a time which includes the period that we have called *détente*." The result was predictable. When the time came to consider seriously the dispatch of a massive conventional force to South Vietnam, it was there to send. The complaint of John Kennedy in 1961, that there were practically no strategic reserves, had been met by himself.

Instead of far-reaching and far-seeing political judgement, instead of considered strategic concepts, the administration of John Kennedy simply prepared the tactical and logistic options between which a rational choice could at any time be made to meet any eventuality. "The range of possible situations in which non-nuclear forces might be employed," writes Adam Yarmolinsky, "also calls for the development of flexible forces like Strike Command, established in 1961, as a central pool of force that could be rapidly deployed to any part of the world." But the likelihood, if it could be deployed, was that it would be deployed; and it was. In its issue of May 1962, the *Military Review* carried a report of a speech made by Paul D. Adams, who had been selected by Robert McNamara as the commander-in-chief of the new Strike Command, with its headquarters at McDill Air Base in Florida. He explained that his command had been created to help to provide "increased flexibility in dealing with outbreaks of various degrees of intensity," and it was this misconception of strategy which persuaded John Kennedy that the power of the United States could be—because it should be able to be—rapidly deployed to any part of the world in the event of any outbreak of violence.

It was a misconception because, by providing the means to meet any eventuality, it made every eventuality seem to be a contingency—a prominent word in the vocabulary of the New Frontier—which must be met by action. The conventional orthodoxy at the time was that the administration had in this way given itself freedom of choice. But it in fact precluded choice— the choice that counts—since it precluded inaction; to some extent, it precluded even action, properly regarded, and reaction became the only course. The President was supposed to have a varied and balanced range of forces from which he could select the most appropriate response. But it was always response to which the United States seemed to be limited. In this manner, policy was subjected to crisis, and the crisis was used in turn to stimulate the response of the people: their appropriate response to the appropriate response of the administration. So they lived for a thousand days in expectation of danger, and of rescue from it.

If great crises produce great men, as John Kennedy said, he and those around him had no doubt that they lived in an age of crisis. In *The Vital Center*, which he reissued in 1962, Arthur Schlesinger wrote:

> If we believe in free society hard enough to keep on fighting for it, we are pledged to a permanent crisis which will test the moral, political, and very possibly the military, strength of each side. A "permanent" crisis? Well, a generation or two anyway, permanent in one's own lifetime. . . . There is no more exciting

time in which to live—no time more crucial or more tragic. We must recognize that this is the nature of our age: that the womb has irrevocably closed behind us, that security is a foolish dream of old men, that crisis will always be with us.

Even if our age is as Arthur Schlesinger describes it, he talks of its condition with a relish that is disturbing. He passes from exaltation to despair, from excitement to tragedy, with an equal indulgence. Yet he is writing a tract to prescribe a moderate course—"the vital center"—which should be pursued in the practical conduct of human affairs. One would have thought that it is the purpose of such a course to attain a measure of security, not to dismiss the possibility of it as a foolish dream; but we are expected instead to dwell on crisis.

We are then offered a further reason for believing that we live in a time of permanent crisis: "science and technology have made the velocity of history so much greater than before." There is obviously an element of truth in the observation, but it is not equally obvious that it has any great practical meaning. It certainly does not follow that an increase in the velocity of history must be accompanied by an increase in the velocity of political decision. The nature of political decision—its occasions, its timing, its calculations, its guesswork—has not much changed since Julius Caesar stood on the banks of the Rubicon and determined to cross it, or since Napoleon Bonaparte decided to lead his army against Russia; indeed, the very same decisions, the march on Rome and the march on Moscow, have been repeated in our own time. But the administration of John Kennedy enjoyed the sensation that they were acting in exceptional times of maximum peril, and that what these required of them was urgency in action. "The tide of events has been running out," John Kennedy said on 30 January 1961, which was perhaps not what he meant to say; but the tides of crisis, at any rate, he would persuade to run in.

Many of the mistakes of the administration in fashioning the Alliance for Progress can be traced to their belief that it was, in a phrase on which they leaned, "one minute to midnight" in Latin America. But it was at one minute to midnight that the administration believed that the hands of the clock always stood, all over the globe; and they were driven by the fear that, if they did not act before the clock struck, they would all seem to be pumpkins. They aspired to greatness, not just occasionally, but all the time. If they had not had the opportunity to be great by one minute to midnight, Eastern Standard Time, at least some of their number sat up most of the night, awaiting the occasion. As the sun rose over the farthermost shores of Cathay and began its slow progress across the heavens, it was one minute to midnight somewhere, and something would happen; a government would fall, there would be a significant outbreak of violence, a *démarche* would be threatened; and the Situation Room would be alerted. All over Washington, men would rise early to answer the bidding to crisis and to greatness, and the still slumbering public would awake in the morning to find that they had been summoned to meet danger once more; and once more to be rescued from it.

An age of permanent crisis, in which the velocity of political decision had been increased; and in which two nations had the power to blow up most of the world. That was the third ingredient. When it was pointed out to John Kennedy that the great Presidents of the past had not sought a condition of national unity in time of peace, he "patiently repeated that this was another time and really another world," as Hugh Sidey reported, "and he pointed to the persistent outside threat of nuclear extinction." Similar phrases are to be found in every memoir. Again and again, the justification of the methods of leadership which were employed was that "the stakes were the highest possible, the lives of hundreds of millions of persons," as Pierre Salinger says of the attempt to control the press during the Cuba missile crisis, that "we were locked in a crisis that could lead to nuclear war." But one must ask why the stakes were so high, not so much in this particular case as in general; why the possibility of ultimate thermonuclear war seemed in those years to be so imminent.

The story of the Cuba missile crisis needs no retelling here. One can only state one's own judgement, after weighing one's words, that the conduct of John Kennedy was an irresponsible exercise of great power, from the consequences of which he was saved only by what Dean Acheson called "plain dumb luck." He was fortunate that he was not pushed down the full length of the course which he had plotted. That he "got away with it" without blowing his own country and the world to kingdom come—a possibility which he openly faced as the ultimate step which he might have to take—is hardly a mark in his favour. The question remains: What if Nikita Khrushchev had not backed down, not before the first step in the escalation of responses which had been planned, not before the second, not before the third, not until the final stage of ultimate thermonuclear war had been reached? The men, cool and rational, laconic and contained, whom he had gathered to his service, planned for thirteen days a strategy of which the accepted end, if the Soviet Union did not react as they wished, was that they would burn the world to a cinder. The scenario was understood, the political game and the military game had been practised; they were now joined, and played for real.

Only two aspects of the story need be noticed in the context of this book: the situation was allowed to develop into a crisis;

the crisis was then magnified. As early as 29 June 1961, William Fulbright had declared in the Senate: "I suppose we should all be less comfortable if the Soviets did install missile bases in Cuba, but I am not sure that our national existence would be in substantially greater danger than is the case today, nor do I think that such bases would substantially alter the balance of power in the world." In fact, much the same was said at the time of the missile crisis by Robert McNamara within the councils of the administration; it was repeated by Roswell Gilpatric immediately after the crisis, when he appeared on "Issues and Answers" on ABC-TV on 11 November 1962; and it is even admitted by Theodore Sorensen in his memoir. But one must notice the date of William Fulbright's observation, because the administration, after the failure of the adventure at the Bay of Pigs, should have considered the possibility—the likelihood—that the Soviet Union would one day attempt to place missiles on Cuba; and it should not, more than two years later, have been taken by surprise, forced to act in secret and in haste, in what seems from all accounts, but especially in that of Robert Kennedy, to have been almost a charade, as the enactment of each syllable of the action was zealously plotted before it was zealously played.

The crisis having been allowed to develop, it was then magnified. When the President finally announced his policy, it was a full week after the Central Intelligence Agency had told McGeorge Bundy of the existence of the missile sites on Cuba. The effect of this silence was that the problem of what to do about them became a public issue only when the situation was acutely critical. During the long days and nights in which the Executive Committee of the National Security Council decided to recommend a blockade as a first step, the Russian ships had been moving deeper and deeper into the Atlantic, until they were already approaching the danger line, where the American ships must stop them, when the policy was announced. Since the blockade was only a first step in a planned escalation of which the final step would be nuclear war itself, and since it would be only a day or two before the efficacy of this first step was tested, John Kennedy had effectively placed his policy beyond immediate criticism. The steps which he had taken had placed the country in imminent danger of nuclear annihilation—a danger which had not existed seven days before—and neither the press nor Congress, on behalf of the people, could in such a situation challenge his leadership.

During the crisis, *The Nation* had commented on "the way in which, through skillful planning, strict security, and artful public relations, the stage was set." But the manipulation of public opinion was not a contrivance of the moment. For almost two years, the American people had been attuned to crisis; they expected little else; they did not question when they were told that it was there. Was it not for this that they had built their fallout shelters a year before, to survive the holocaust, ninety-seven out of each one hundred of them? Would their leaders not guide them once again safely through the storm? Nerves would be tightened, eyes would be lifted anxiously to the White House hoping for deliverance, hearts would falter and then grow stronger. Since 20 January 1961, the American people had known no other way of living. In particular, had they not been taught to believe that the unthinkable was in fact thinkable: that ultimate thermonuclear war was a possibility which could be rationally faced?

"The Great Debate" about nuclear strategy, which occupied so many minds during the decade after 1955, was complicated and mesmerising. It is hard to return to it now without a sense of unreality: the flurry of argument about "massive retaliation" and "spasm war" and "overkill" and "invulnerable deterrent" and "second-strike capability" and "controlled response" and "counterforce strategy" and "nuclear threshold." It was the period in which men such as Herman Kahn earned what one would have thought were unenviable reputations by asking people to think the unthinkable: to envisage, as he suggested, forty-four rungs on the escalation ladder to ultimate thermonuclear war, twenty-nine of these stages to involve the use of nuclear weapons. But at least one prominent voice before 1961 had spoken against this madness: that of Dwight Eisenhower, who said that the idea of general war was "preposterous" in the nuclear age. "In spite of John Foster Dulles's bluster about massive retaliation," wrote Charles Bolton in *The Nation* of 17 November 1962, "President Eisenhower unfailingly held before the American people the image that international war is obsolete and the initiation of nuclear war unthinkable for sane people." But the voice had been replaced.

It had been replaced by the voices of Robert McNamara, enunciating the strategy of "counterforce" in his famous speech at Ann Arbor on 16 June 1962, and of John Kennedy expounding it. Did it imply that the United States would, in some circumstances, make a first strike? If there was any doubt, it would seem to have been eliminated by the President himself. In the message which accompanied his first defence budget on 28 March 1961, he said: "We are not creating forces for a first strike against any nation." But exactly a year later, in the issue of the *Saturday Evening Post* of 31 March 1962, he gave an interview to Stewart Alsop, in which he openly declared: "Of course, in some circumstances, we must be prepared to use the nuclear weapon at the start, come what may—a clear attack on Western Europe, for example. But what is important is that, if you have these weapons, you have control over their use." He was here introducing the complementary doctrine of "controlled response," and it was reiterated by Robert McNamara at a press conference on 6 July 1962, when he said that "we can't be certain how a nuclear war will be fought. We must have a flexible strategy."

If one of the elements of the atmosphere of crisis in which the administration acted, and the country lived, for a thousand days was the fear of nuclear war, then one must ask who had created the fear; who was not only entertaining the possibility, but anticipating the reality? Robert McNamara spoke of the country's nuclear capability, during these years, not only as a deterrent, but also as an offensive force in the event that "war should nevertheless occur." In short, the idea of a rationally controlled escalation towards ultimate thermonuclear war had been accepted; and it was in terms of this escalation that every difficult international situation was perceived as a crisis, and presented as such to the people.

At about 2 A.M. on 13 August 1961, in spite of the atmosphere of crisis which John Kennedy had created round the question of Berlin, the East Germans began to build the Berlin Wall; and they went on building it for several days. There was a flurry of activity. A melodramatic dash was made on 20 August by the 1st Battle Group, 8th Infantry, across the more than one hundred miles of East German territory between West Germany and West Berlin; they were allowed to make the crossing unmolested, but "if a single day can be pointed to when the President felt the nation was entering the danger zone," reported Hugh Sidey, "it was this." He did not fly to Cape Cod that weekend, one of his advisers having said to him: "I'll never forget that General Marshall couldn't explain where he was on Pearl Harbor Day. We shouldn't declare war from Hyannis

Port." But, if war had come, on whom would the responsibility have lain? Who was going to the edge of it?

For what was the purpose of the flurry of activity? What was the dash of the infantry meant to accomplish? They could not stop the Berlin Wall from being completed; and it is still there today. "We . . . gave up, although we never said so," said Walter Lippmann in a televised interview on 7 June 1962; and six months earlier he had put the awkward question: "We are not in a position in Berlin to say, 'Remove the wall or else.' Because what's 'else'?" It was the question which had been left unanswered by all of John Kennedy's preparations; and it is at this point that the politics of crisis and the politics of expectation can be seen to be joined. By generating an atmosphere of crisis, in which he could give a spectacular display of personal leadership, he exaggerated in the public mind the military strength of the United States, and obscured its actual impotence in many situations. What was the "else" in the country's armoury, in spite of the flexibility which he boasted he had given himself, unless he was ready to think the unthinkable, and carry the country with him? He "prepares the public mind to gamble all, if necessary, on Berlin," wrote I. F. Stone in his newsletter of 25 September 1961. "This is the real mobilization. Our moral scruples and our good sense must first be conscripted." But, when the American people had been so galvanized, what was there then to show? Wherever one looked, at the end of the thousand days, the situation in the world was at least as threatening, and in many cases more threatening, to the United States than when he took office.

His legacy was that he had accustomed the American people to an atmosphere of crisis, and taught them to seek confrontation, eyeball to eyeball, within it. On 28 October 1962, after the Cuba missile crisis, the Los Angeles *Times* published a column by Matt Weinstock describing a scene "common throughout the United States." In the high schools, junior and senior, of Los Angeles, he said, students had broken down and sobbed aloud: "I don't want to die." In some schools, the situation "became so bad that principals had to go on the public address system to calm students with facts and commonsense." If this reaction is regarded by some as exaggerated or exceptional, then one must put beside it, not only the observation of the college president, already quoted, that "youth's decreasing identification" with John Kennedy was caused in part by their "shock and terror" during the Cuba missile crisis, but also the personal testimony of many American people of one's acquaintance. The memories are vivid and painful; when recalled, they are still unsettling; the shock and the terror can even now be felt.

But above all, if one gazes back on the turbulence of the United States during the second half of the 1960s, is not at least a part of the explanation to be found in the pitch of feverishness at which the American people had been kept for three years by the politics of crisis—its expectations and its confrontations—raised to an exalted level? When one has listened to the flower children and the hippies and the freaks, has one not also heard the barely suppressed echoes of a childhood in which they were told to think the unthinkable and, for a week in the fall of 1962, believed that the thinkable was about to happen to them? On the one hand, the seeker after confrontation; on the other hand, the drop-out from confrontation. The country, and especially its youth, had been imaginatively prepared only for crisis, either to rush eagerly towards it, or to flee already weary from it.

CHAPTER THIRTEEN

The Displacement
of Politics

WE ENGAGE IN political activity so that we may, as societies of men, deal with the world as it is. This is not a slight endeavour; the world as it is, as experience teaches us, is not easy to deal with. Some men all of the time, and almost all men some of the time, try to escape from it, into dreams or fairy stories or myths, the sub-creations which J. R. R. Tolkien has named Secondary Worlds; and even try, in some cases, to carry these Secondary Worlds directly into the Primary World, the world as it is, and impose them on it. What many of the most vocal and most disruptive of the political movements in the United States had in common during the second half of the 1960s was a radical failure to distinguish between these two worlds. People carried their Secondary Worlds directly into the Primary World which is the proper care of politics, and tried to impose them on it. The politics of the United States became theatre—at its worst, psychodrama—and they have not yet recovered.

It was for much these reasons that Michael Oakeshott, in an essay which he wrote in 1956, said that politics are "an activity unsuited to the young, not on account of their vices, but on account of what I at least consider to be their virtues." Everybody's young days, he said "are a dream, a delightful insanity, a sweet solipsism. Nothing in them has a fixed shape . . . everything is a possibility. . . . Nothing is specified in advance; everything is what can be made of it. The world is a mirror in which we seek the reflection of our own desires. . . . Since life is a dream, we argue . . . that politics must be an encounter of dreams in which we hope to impose our own." But, as we grow, and pass what Joseph Conrad called the shadow line, there is disclosed to us "a solid world of things, each with its fixed shape, each with its point of balance, each with its price; a world of fact, not poetic image, in which what we have spent on one thing we cannot spend on another; a world inhabited by others besides ourselves, who cannot be reduced to mere reflections of our own emotions." It is coming to be at home in this commonplace world that qualifies us, "if we are so inclined, and have nothing better to think about," to engage in political activity; and coming to be at home in it—"to rein in one's own beliefs and desires, to acknowledge the current shape of things, to feel the balance of the world in one's hands"—is a difficult achievement, not to be looked for in the young.

This is a classic statement of one attitude to politics; and it is the attitude which underlies much of the argument of this book. One cannot blame the Kennedys—either the brothers themselves or those who served them—for the whole of the displacement of politics which took place in the 1960s; and one cannot blame them only for any of it. But the fact remains that they had an unusual impact on the social imagination of the American people during the years in which they acted—beyond the meaning of anything which they did—and that the force of that impact was to persuade the people either that the limits of politics could be transcended or that politics could transcend the limits of the commonplace world; one or the other, or both. The one place where they did not feel at home, where they were not content to act, was in the world as it is. Even when, in their practice of conventional politics, which was also a part of their method, they had to bow to the world as it is, they still implied that it should, and that it could, be transcended. This was at the root, not only of the politics of expectation, but of the politics of confrontation which these in turn spawned. From a commanding position of influence, they created a Secondary World, of poetic image, not of fact, and carried it directly into the Primary World which is the sphere of politics. Is this not the meaning of the graves? Do they not celebrate a time when politics became an encounter of dreams?

It is one of the uses of political activity that it enables us to listen to the conversation of a society. Part of the justification of politics, therefore, lies merely in the continuation of the activity itself, the carrying on of the conversation. These—the activity and the conversation—take place in the political institutions which are today regarded, not least by those who should know better, with an ignorance and an impatience which are unprecedented. The character of a political institution seems no longer to be comprehended. No matter that the draft of its keel is deep; people expect it—trade union or party or legislature or department—to respond to fashionable cries. But a political institution of true value does not answer to these ripples; it feels the tow of public opinion on great issues, slow and undramatic, beneath the surface. One cannot neglect the fact that the total effect of the political method of the Kennedys was to bring the political institutions of the country into disrepute by the promise to transcend them.

One is told that the American people at the time applauded John Kennedy when he described the Department of State as a "bowl of jelly"; in that case, ignorance was being cultivated in them, and it was their own ignorance which they were appreciating. We have what are known, a little speciously, as "The Pentagon Papers," but we do not yet have "The State Papers." But there is sufficient evidence to suggest that, throughout the administration of John Kennedy, the Department of State was more wise and more patient than the White House. If its influence was less than it should have been, this was in part because John Kennedy did indeed disdain it as a bowl of jelly; and in part because the Secretary of State, wise and patient as he personally was, did not press its point of view.

On 20 February 1961, Dean Rusk addressed the policy-making officers of the Department of State. "We have a President," he said, "with a great interest in foreign affairs"; and there was "an active expectation on his part that this Department will in fact take charge of foreign policy"; but this was not how it was to happen. Roger Hilsman tells us that he asked his secretary to type Dean Rusk's words on a card, which he then kept on a corner of his desk. A few days later, Richard Neustadt noticed it. "'My God, I hope it does,' Neustadt said with an intensity that startled me. 'If the Secretary and the Department don't run with his ball, we will all be paying for the failure.'" Yet, within a few weeks, Roger Hilsman was noticing that "Power was not going to the State Department, but away from it," and others were making the same observation. In his address to the policy-making officers, Dean Rusk had declared: "It is the concern of the Department of State that the American people are safe and secure; defense is not the monopoly of the Department of Defense"; but the battle went the other way.

The inclination is to put the blame on Dean Rusk, and he cannot be exonerated. But we must remember the kind of President whom he was serving: one who had a great interest in foreign affairs, which tempted him to take not only a direct but an immediate command of them; who was inclined to see international events as crises, and to seek military solutions to them; and who demanded in the conduct of his foreign policy not only action but quick action. These are not the manners of a bureaucracy, unless it has been transformed, as had happened at the Pentagon, into the instrument of a single will; they are not the ways, in particular, of a foreign office; above all, they are not the biddings to which diplomacy is intended to answer. John Kennedy was asking the Department of State to act as if the peculiar simplifications of war in fact existed.

If he wished the Department of State to take charge of foreign policy, it was as *his* Department of State, even though he had already established his own "little State Department" within the White House. Robert McNamara, when he was nominated, was given the freedom to choose his subordinates, to be approved by the President. By an action that gave a clear indication of what was to come, John Kennedy made several appointments to the Department of State before he had nominated Dean Rusk, and then continued to do so: Chester Bowles, to be the Under Secretary of State; Adlai Stevenson, to be the ambassador to the United Nations; Mennen Williams, to be the Assistant Secretary of State for African Affairs; George Ball, to be the Under Secretary of State for Economic Affairs, and Averell Harriman, to be the roving ambassador of the Department. There could hardly have been a more explicit downgrading of the Secretary of State, his prestige and his authority, from the start, or a clearer signal to his subordinates.

This attitude was dramatically reaffirmed in the "Thanksgiving Day Massacre" of 1961, when the following changes in the Department of State were announced: the removal of

Chester Bowles from his post as Under Secretary of State, to the "meaningless position," as Roger Hilsman describes it, of Special Representative and Adviser to the President on African, Asian, and Latin American Affairs; the removal of George McGhee, one of the few important appointments originally made by Dean Rusk, from his post as Chairman and Counselor of the Policy Planning Staff, to become the Under Secretary of State for Economic Affairs; the elevation of George Ball from the post of Under Secretary of State for Economic Affairs to that of Under Secretary of State; the transference from the White House of Walt Rostow, whom Dean Rusk had originally refused to accept, to become the Chairman and Counselor of the Policy Planning Staff; the transference from the White House, to be the Assistant Secretary of State for Congressional Relations, of Frederick G. Dutton; the transference from the White House, to the position of Deputy Assistant Secretary of State for Latin American Affairs, of Richard Goodwin; and the promotion from the vague post of roving ambassador of Averell Harriman, to be the Assistant Secretary of State for Far Eastern Affairs. In none of the four accounts that we have—Theodore Sorensen's; Arthur Schlesinger's; Roger Hilsman's; Chester Bowles's—is there any indication that Dean Rusk was seriously consulted. His authority in his department was being cut from under him; a man of the mettle of Harold Ickes would not have stayed a day longer in the job.

We need only notice that every man who was promoted had originally been a direct appointment of John Kennedy; and that Chester Bowles, although he had also been a direct appointment of the President, was intended to be the sacrifice. The avowed object of the exercise was that John Kennedy "required people in the State Department," as Arthur Schlesinger says, "whose basic loyalty would be to him"; and on 10 January 1962, he explained his reasons to Roger Hilsman, who has given us an account:

> He had found that he was going to have to work with people at the action level in the State Department, and there were now a number of people at that level with whom he would be working closely. Hopefully, in this way, we could get on with the job.
> What the President suggested was moving toward a more direct and personal supervision of foreign affairs. . . . he had convictions where the world ought to be headed and a determination to move it in that direction.

Roger Hilsman had been intending to resign from the administration, to accept a position at a university; but John Kennedy retained him at this interview, to become yet another of the President's men within the Department of State.

The criticism that is being offered here must not be misunderstood. There can be no objection to a President organising within the White House a staff capable of bringing his wishes to bear on the Department of State. The task of such a man as Carl Kaysen, on the staff of the National Security Council, was correct and valuable; and, being a correct and valuable man, he performed it well. He was "the man from the White House" identifiable as such, pushing and pulling at the departments and the agencies, bringing them together, whether in pursuit of a test-ban treaty, of a satisfactory solution of the conflict in the Congo, or of a sensible revision of the world's monetary mechanism. But the important point is that Carl Kaysen was acting on the departments and the agencies from outside, in an attempt to accomplish the will of the President; he was not the will of the President embodied within the departments and the agencies themselves.

John Kennedy, in the conditions of peace, sought to use the Department of State as an instrument of his will, instead of as an instrument which, in serving the purposes for which it exists, would refine his will. Edward Weintal and Charles Bartlett notice his habit of consulting directly with Llewellyn Thompson, his ambassador to the Soviet Union, and then shrewdly observe:

> However, Kennedy's curiosity also had its drawbacks. He was in the habit of by-passing the Secretary and Under Secretary to call Thompson directly, asking point blank: "What should I do about this problem?" The weakness of this system was that, with the best will in the world, Thompson could not always fill in his chief in time, and was in constant fear of making his own policy rather than reflecting the Secretary's views.

In these casual sentences, there is a severe indictment: of a man who was confusing the loyalties of his subordinates; who wished quick responses from his emissary in the field, even if it was impossible to give them; and who was, above all, ignoring the fact that the Secretary of State, regularly in touch with his ambassador, might know better then he how to evaluate the advice which was given. The complicated machinery of the Department of State was to be organised to simple ends.

Dean Rusk had a profound sense of the complication of the globe and the intractability of human affairs, and of the patience with which diplomacy must pursue the accommodations which it seeks. He was not entranced by power; he knew its limitations. When he was asked by Eric Goldman whether he agreed that, if a question gets as high as the Secretary of State or the President, it is likely to be insoluble anyway, he answered: "Well, there's a good deal in that; there is a good deal in that." On another occasion, he told a story of John Sherman Cooper who, when he was asked in 1952 whether he expected any major new foreign policies from the new administration, replied that the world was still pretty much the same place as it was yesterday, therefore few changes in foreign policy were likely. One is not denying that this stoicism can be carried too far; but it has its place, and its voice was desperately needed in the administration of John Kennedy; it is hard to excuse Dean Rusk for not raising it more persistently at the White House.

It is clear where one of the faults lay: in the exalted view of the Presidency to which, as we saw earlier, he had given forceful expression in his article in *Foreign Affairs*. "The crucial, indispensable contribution which the President can make to the conduct of our foreign affairs," he had written, "is to enter fully into his office"; and he repeated to Eric Goldman that "the President, under our constitutional system, is primarily responsible for the conduct of our relations with the rest of the world." Such a responsibility, he said in an interview in the issue of *Newsweek* of 16 July 1962, "is a political necessity, for it is he who mobilizes political support in the country and in Congress." These statements are faultless as statements of the constitutional position and of the political necessity; but they are sadly limited as statements of the President's own need and of the Secretary of State's responsibility in supplying it. Throughout the administration, Dean Rusk restrained his counsels of restraint; he assisted in his own subjection.

He had told the policy-making officers that "Power gravitates to those who are willing to make decisions, and live with the results." During the next eight years, he was to display a monumental capacity to live with the results, often of decisions which he had not made. But, if he was to blame, was not John Kennedy even more at fault? He did not like the methods of the Department of State, and he did not enjoy counsels of restraint. During the summer of 1961, there were many people who did not think that the situation in Berlin was critical. Bruce C. Clarke, the commander of the United States Army in

Western Europe at the time, refused to consider it as a crisis, "as I would define a crisis"; and Richard Rovere observed in *The New Yorker* of 25 July 1961, "For the first time, the administration seems less a victim of circumstance than a creator, or contriver, of it." But the President was eager to regard it as a crisis. He was in a hurry, but the Department of State was not.

He was irritated by the slowness of the department in drafting a reply to the Russian *aide-mémoire*. When he at last received it, he was further irritated by its lack of crispness, by its reliance on the legalistic language of diplomacy. He asked Theodore Sorensen to produce on a single afternoon a version which was shorter and simpler. But, when this had been done, he found to his chagrin that this new draft could not be substituted for the formal note without consulting once more with the departments concerned and with the interested allies. The man who, in his election campaign, had said that he would act as "the Commander-in-Chief of the grand alliance" had forgotten his allies. But it is precisely the duty of the Department of State to remember the country's allies, as it is also its duty not to send hurried notes when there is nothing much to be said, because there is nothing much that can be done.

Yet it was the behaviour of the Department of State on this issue, among other causes, which convinced him that the "Thanksgiving Day Massacre" was needed, and persuaded him, not only to appoint a task force to handle the situation, but to reach past the Department of State and choose as its chairman Paul Nitze, who was the Assistant Secretary of Defense for National Security Affairs, just as, when the Secretary of Defense —let it be noted—proposed that a task force should be appointed to handle the situation in Vietnam he again reached past the Department of State and chose as its chairman Roswell Gilpatric, who was the Deputy Secretary of Defense. At this point,

Dean Rusk should have sought a confrontation with the President, who was both filling the Department of State with his own men and, when these were not sufficient, draining power away from it. But he did not.

The officers of the Department of State, wrote Louis Halle in the *New Republic* of 5 June 1961, "are conscious of a widespread disposition to accuse them of always holding back from action, of being pettifogging about points of form and usage"; and this was indeed the attitude of John Kennedy. "They never have any ideas over there," he said; "never come up with anything new." But "anything new" is not necessarily, and certainly not always, the advice that a President should be seeking from his bureaucracy. Early in the spring of 1962, he spoke for forty minutes, off the record, to some eight hundred officials of the State Department, and he emphasised what he expected of them: that they should provide the answers to problems—and not memoranda which were erudite but inconclusive—and that they should deliver these in a hurry. But international problems do not always have ready answers, even any answers, and it is not the duty of a foreign service to manufacture them; he was asking the Department of State to abandon the reason for its existence, and its value to him.

Here and there, in the memoirs, the asperity with which Dean Rusk is usually mentioned is relaxed. It is admitted that, in negotiation with the Russians, he was tireless and skilful in avoiding headlines and the crises which accompany them. In a television interview on 7 June 1962, Walter Lippmann had been even more pointed: "Well, Dean Rusk has proved himself . . . since, roughly speaking, last summer, to be a really first-class negotiator with the Russians. He's got one quality that is indispensable for dealing with the Russians. He never gets bored. He can say the same thing and listen to the same thing.

. . . His negotiations with Gromyko, at the end of August I think it was, after the wall business, resulted really in taking the ultimatum out of the Berlin situation." That is indeed the business of diplomacy. It requires not only professional experience but the professional attitude that is embodied in a foreign office such as the Department of State, whose conversation is a part of the conversation of politics.

There can be no question, as Bernard Brodie put it in the July 1965 issue of *World Politics,* that Robert McNamara was *un phénomène.* Even when one met him, formally or informally, interviewed him as a journalist, or listened to him converse, it was hard to avoid the impression that he was unaccountable, which is one of the characteristics of a phenomenon. What did he want to do, what did he think he was doing? Even from those who have worked closely with him, no convincing answer is forthcoming. Yet he established an unusual dominance over his President, over his department, over his colleagues, and over the journalists in Washington, who until the very end would not believe that his policies were mistaken, that his management was inefficient, and sent him off to the World Bank, heaped with praise in which there was no hint of qualification.

Robert McNamara, throughout his long administration of the Department of Defense, was consistently praised for establishing civilian control within it. Although the method of his control has been severely criticised by many dispassionate authorities, it was not just the method which was at fault; it was the objective. The civilian authorities—especially the Secretary of Defense and the President beyond him—should in peacetime, at least, stand in opposition to the military leaders; they should be in an adversary situation, their opposition to each other carried through every level of defence planning to the top. The predictable result of the civilian control which Robert McNamara enforced was that the civilian antagonism ceased at too low a level. Through his civilian Assistant Secretaries, he did indeed establish a firm personal hold on defence planning at an early stage; and the policies which emerged could, from an early stage, be described as his own. But, because they were his own, they were then beyond further challenge; his Assistant Secretaries and his Deputy Secretary could not challenge them; and his personal dominance meant that the President would not challenge them. This may be a sensible way to produce an automobile or even to run a railroad. But it is a dangerous way to produce armaments, and an even more dangerous way to decide if, and when, and how, they should be used. The civilian—the political—check was operating too far down, too far back, to perform its function.

Robert McNamara had only a slight—and, even then, impatient—conception of the nature of a political decision. One of his apologists, Henry L. Trewhitt, tells us that the techniques which he used "were those that had always carried him to the top. . . . the challenges, as he saw them, were the same. Ford Motor Company was a fair-sized undertaking, he reminded questioners, and once you passed a certain level mere size became irrelevant." As early as 17 February 1961, he said in a television interview, "I think the role of the private manager is very similar to the role of the public manager"; and he described the managerial role, as he conceived it, in the New York *Times Magazine* of 26 April 1964: "When I became Secretary of Defense in 1961, I felt that either of two broad philosophies of management could be followed at the head of a great establishment. He could play an essentially passive role—a judicial role. In this role, the Secretary would make the decisions required of him by the law, by approving recommendations made to him.

On the other hand, the Secretary of Defense could play an active role providing aggressive leadership—questioning, suggesting the alternatives, proposing objectives, and stimulating progress. This active role represents my own philosophy of management." But the words "passive" and "aggressive" beg the question. He may have provided aggressive leadership in the early stages of the formation of policy; but, when the policy became his own, still at a comparatively early stage, the aggression in fact ceased, and he became a passive manager of his own decisions, too closely identified with them.

As James M. Roherty says in his study *The Decisions of Robert S. McNamara,* the system of management which he established in fact meant that "a policy framework is set by the Secretary; much of the data is provided by the Secretary; judgments are invited by the Secretary; decisions are made by the Secretary." This may be what is meant by active management in the world of the corporation, but it is a misleading objective in the world of politics. Even if there were an agreed goal in politics, it would still have to be discovered—and pursued—by a process of indirection: the way to a political decision is very like that described by G. K. Chesterton in his poem in which he praises the rolling English road, and boasts of "the night we went to Birmingham by way of Beachy Head."

Instead of providing leadership within the military establishment, Robert McNamara sought to eliminate the need for it by smothering the traditional rivalries under his system of unified control. Indeed, he came near to eliminating the Presidential leadership which should be the ultimate civilian control. "You don't go to the President until you are ready for a decision," Edward Weintal and Charles Bartlett quote him as saying; but what this really means is that you do not go to the President until you are ready for his approval. In short, the President is reduced to the passive role which Robert McNamara said that *he* would not tolerate in his own department. The opposite point of view was put by Dean Rusk:

> Now, I think that a Secretary of State has a responsibility . . . not to screen out differences of point of view so that, when the advice goes to the President, the President will know that here is a situation requiring a decision, that there are alternatives, there are choices to be made—including doing nothing—and that there may very well be on-balance judgments.

But, in spite of the myth that he invited differing opinions, John Kennedy did not really like inconclusive advice; and he was content that Robert McNamara effectively filtered the military advice that he would receive, bringing to him a custom-made policy for his approval.

Given the force of his personality, Robert McNamara was likely to obtain that approval. His articulation and his persuasiveness, said Robert Kennedy, made him "the most dangerous man in the Cabinet," a remark uttered in admiration, but with so hard a core of truth in it that he would have been nearer to the point if he had uttered it as a criticism, and as a warning to his brother. "Kennedy could comfortably let McNamara be 'Secretary of Defense,'" says Roger Hilsman. In fact, he confined himself, in defence policy, not merely to one set of advisers, but to one adviser, with the unhelpful exception of Maxwell Taylor, and the total effect was that, although Robert McNamara may have established a form of civilian control over the military services, he had in the process put the Department of Defense beyond effective political control. Military policy had been given an independence on which there was little check; and it was for this reason that *The Nation* could observe on 26 January 1963 that "The defense program has acquired a rationale, purpose, and momentum of its own."

We have noticed earlier the abruptness with which John Kennedy met a display of independence from the Secretary of the Air Force; and the story is significant because it emphasises the support which was given to Robert McNamara as he subjected the service secretaries to his unified command. Elvis T. Stahr resigned from the post of Secretary of the Army in the early summer of 1962. In an interview which was published in the New York *Times Magazine* on 8 July, he said that, "more and more, the decisions once made by the service secretaries and the military chiefs, as individuals, are made by the Secretary of Defense and his staff," and he described the personal control which Robert McNamara had established as "over-reaching." Elvis Stahr was promptly replaced by one of Robert McNamara's own men, Cyrus R. Vance; and, in exactly the same way, when the opportunities were available, two other members of his own team were moved to take control of the other two services: Paul Nitze, to be the Secretary of the Navy, and Harold Brown, to be the Secretary of the Air Force.

Interservice rivalry is not only a traditional, but a healthy, part of the military establishment of the United States. In the early summer of 1963, Hanson Baldwin wrote in the *Saturday Evening Post*: "The 'unification' of the armed services sponsored by McNamara poses some subtle and invidious danger—creeping dangers . . . that could present, in their ultimate form, almost as great a threat to a secure and free nation as an attempted military coup." In combination with the powerful committees of Congress where they exercise their influence, and with the press to which they leak the information that they believe will assist them, the rivalry of the armed services ensures that the operations of the military establishment are far more open to scrutiny than in any other country. Interservice competition, as Adam Yarmolinsky says in *The Military Establishment*, "may be an important tool in preserving civilian control." But it was the object of Robert McNamara, supported by John Kennedy, to confine this rivalry to the earliest stages of policy-making, and to prevent it, as far as was possible, from being advertised in public.

In fact, the smothering of interservice rivalry defeated the objective of civilian control in other ways. Because of the conflict between the services, wrote Samuel Huntington in the March 1961 issue of the *American Political Science Review*, at no point after the establishment of the Department of Defense in 1947 "were the President and the Bureau of the Budget confronted with a truly joint, integrated military program, publicly announced and supported by all military men." On the contrary, "inter-service rivalry . . . strengthened civilian agencies, enabling the Department of State and the Bureau of the Budget to pick and choose between proposed defense policies." In the same issue of the review, Gene M. Lyons argued that the divisions among military leaders "are crucial in a political process within which priorities must be established"; if they cannot agree on their priorities, "there is little reason to expect that the military can control government policy." He proceeded to make two valuable points: that "military disagreement, if exposed, is an invitation to civilian intervention"; and that "it is very often the military who put defense policy to the test of public accountability by exposing the bases for decisions." For eight years, this wisdom was ignored.

Under the system established by Robert McNamara, and reinforced by his relations with the President, agencies such as the Bureau of the Budget were precisely confronted by "a truly joint, integrated military program"; and by 1965 he was vigorously claiming that the bureau took no decision which affected his Department. His own opportunity—the bureau's opportunity—the Department of State's opportunity—the President's opportunity—to pick and choose between alternative defence policies were all reduced almost to vanishing point. The civilian control over the individual services may have reduced their influence, but it elevated the influence of the military establishment as a whole, of the Department of Defense under his command, to a position which it had never occupied before, and which Melvin Laird has consciously sought to reduce. Once again, the conversation which political activity is intended to elicit, was being silenced or, at best, deflected. One voice would pronounce the military policy of the country, and it would not be challenged.

When the New York *Times* first published its almost unintelligibly abbreviated version of "The Pentagon Papers," many observers were horrified at the manner in which the policymakers in the administration described their plans for the war in South Vietnam in terms of "games" and "models" and "probabilities" and "options." They were right to be horrified, but they left it there. They did not inquire into the origin of this vocabulary, and the kind of thinking which it represented. They were satisfied to lift their hands in pious indignation at the picture, as they represented it, of grown men playing in a sandbox. But the grown men had a reason to be in the sandbox; it was there; and it had been made for them by none other than the social scientist in the United States at the end of the 1950s. To cut a long story very short, the behavioural revolution that had not only swept the social sciences in the United States during the 1950s but swept them together was carried at the end of the decade into a field which immediately concerns us: the study of international politics. By the time that John Kennedy took office, the academic study of international politics in the United

States was dominated by "the techniques of systems theory, game theory, simulation, or content analysis."

We may concern ourselves with only one of these techniques, "political gaming," of which there were two forms, the "theoretical approach" and the "reality approach." In both of them, the individuals who were participating were given roles to play, in which they represented the countries and the organisations and the forces that might be involved in a given international situation. In the theoretical approach, which was pioneered by Harold Guetskow at Northwestern University, no actual country was represented, so that the result of the game would illuminate only the theoretical structure of the study of international politics. But, in the reality approach, which was pioneered by the RAND Corporation, the individual players were identified as realistically as possible with the strategies and policies of actual governments.

In the *United States Naval Institute Proceedings* of September 1960, Lincoln P. Bloomfield gave an account of a political game which had been played in the fall of 1958 at Endicott House, the country estate which the Massachusetts Institute of Technology converted into its own sandbox: ". . . the problem was a crisis caused by an anti-regime coup in Poland. We therefore had to assign maximum strength to the American, Soviet, and East European teams. But at the same time, since we anticipated that the problem would go before the United Nations, it was necessary to have teams representing aggregate countries in Africa, Asia, and Latin America." On the other hand, Lincoln Bloomfield continued, the games were sometimes not confined to a single crisis, but "take the whole world for their arena, with all teams making moves and reacting right across the board." Indeed, he argued, "the chief characteristic of the political exercise is that it can be global in scope, stimulating not only the global political community, but also the detailed interaction of governments on a global scale." One can only rub one's eyes at this pretension: the world had become a sandbox.

The political games were—they are hardly as fashionable today—more complex than this brief description allows, as are the systems theory, the game theory, the simulation, the model-making, from which they were derived. If they had been confined to the intellectual community—to the Secondary World where they belonged—the political games might have enjoyed a voguish existence, encountered the opposition of a more traditional approach, and eventually faded away, perhaps leaving a small deposit of such insights as they offered. But they were not confined to the academic world as an educational aid. Actual diplomats and actual officials were invited to play them; and they spread in the 1960s from the universities and the "think-tanks" to the Primary World of human affairs. With the election of John Kennedy—in particular, with the elevation of Robert McNamara—the methodology was enthroned in the seat of government.

The political game as such was actually installed in the Department of Defense. The origin of Robert McNamara's ideas on strategy, wrote Bernard Brodie in the July 1965 issue of *World Politics* "was a relatively small group of persons formerly associated with RAND, but with an exceptionally strong in-group cohesion among themselves, and thus a sometimes marked degree of personal and intellectual separation from most other members of that organization that developed a philosophy extremely close in detail to that which Mr. McNamara has since made his own." The leader of his group was Albert Wohlstetter, who was invited to join the Department of Defense, but preferred to remain outside it, available for consultation, and in close contact with his former associates; and Robert McNamara awarded him the medal for Distinguished Public Service, which is the gift of the Department of Defense.

There were other sources—for example, the Livermore Laboratory—but their nature was the same; and the Secretary of Defense locked them into positions immediately below him, where they contributed, as James Roherty puts it, "support rather than influence." The character of their support was formed by their own self-support as a coherent group, and the much advertised civilian control that Robert McNamara was supposed to have established consisted in this: a group of intellectuals who were bemused by their instruments and their techniques pursued their methodology as if it were a method, and were possessed by an arrogance—particularly noticeable in the key figures of Charles J. Hitch and Alain C. Enethoven—which made their own ideas inaccessible to correction.

They were not only intellectuals but of the particular breed of intellectuals who may be generically described as social scientists; even more particularly, they were in the main trained as economists. They had little sense of, as they had enjoyed little training in, either politics or history. In the "Great Debate" on nuclear strategy, they were insensitive, as Raymond Aron commented, to "the susceptibilities of their European allies." On the other hand, those analysts, fewer in number, who had been trained in political science, such as Henry Kissinger and Bernard Brodie, were consistently alert to the feelings of proud nations which had been accustomed for many centuries to recognising and defending their national interests. This distinction is helpful, because they were serving a man who also had enjoyed no instruction in history or in politics. "There was nothing in his previous career," says James Roherty of Robert McNamara, "to provide him with a grasp of high strategy and international political-military relations." Each reinforced the other.

The conversation of politics, which pays attention to the actual world, historical and political, its untidiness and its intractability, was overwhelmed by the patter of a particular kind of intellectual who finds it hard, in the words of Hedley Bull, a severe critic of political gaming, "to sort out what is happening in the game and what is happening in real life." He will not pay attention to even the simplest of historical facts. Remarking that Americans were not the pioneers in the political game, Lincoln Bloomfield pointed to the evidence that "both Germany and Japan indulged in serious political gaming" before the Second World War. One would have thought that such evidence was enough: after all, both Germany and Japan then lost their wars. If such men were to be brought into government at all, it should have been on a tight rein, not serving a President who was fascinated by the intellectual method and a Secretary of Defense who was obsessed by the scientific methodology. But that was their situation and, as such, they became the "fashionable madmen" of the administration; and the rule of thumb of the politician, feeling the cloth of human affairs by his touch, and the balance of things in his hands, was overridden by them.

The activity of politics, which listens to many voices, was thus downgraded even in the conduct of the administration itself. Someone knew best—someone would be found, who it was said knew best—and the making of policy would be placed in his hands: the President's men would override the Department of State; the Secretary of Defense would override the services within his department and the agencies outside it which might have challenged him; the theorists of systems and of models would override the practical judgement of men of affairs. It is characteristic and revealing that, with the exception of one or two incidents such as the "Thanksgiving Day Massacre," there is almost nothing in the memoirs about the politics of the administration, the struggles which went on within it. One catches the smell of them here and there: in the refusal of the President to give any support to Luther Hodges in his attempt to impose some sense of public responsibility on big business; in the inability of Abraham Ribicoff to extract from the White House any clear indication of the extent of its commitment to the bill to increase the amount of federal aid to public education, or of the strategy by which it hoped to carry the bill; in the running battle on economic policy, between "the liberals" and "the technicians" in the government, which was still being fought at the time of the assassination. But the impression which is always left is that, although there may have been some smoke, there was not necessarily any fire.

Instead of being told of the politics of the administration, we are told of its process, the word from which there is no escape. Joseph Kraft quotes one of the assistants of McGeorge Bundy: "There are three kinds of people in the policy game. There are those with options who are looking for positions. There are those with positions who are looking for options. There are those with options who are looking for options. Bundy is a creature from the third species." It is an endlessly revealing statement, not least in its manner: intellectual hubris and intellectual playfulness in equal parts. "There's nothing like brains. You can't beat brains," John Kennedy was often quoted as saying. But it depends on what kind of brains they are, on the manner in which they have been educated, and on the humility with which they are employed. Otherwise, as Hans Morgenthau said in the *New Leader* six months after John Kennedy had taken office, criticising the heavy emphasis on academic experience and intellectual expertise in his appointments, "anything goes that is presented cleverly and with assurance." As an acquaintance of many of them once remarked: "They always seemed to be playing with their toes." Perhaps there is nothing more to be said.

But what is most seriously absent from the process, as this passage describes it, is any genuine concern for values or interests, although it is these alone, one or the other or both, which can give any meaning to the options which are chosen or the positions which are adopted. Values and interests are what the voters take with them to the polling stations. It is by these that they judge, and, over the stretch of the years, they judge with a steadiness of perception that is in itself a sufficient justification of democracy. They have no way of knowing whether one option is more appropriate than another; and between one position and another there is often no useful distinction to be made. But they can set their values against other values, and their interests against other interests, and on these grounds judge for themselves. If the conversation of politics is not conducted in terms of values and interests, they have been deprived of the opportunity to make their own measurements. In the choice of options and positions, they cannot intervene, and they are left open to the suggestion that they should surrender that choice to men with the intellectual equipment and the rational disposition to make them on their behalf in an alleged general interest.

If this were another book with a different purpose, it would be pertinent to describe the all but absolute failure of the administration in the field of domestic policy: whether the failure even to carry its own measures; or the failure to define the problems which faced the country in any but the conventional terms of the past; or the failure to find the basis of a coalition on which it could rely in any effort which would be made. But the facts are known, and no matter how often they are rehearsed, they always tell the same story, of a method of politics that expected to succeed without the use of politics: to accomplish what it wished to do without the assistance of political institutions; to determine what it should do without the guidance of political values; to sustain its effort in what it attempted without the co-operation of political interests.

It was at this point that process failed, for it is not by process that Congress can be managed, or that priorities can be determined, or that interests can be engaged. The most striking domestic failure—the defeat of the education bill which he so frequently promised during his campaign—was a failure to exploit the initial advantage which had been gained when the composition of the Committee of Rules of the House of Representatives was significantly changed; a failure to demonstrate that the priority which had been given to the bill was dictated by a political value which was at the very core of the administration's reason for existence; and a failure to enlist the interest of the Roman Catholic Church on the side of the bill, or the support of another interest to offset its influence. A political institution, a political value, a political interest: without them, the emperor had no clothes, and neither the plumage of national purpose nor the weapons of "consensus politics" could conceal his nakedness.

"See the New Frontiersman run. He is running to the Capitol to save the program," wrote Russell Baker in the fall of 1962 as, for the second year in succession, John Kennedy failed to carry the substance of his proposed domestic legislation; and this was in fact the level to which his political leadership in Congress was reduced throughout his administration, except in support of his foreign policy and the legislative measures to support it. "At the heart of President Kennedy's troubles with Congress is lack of clear direction," Ted Lewis said in *The Nation* of 14 July 1962. "If Congress is to function purposefully, it needs marching orders aimed at achieving a firm objective. There is actually nothing wrong with the present Congress that direction would not cure." But there was no conceptual strategy of this kind in his political leadership. He would send a message to Congress in support of a measure, both of them lit with promise; he would then forget about it until the time for the crucial vote had arrived; then Lawrence O'Brien would be found, trying to stitch together the votes which were needed to carry a bill which no one had been given any reason to know was considered by the administration to be important.

When the display of leadership is so convincing, and the reality of leadership is so slight, the people will cease to understand the working of their political institutions. John Kennedy proclaimed in measures and in messages that he wished to do so much; but he in fact achieved so little that the people could hardly be blamed if they concluded that their political processes were inadequate to their tasks. If a leader of such exceptional vigour, commanding an administration of such unusual talents, could not achieve his purposes, there must be something at fault with the political institutions which balked him. The fact that he was not, from day to day, exercising any political leadership within those institutions went unnoticed. The poetic images of the popular leadership on which he relied were so dazzling that his neglect of the solid world of things in which politics must make their useful adjustments was hardly contemplated. In place of the conversation of society, the people had been persuaded that they should hear in their politics "that ring of command . . . that intrepid assertiveness" which the *New Republic* had found in the inaugural address; in the end there is nowhere for a people so bemused to go but into the streets.

CHAPTER FOURTEEN

As a City Upon a Hill

HE DIED WHILE he was campaigning, and it was while he was campaigning that his brother died also: a fact of which the meaning is not clear, but in which one suspects that there is a meaning. A year before the election, he was once more bearing himself before the American people; for a method of politics that relies on personal leadership, that has no other stay in the actual world of politics, must display that personal leadership. He had believed in the campaign-before-the-campaign when he ran for the Senate; he had believed in it when he ran for the Presidency; even as President he still believed in it. In five days, at the end of September of 1963, he had already travelled in a wide arc from Milford, Pennsylvania, to Ashland, Wisconsin, to Duluth, Minnesota, to Grand Forks, North Dakota, to Cheyenne, Wyoming, to Billings and Great Falls, Montana, to Hanford, Washington, to Salt Lake City, Utah, back to Tacoma, Washington, to Tongue Point, Oregon, to Whiskeytown, California, to Las Vegas, Nevada. He was the President, as it was advertised, talking about conservation; he was in fact the candidate on the stump.

In the last week of his life, he had resumed his journeying, and we must attend to his words; they are the only clue we have to what the character of his second term in office would have been. On the Monday he flew to Tampa, Florida, bearing with him a new image of excellence, the decision to build a supersonic plane: ". . . we are going to be laying the groundwork which will permit people to fly at five times the speed of sound, and before the end of the century many more times than that." Within a paragraph, the excellence had proclaimed the power: the United States was helping countries "all around the globe" to maintain their freedom. "It involves us in alliances with dozens of countries. It involves Americans in combat 10,000 miles away. It has taken a country like the United States, which lived a hundred and fifty years of its history in isolation, and has made it for the last twenty years the keystone in the arch of freedom."

Still in Tampa, he moved on to the Chamber of Commerce: to seek again a "consensus" with business—"Businessmen are welcome at the White House"; to hedge a little on civil rights— "What the Congress passes, I will execute"; to proclaim that Fidel Castro "still remains a major danger to the United States." Journeying on to Miami, he began by admitting that the problems of Latin America "will not be solved simply by complaining about Castro, by blaming all problems on Communism," but went on to say that "Communism is struggling to subvert and destroy the process of democratic development, to extend its rule over other nations of this hemisphere." The leaders of Cuba had made it "a victim of foreign imperialism. . . . As long as this is true, nothing is possible." With that he returned to Washington. There had been some indications of chastening as he spoke of the Alliance for Progress, but they were transcended in familiar vocabulary: ". . . if we do not lose heart, the gloomy prophecies of today can once again fade into the achievements of tomorrow. For although the problems are huge, the greatest danger is not in our circumstances or in our enemies, but in our own doubts and fears . . . ultimately we will hold a continent where twenty strong nations live in peace, their people in hope and liberty."

Two days later, he flew to San Antonio, Texas, to begin: "For more than three years I have spoken about the New Frontier," and he defined it: "It refers . . . to this nation's place in history, to the fact that we do stand on the edge of a great new era, filled with both crisis and opportunity, an era to be characterized by achievement and by challenge. It is an era which calls for action and for the best efforts of all those who would test the unknown and the uncertain in every phase of human endeavor." Excellence and power were joined in the symbol of the space programme, which "stands on its own as a contribution to national strength"; the new Saturn C-1 rocket booster would be "the largest booster in the world, carrying into space the largest payload that any country in the world has ever sent into space." The justification was not hard to predict: "I think the United States should be a leader . . . second to none. . . . This space effort must go on. The conquest of space must go on. That much we know. That much we can say with confidence and conviction."

He rose on 22 November 1963, to proclaim in front of the Texas Hotel in Fort Worth that "the new environment, space, the new sea," was an area "where the United States should be second to none," and inside the hotel he took breakfast with the Chamber of Commerce. He there proclaimed the achievement of his administration in strengthening the country's defences: "In the past three years we have increased the defense budget of the United States by over twenty per cent; increased the program of acquisition for Polaris submarines from twenty-four to forty-one; increased our Minuteman missile purchase program by more than seventy-five per cent; doubled the number of strategic bombers and missiles on alert; doubled the number of nuclear weapons available in the strategic alert forces; increased the tactical nuclear forces deployed in Western Europe by over sixty per cent; added five combat ready divisions to the Army of the United States, and five tactical fighter wings to the Air Force of the United States; increased our strategic airlift capability by seventy-five per cent; and increased our special counter-insurgency forces which are now engaged in South Vietnam by six hundred per cent." Such a boast could only astound.

"This requires sacrifice by the people of the United States," he continued; the accent was familiar. "But this is a very dangerous and uncertain world. As I said earlier, on three occasions in the last three years, the United States has had a direct confrontation. No one can say when it will come again. No one expects our life will be easy, certainly not in this decade, and perhaps not in this century." The summons to crisis and confrontation was being given its customary expression. "I don't think we are fatigued and tired. We would like to live as we once lived. But history will not permit it." It was the last call to the American people that he made. Three and a half hours later he was dead.

But there are included in the official volumes of his public papers the two speeches which he had prepared to deliver in Dallas and in Austin on that same day. He was to have talked at the Trade Mart in Dallas of the "link between leadership and learning. . . . America's leadership must be guided by the lights of learning and reason." He was to have talked of the "painful, risky, and costly" effort which was being made in South-east Asia, and to have added: "But we dare not weary of the task." He was to have talked of "our mission in the world," and of the need to "carry our message of truth and freedom to all the far corners of the earth." He was to have talked of "the righteousness of our cause," and to have proclaimed at last: "We in this country are—by destiny rather than choice—the watchmen on the walls of world freedom." He was to have travelled then to Austin, to proclaim again that "this is a time for courage and a time for challenge," and to appeal finally for the elevated sense of national purpose on which his popular leadership was built: "Let us not quarrel amongst ourselves when our nation's future is at stake. Let us stand together with renewed confidence in our cause—united in our heritage of the past and our hopes for the future—and determined that this land we love shall lead all mankind into new frontiers of peace and abundance."

A little more than four years later, Robert Kennedy was to take to the streets with the promise to reverse the policy of his brother, and of the administration of which he had been a member, at least in the most obvious of its manifestations. Early in 1962, he had said in Hong Kong that the solution of the war in South Vietnam "lies in our winning it. This is what the President intends to do"; and at the same time in Saigon he declared, "We are going to win it, and we are going to stay here until we win." Now at Kansas State University, on 18 March 1968, he proclaimed, "If the South Vietnamese government feels Khe Sanh is so important, let them put South Vietnamese troops in there, and let them take the Americans out." Yet at the moment at which he had announced his candidacy had he not said that what was at stake in the election was the right of the United States "to the moral leadership of the planet"? There was again a geological fault.

The campaign seemed to be different; the issues seemed to be different; the man seemed to be different; and to some extent they all were. But the method was the same; and it follows from the argument of this book that the method must have had the same end—in a tragic sense, it did—and that, if Robert Kennedy had been elected, the American people would have been called to four more years, or to eight, of the politics of expectation: of zeal and of turbulence, of crisis and of confrontation, of danger and of the rescue from danger. He had to seek different constituencies in 1968 from those to which his brother had appealed in 1960; or so it seemed, for even on this point we must be careful. We must remember that we did not see him in the arena of the Democratic Convention; we did not even see him begin the serious business of calculating how many more votes he would need at Chicago, and where he could best look for them. We must remember that we saw him only in the campaign for the nomination, and not in the campaign for the election; and we must ask ourselves whether, if he had been nominated, he could have afforded to conduct the kind of campaign which had been useful until then, and in which he is today remembered. Perhaps above all, we must remember that, as in the case of his brother, he became a different political figure as the result of his assassination; the candidate when he was alive was less powerful than his shade at once became. He was not in a strong position when he died; between California and Chicago, he would have had to bend in many ways.

It is difficult to write sensibly of the man, even though one met him, and watched him, and listened to him; and one of the reasons is that the man keeps getting in the way of the politician. There was an impersonal quality in the public appearances of John Kennedy; aware at all times that he stood on a conspicuous stage, the world marking his demeanour, he always took to it apparelled; even his attractive qualities were those of an attractive public figure; one gazed on the compleat politician, accepted him as such, and did not much consider the man; one did not ask what made him tick. But everyone was always wondering what made Robert Kennedy tick, as if he were a timebomb, as some indeed regarded him; and we must clear the man away if we are going to consider him sensibly as a politician. It is not often that we find in the man the explanation of the politician; and one of the reliefs of political biography is that psychological interpretations do not really assist it, and one is therefore saved from a lot of hazy speculations about character.

One reason why the man in Robert Kennedy gets in the way of the politician is that his career as a politician was so short, and his achievements were so slight. A thousand days as the Attorney General of the United States, and not much longer as the junior senator from New York: that, and his brief campaign for the nomination, are almost all we have to talk about. The record is so slender; the impact was so great. This does not, to some, appear to be a difficulty; then judge him, they are satisfied to say, by the impact. This is fair up to a point, but where does one look for the impact, and how does one measure it? One will usually find that they are talking about the impact of the man on themselves. It is hard to think of another politician into whose life so many people read themselves with such indulgence. The fact that he to some extent invited this identification is no excuse.

Some time before Robert Kennedy was assassinated, William V. Shannon wrote of him that he "wishes to be an existential hero," a tempting phrase which Jack Newfield elaborated into a theme:

> He had an existential dimension. He defined and created himself in action, and learned about everything from experience. His end

was always unknown. He dared death repeatedly. He was pre-
occupied with suffering and despair. When his brother died, he
passed through a night of dread, and learned about the absurd.

One must be harsh. Either this passage is accurate, in which
case the man was too dangerous to hold responsible political office; or the passage is fiction, itself its own theatre, the psychodrama, not even of the politician, but of the journalist himself.

There is something, on the surface, to be said for both points
of view. The man who could say to Arthur Schlesinger, "I
wish I never was born," and who replied to a questioner that,
if he had not been a Kennedy, he might have been "a juvenile
delinquent or a revolutionary," would seem to have read too
much of Albert Camus too late in life and to the wrong purpose;
and he is certainly not the obvious figure to whom one would
entrust the safety and sure governance of a people. On the
other hand, one cannot help forming the impression that Robert
Kennedy was more and more trapped into making such remarks and acting such a role, by a throng of hangers-on who
had never been Kennedys or juvenile delinquents or revolution-
aries but were only journalists. It seems to be worth pointing
out that, when Robert Kennedy died, he was trying to win the
highest political office in the world in a most un-existential way.
He showed no sign of wishing to stand by the last tree, the last
fighter, and die in silence. He was shot while the applause rang
in his ears as a victor.

The existential hero calculated at length whether he should
run against Lyndon Johnson; the existential hero travelled to a
fund-raising dinner in Philadelphia and found the words to
celebrate James Tate as "one of the greatest mayors in the
United States"; the existential hero, as he estimated his chances
in the small towns of Indiana, estimated that they would like
to hear what the small towns of Indiana think; the existential

hero was prepared, according to his advertising agency, to spend $18 million to secure his election; the existential hero wished to follow his brother to the White House, not to the grave. Above all, there is not a shred of evidence that the man defined himself in action; on the contrary, all the evidence is that he went to great pains to define beforehand any action which he might take, and to define himself in readiness for that action. In the taking of every major decision that is described by Theodore Sorensen in *The Kennedy Legacy* he was as circumspect as a cat, circling a problem before deciding to grasp it.

Perhaps it is more a matter of Jack Newfield trying, as did many others, to define himself in Robert Kennedy. There is a thrill of self-discovery in his reaction to the assassination:

> Now I realized what makes our generation unique, what defines us apart from those who came before the hopeful winter of 1961, and those who came after the murderous spring of 1968. We are the first generation that learned from experience, in our innocent twenties, that things were not really getting better, that we shall *not* overcome. We felt, by the time we reached thirty, that we had already glimpsed the most compassionate leaders our nation could produce, and they had all been assassinated. And from this time forward, things would get worse; our best political leaders were part of memory now, not hope.

Things would no longer get better, they would only get worse: this was exactly the attitude which the sociologists had noticed in schoolchildren after the assassination of John Kennedy, an anxiety that other bad things would happen. "The stone was at the bottom of the hill, and we were alone," Jack Newfield at last ends. It is at this point that we must ask *who* wished to stand by the last tree, the last fighter, ready to die aloud in three hundred pages of advertised print.

The brothers were of course different men, and so were the

situations in which they acted. But, if we stand back for a moment, and keep some coolness in our judgement, we will notice that many of the qualities which in Robert Kennedy were said to provide the existential dimension could be found also in John Kennedy. Action was important to both of them; as we have noticed of John Kennedy, he sought the consolations of activity. Both of them responded to the myth of the guerilla; and were inclined to use his method even as they made their adjustments to conventional politics. To both of them experience was more important than concept; so that they reacted to poverty as they saw it rather than to any notion of human equality as they conceived it. Both of them were persuaded of the value of personal gesture; committing themselves to a cause by symbolic acts, such as their personal association with Martin Luther King, rather than by developing a political strategy to achieve it. By their deeds, both of them said, they would be known.

Both of them might have taken as their motto the sentiment of Theodore Sorensen, "To prove ourselves, we must improve the world." To leave any day simply as they found it, untouched by their zeal, unimproved by their doing, was a default. Idleness in any day they counted as a failure and, if they had expressed themselves in such language, a sin. If either of them had been a fisherman, he would have counted the pleasure of his day by the size of his catch, not by the hours spent at leisure on a river bank. "At all times he was in motion," Joseph Kraft had written of John Kennedy. "Inside and out," he wrote of Robert Kennedy, "he was a man in motion." If the zeal burned in Robert Kennedy in 1968 for all the world to see, in a way in which it had not done in his brother, we must at least remember the difference in their situations. Robert Kennedy went to the people in 1968 when urgent national concerns seemed to call for a passionate political response. We have no way of knowing whether, in similar circumstances, the zeal of John Kennedy would not have broken through its containment, just as we have no way of knowing how contained, if he had been elected, Robert Kennedy would have been in the White House; we can only speculate.

By 1968, the poor had been discovered, and the young had discovered themselves. They were both more visible than they had been eight years before, and they were treated in the oratory of the campaign in much the same manner as were the guests at the wedding feast, brought in from the highways and the byways. One is not, in this, being cynical, although the accusation will no doubt be made. Robert Kennedy in 1968 faced the same problem as John Kennedy in 1960—the problem that, as was suggested at the beginning, confronts any politician who is compelled by a high ambition to construct a coherent national appeal—and he managed it with the same imagination as his brother. He became necessary—known to himself, and seen by the people, to be so—to the groups that appeared at the time to be defining the nation's concerns, the poor and the young. Our interest must be in the political character of the relationships that he formed with them.

In 1960, the nation's concerns had been defined, as we saw, by the intellectuals and the academics; and John Kennedy closely followed their lead. But these were not defining the concerns of 1968, and Robert Kennedy did not look to them to find what he should be saying. They had been representatives of a privileged elite, already in positions of influence in the existing society; but in 1968 the concerns that were defined were those of the unprivileged, whether like the poor they actually were so, or like the young they felt themselves to be; and neither of them were in positions of influence. The campaigns were therefore different, but the method and the purpose were the same: to appeal from the apparent urgencies of society, as these had been presented by special groups, to the creation of an essentially unpolitical will, a sense of purpose, by which they might be met and overcome.

But what is to bind a politician who is returned to power by such an appeal? The answer is, precious little. The poor and the young may make themselves visible and audible during an election campaign; even in their day-to-day lives, the streets are their arena. But, when the election is over, no groups carry less political weight, or are less able to use effectively whatever weight they may have. Visible in an election, they are all but invisible between elections. The spontaneous activity that is their strength on the streets is no substitute for the organised action that can force a concession from the government. In fact, no constituencies can be bought more cheaply than the poor and the young. There is almost no promise which cannot be made to them; there is almost none which they can insist must be redeemed by the leader whom they helped to return to power.

The point was made with a telling precision by Stokely Carmichael, when he said to Theodore Sorensen, speaking specifically of Robert Kennedy: "I would not want to see your man run for President, because he can get the votes of my people without coming to me. With the other candidates, I'll have bargaining power." This is one of the dangers of personal leadership in a democracy. The unorganised voters are easily attracted by it; they imagine that they are effectively participating in politics if a leader pays them unusual attention during a campaign, and if they respond to his attentions with their votes. But no bargain between them has been struck. When the campaign is over, the elected leader at once withdraws from the accessibility of which he had boasted, and is guarded by doorkeepers. The crowds cannot follow him, to ask what he has done for them, unless they can send a leader who is in the position to say: "I have these votes; if you do not bargain with me, I will withhold them from you."

Many of the reporters, including some who were sympathetic to him, who followed the campaign of Robert Kennedy in 1968 began to talk of the crowds on the streets as mobs; and they were right. They were mobs, not just because of their behaviour, but because of their formlessness. Sixty thousand people at a football game are not a mob, because they arrange themselves so that each of them may satisfy the purpose for which they all have come, to watch the football, and they do not then try to change the purpose. But a mob has no purpose other than to be its own theatre; when it has done its own thing, it has nothing else to do. It does not then split into groups which decide if they agree with what the candidate said, or whether they should give him their support, or how they can bind him to serve their interests. Unlike a crowd, which is a society, a mob has no after life. It was Chaos while it existed, to the Void it returns, as unpolitical in its intent as it is unsocial in its character; and the communion between Robert Kennedy and the poor and the blacks in 1968 was also unpolitical.

There can be little doubt that as a man he was engaged in his own theatre as he took to the streets, and one can well understand it. He was assuming the mantle of his brother, which might have been difficult in any circumstances, but he was assuming it in unfavourable conditions. He was deeply aware that, by his initial refusal to run against Lyndon Johnson, he had forfeited in many people's eyes the claim to represent the idealism and the excellence which he must promise to restore to the nation's life; and that he had forfeited it especially among the young, who had come to matter to him and who at the time seemed to matter. At last a candidate, there was something which he needed to prove, and to prove as quickly as possible; and he chose the theatre of the streets. There he could make a spectacular display of his personal leadership. He had to make no bargains. He had merely to say, "I am."

He appeared not to have given the proof when he was defeated by Eugene McCarthy in the primary election in Oregon; but it was different in California on the night of his assassination. "We can win this thing now," he said to Theodore Sorensen when his victory was clear; and, as he turned from the primary elections, to put together "a sizable majority of delegates" from the large states of Pennsylvania and Ohio and New Jersey and Michigan and Illinois, who can doubt that he would have moved off the streets? One of his strongest allies at Chicago—an ally whom he needed, and whom he wooed—would have been Richard Daley. On the last night of his conscious life, having swept California well enough, he talked of "the politics of reality." We should remember it. On the streets there had been an encounter of dreams; reality was once more available to him.

The reality would not have pleased many of his followers. A false admirer of Robert Kennedy such as Jack Newfield says of him that he was "a good and decent man . . . , but he allowed himself to be trapped in the venal and compromising snake pit of American politics." It is not clear to an outsider that the venality and the compromise in American politics are much worse than elsewhere. The difficulty the United States has is that it appears to know only two ways of coping with them: either by sweeping them under the rug, or by trying to transcend them in a moral revival. The fact is that Richard Daley represents both interests and values (including anxieties about those values) which compose an important part of American society, and which have at least as much claim to its attention as any others; and, unless a Robert Kennedy is so good and decent and a Richard Daley is so venal and compromising that neither of them should be in politics at all, a conversation between them can only be rewarding to a society which already converses too little in its politics.

But although, when he died, the politics of reality were once more available to Robert Kennedy, and he would have begun to converse, not with one Richard Daley, but with a thousand Richard Daleys, as his brother had done before him, the intention would again have been to conceal the reality, to suggest that it had been transcended by personal leadership of an exceptional character. "We are in a time of unprecedented turbulence, of danger and questioning," he proclaimed at Kansas State University on 18 March 1968. "It has at its roots a question of the national soul." It had nothing of the sort at its roots, but no matter. "There is a contest on," he continued, the rhythm of his sentence carrying the clearest echo from the past, "not for the rule of America, but for the heart of America"; which was again not true. But what one must notice is that the language that he was using to summon the American people to meet the turbulence of 1968 had been used eight years before to summon them to meet the passivity of 1960; and one is entitled to ask whether the passivity had not been replaced by the turbulence at least in part because just such language had aroused expectations of politics which could not be fulfilled. When he spoke in 1968, at Los Angeles airport, of "the failure of national purpose," was he not right in a way which he did not intend: that there had been a failure, which was costing the country dear at home and abroad, of a method of politics that was based on the excitement of too strenuous a purpose, by too exalted a manner of leadership?

For, if his brother had first made the connection between excellence and power, he was now able to make a further connection. When he was asked by Benjamin Bradlee, in an interview in *Newsweek*, if he would accept the Vice-Presidential nomination in 1968, he gave a revealing answer: "It is important that the striving for excellence continue, that there be an end to mediocrity. . . . The torch has really passed to a new generation. People are still looking for all that idealism. It permeated the young people all over the globe." The implication was as clear as it was intended. The striving for excellence and the idealism of a whole people had found expression in the leadership of one member of the family; an interval of mediocrity had intervened; they could now be revived by a second member of the family. In short, the American people were being promised the restoration of a dynasty.

As his oratory expanded in the campaign, there seemed to be almost no excellence that the nation had not attained during the regime of his brother, almost no degradation to which it had not sunk in the intervening years, almost no restoration that he could not promise. When at Vanderbilt University he appeared to blame Lyndon Johnson for the alienation of the young and their addiction to drugs, it was not only Richard Harwood in the Washington *Post* who protested that he was going too far. As the result of the divisions in the country, he had said, young people were turning away from their "public commitment of a few years ago to lives of disengagement and despair, turning on with drugs and turning off America." The presumption of this remark must be noticed: that people may not have private reasons for the lives which they choose to lead, that the alienation and the addiction of the young may not be responses to anxieties, possibly even to aspirations, which cannot be touched by, as they have not been inspired by, the doings of politicians. In short, politics are made co-extensive with life, and people are regarded as creatures of them. A politician can turn them off, a politician can turn them on, will-less in the hands of a leader.

"There's affluence, yet a feeling of unhappiness in the country," he said at breakfast with a group of political writers at the National Press Club in Washington on 30 January 1968. "If someone could touch that." This is to carry politics far beyond their proper realm. It may be the concern of politics to make the arrangements in which an individual may pursue his happiness if he so wishes, which is the promise of the Constitution of the United States of America; it cannot be their concern to endow each individual with happiness, even though this is the promise of the constitution of the state of Colorado. When a politician seeks to touch the happiness or the unhappiness of a people, politics are being translated into religion and, since they cannot give the assurances of religion, the only consequence can be, at first too high an expectation, and then too deep a disillusion. The disillusion had in fact come by 1968. Robert Kennedy promised to restore the expectation which had caused it.

The expectation was on each occasion the same, "that we shall be as a city upon a hill: the eyes of the world are upon us." This was the loftiness of the purpose and the elevation of the promise which men such as John Winthrop indeed brought to the New World: the puritanism which would in turn yield the evangelism of the Great Awakenings, a response to "the challenge of the vast territory, its limitless prairies, its great rivers, its sublime mountains," as Elizabeth W. Miller says, "all waiting to be explored, to be mastered, to be mined," but also to "the uniqueness of the new man, the American republican, who would indubitably achieve marvels in the governance of society, in science, in letters and the arts," who could "legitimately aspire to the moral sublime." The same influence, said the *Christian Spectator* as the Second Awakening spent its force, "which in revivals of religion descends on families and villages . . . may in like manner . . . descend to refresh and beautify a whole land," the whole beautiful, terrible, awesome land, as Perry Miller exclaims. Even in a secular age, the longing can still persist that America will be greened again.

One can hardly doubt that the American people are at last coming to terms with the limits of their power: not of their political power and their military strength alone, which would be a small lesson to learn, but of their capacity to master nature itself. The positivism of the American mind, marching with the puritanism of the American spirit in a fearful combination, has suffered a severe jolt. Its ability to control the actual world has itself been found to be out of control. One cannot study the administration of John Kennedy, the men and the measures, without deciding that it was a last confident—almost braggart—assertion of the capacity of American positivism to fulfil the prophecy of American puritanism: that the city of man can be built in the image of the City of God on this earth, and that the response of the American people to this assertion was that of men who wished to believe it. When it failed, there was an assassination to blame; when it failed again, there was yet another assassination; and it is out of this that yet another myth can be constructed.

The weakness of the positivism of the American mind is that it can too easily degenerate into what Abraham Kaplan calls a vulgar pragmatism, which he is at pains to dissociate from the philosophic pragmatism of Charles S. Peirce and William James and John Dewey, although he acknowledges that "there is something in pragmatism which lends itself to this vulgarization." The characteristics which he attributes to vulgar pragmatism may be briefly summarised: the ideal of success, in which "competitive success is taken to be at once the sign and substance of worth"; the ideal of efficiency, in which "important values are left out of the accounting"; the ideal of scientism, in which "special instruments and techniques [are] taken to be the method itself"; and the ideal of quantification, in which "nothing is so real as a measurable quantity." He continues to link this vulgar pragmatism with the emphasis on "toughness" and "tough-mindedness" in American society: "To be a man is to be successful, efficient, even ruthless. . . . The political leader must above all never be naive or a soft touch . . . he may not under any circumstances go soft on matters of policy." The total effect, he concludes, is that morality is transformed into no more than morale.

Those who have read the argument of this book cannot fail to respond to this picture. It was all there in the administration, in the method of its politics and in its approach to any problem, until the decision to shoot for the moon, which was indeed a problem that vulgar pragmatism was capable of solving, was translated into a metaphor. Science, it was proclaimed, was the breastplate of the New Frontier; if only it had been, the scientism of the intellectuals at the Department of Defense would not have been allowed to reign; and no one would have imagined that efficiency could be found in process; options would not have been confused with choice, and success, which is easy to come by, would not have been understood as achievement; quantification would not have been thought to be the measurement of a problem; and tough-mindedness would not have been regarded as a proof of strength.

One returns to the graves, remarks the words on their walls and the tourists as they pass by, and remembers the brothers themselves as valiant; no one is going to deny that. But we cannot, in the conduct of our affairs, rely on valour alone, because there have been valorous men, in the whole of the history of man, in causes which have been mistaken and even evil. The cause to which the brothers, and the men who served them, set themselves, was not evil, only mistaken; and the American people themselves must make their own terms with the error. There is a place for the arousal of expectation in politics; without it, man would hardly have progressed. Politics is not only the art of the possible, which is too often a thoughtless commonplace in small minds; but neither is it the art of the impossible to which the American people were called in 1960, and were about to be called again in 1968. Politics can be made the art of the necessary. A people can be nourished to believe that there are necessary things to be done, which they have overlooked, and that they have the necessary capacity to do them. That was the art practised by Franklin Roosevelt, the greatest political leader of this century, and an American beyond any dispute.

It is expectation enough, and the American people, beyond all people in our time, have the genius, when they have recovered a sense of propriety in the conduct of their affairs, to teach the world again that the necessary can be accomplished.

Index

INDEX

(of main references to persons and publications)